TANGIER

The fact that this book has been published is a tribute to the encouragement and unstinting help I have received from my wife Jane and my children Jemima and Luke.

Thank you all for your endless hours of reading my countless drafts, your many and varied suggestions and your patience in participating in my consuming passion.

TANGIER
THE EARLIEST BATTLE HONOUR

JOHN HAWKINS

Pen & Sword
MILITARY
AN IMPRINT OF PEN & SWORD BOOKS LTD.
YORKSHIRE – PHILADELPHIA

First published in Great Britain in 2023 by
PEN AND SWORD MILITARY
An imprint of
Pen & Sword Books Limited
Yorkshire – Philadelphia

Copyright © John Hawkins, 2023

ISBN 978 1 39907 306 6

The right of John Hawkins to be identified as Author of this work has been asserted by him in accordance with the Copyright, Designs and Patents Act 1988.

A CIP catalogue record for this book is available from the British Library.

All rights reserved. No part of this book may be reproduced or transmitted in any form or by any means, electronic or mechanical including photocopying, recording or by any information storage and retrieval system, without permission from the Publisher in writing.

Typeset in Times New Roman 11/14 by
SJmagic DESIGN SERVICES, India.
Printed and bound in the UK by CPI Group (UK) Ltd.

Pen & Sword Books Limited incorporates the imprints of Atlas, Archaeology, Aviation, Discovery, Family History, Fiction, History, Maritime, Military, Military Classics, Politics, Select, Transport, True Crime, Air World, Frontline Publishing, Leo Cooper, Remember When, Seaforth Publishing, The Praetorian Press, Wharncliffe Local History, Wharncliffe Transport, Wharncliffe True Crime and White Owl.

For a complete list of Pen & Sword titles please contact
PEN & SWORD BOOKS LIMITED
47 Church Street, Barnsley, South Yorkshire S70 2AS, United Kingdom
E-mail: enquiries@pen-and-sword.co.uk
Website: www.pen-and-sword.co.uk

Or
PEN AND SWORD BOOKS
1950 Lawrence Rd, Havertown, PA 19083, USA
E-mail: Uspen-and-sword@casematepublishers.com
Website: www.penandswordbooks.com

Contents

Maps		vi
Characters		vii
Introduction		xi
Prequel		xv
Chapter 1	King and Colony	1
Chapter 2	King and Warlord	12
Chapter 3	Bastions and Redoubts	25
Chapter 4	Broken Treaty	39
Chapter 5	The Navy Distracted	58
Chapter 6	Waning Warlord	66
Chapter 7	Waxing Sultan	82
Chapter 8	Spendthrift King	99
Chapter 9	Betrayal	112
Chapter 10	Ottoman Tactics	132
Chapter 11	Tangier Besieged	141
Chapter 12	Tangier Relieved	154
Chapter 13	Military Success	169
Chapter 14	Diplomatic Failure	181
Chapter 15	Tangier Dénouement	193
Appendix 1	Witness Characters	205
Appendix 2	Morocco and Moroccans	207
Appendix 3	Maps, Views and Fortifications	209
Acknowledgements		211
Glossary		212
Bibliography		217
Index		221

Maps

Tangier at the centre of seventeenth century trade

Morocco, 1660

North Fez

The locality of Tangier

Tangier city locations

Characters

Tangier Governors dates serving in Tangier

*Lieutenant Governor / Acting Governor during Governor's absence

Jan. '62 – Jun '62	Henry Mordant, 2nd Earl of Peterborough
Jun '62 – Aug '62	*Colonel John Fitzgerald* *
Aug '62 – Oct '62	Henry Mordant, 2nd Earl of Peterborough
Oct '62 – Dec '62	*Colonel John Fitzgerald**
Dec '62 – May '63	Henry Mordant, 2nd Earl of Peterborough
May '63 – Sept '63	Andrew Rutherford, 1st Earl of Teviot
Sept '63 – Jan '64	*Colonel John Fitzgerald* *
Jan '64 – May '64	Andrew Rutherford, 1st Earl of Teviot
May '64 – Oct '64	*Colonel Sir Tobias Bridge**
Oct '64 – Apr '65	*Colonel John Fitzgerald* *
Apr '65 – Apr '66	John Belasyse, 1st Earl of Belasysye
May '66 – Oct '69	*Colonel Henry Norwood**
Oct '69 – 'July '74	John Middleton, 1st Earl of Middleton
July '74 – Mar '75	*Major Palmes Fairborne* & Lieutenant Colonel Roger Alsop*
Mar. '75 – May '76	William O'Brien, 2nd Earl of Inchiquin
May '76 – May '78	*Major Sir Palmes Fairborne**
May '78 – May '80	William O'Brien, 2nd Earl of Inchiquin
Jun '80 – Oct '80	*Lieutenant Colonel Sir Palmes Fairborne**
July '80	Thomas Butler, Earl of Ossory died in England without taking up post

TANGIER: THE EARLIEST BATTLE HONOUR

Oct '80	Charles FitzCharles, 1st Earl of Plymouth died of dysentery before receiving his appointment
Jun '80 – Oct '80	Fairborne* killed in action before receiving his appointment
Oct '80 – Dec '81	*Lord Sackville**
Dec '81 – July '83	Sir Percy Kirke
July '83 – Feb '84	George Legge, 1st Baron Dartmouth

Other Characters

Allin, Sir Thomas	Admiral of Mediterranean Fleet 1668-1671
Barlow, Edward	sailor, author of a journal of his life and voyages
Belasyse, Lord John (1614-89)	Tangier Governor, see above
Ben Abu Bakr	Sultan of Fez 1659 – 1673
Bennett, Henry 1st Earl of Arlington	Secretary of State for the Southern Department 1662 - 1674
Bridge, Colonel of Horse, Sir Tobias	Tangier Acting Governor 1664 following Teviot's death in Fitzgerald's absence see above
Cholmley, Sir Hugh	contractor for mole 1662 - 1676
Dartmouth	Tangier Governor
Dover	whore mentioned by Pepys
Fairborne, Colonel Palmes	Captain promoted to Major 1663, knighted 1675, Acting Governor, see above
Fairborne, Marjory	Palmes' wife, also Margaret or Margery
Fairborne, Stafford	Palmes' oldest son
Fitzgerald, Lt Colonel Edward	garrison soldier fought duel with Palmes Fairbourne
Fitzgerald, Lieutenant James	garrison soldier provoked duel

CHARACTERS

Fitzgerald, Colonel John	Tangier Lieutenant / Acting Governor
Ghailan	Warlord of many of the tribes and cavilas of the Gharb 1659 - 1673
Halkett, Major James	Dumbarton's Scots Regiment
Hamut	Moor bought as slave by Lord Belasyse, gifted to Duke of York
Inchiquin	Tangier Governor, see above
Ismail, Mulay Ibn Zerif	Sultan of Morocco 1672 - 1727
Kirke	Tangier Governor, see above
Luke, John	Judge Advocate 1662-1675; Secretary to Governor 1664-1675
Luke, Nathaniel	Secretary to Tangier Governor 1662-1664
Medina, Duke of	Spanish Duke, vehemently opposed to the English in Tangier
Middleton	Tangier Governor, see above
Norwood	Tangier Acting Governor see above
Omar	Omar Ben Haddu, Qaid of El-Kasr
Pepys, Samuel	Clerk of the Acts to the Navy; Secretary, then Treasurer of Tangier Commission
Peterborough	Tangier Governor, see above
Al-Rashid, Mulay Arsheid Zerif	Sultan of Morocco 1666 - 1672
(Ossory)	(Tangier Governor), see above
Sackville	Tangier Governor, see above
Sandwich, 1st Earl of	Admiral of Mediterranean Fleet 1665 -1667
Shere	Chief Contractor for the mole at Tangier 1676 - 1683
Teviot	Tangier Governor, see above

TANGIER: THE EARLIEST BATTLE HONOUR

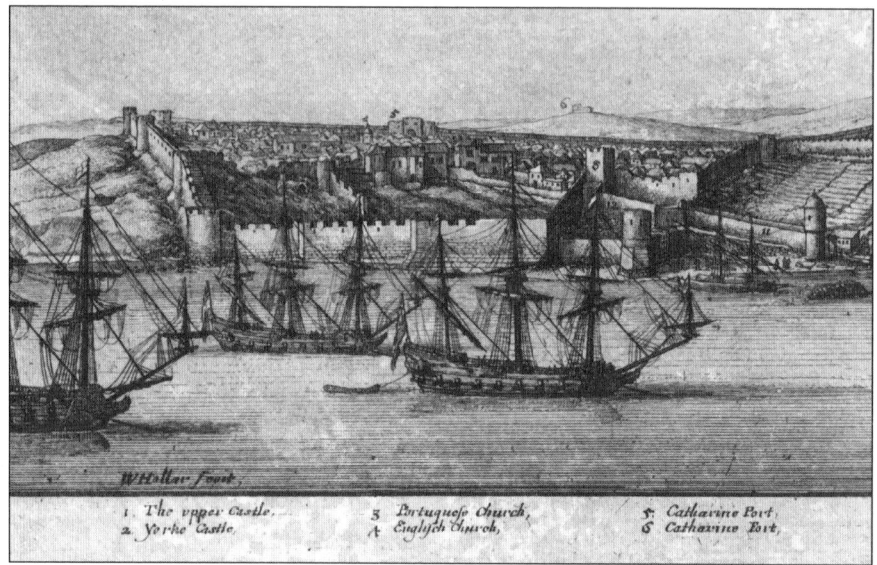

Tangier city from the bay. (Detail from 'Prospect of Tangier from the East' Wikimedia Thomas Fisher Rare Book Library from Univ of Toronto Wenceslaus Hollar Digital Collection)

Tangier York Castle and the citadel from the bay. (Detail from 'Prospect of Tangier from the East' Wikimedia Thomas Fisher Rare Book Library from Univ of Toronto Wenceslaus Hollar Digital Collection)

Introduction

Tangier is a narrative history of the English occupation of the city of Tangier, told through the experiences of characters who lived at the time.

The descriptions of life in Tangier, the locations and people, the details of military engagements and the regiments and personnel involved are all gleaned from the extensive collection of contemporary official documents and letters held in the National Archives, the British Library and the Bodleian.

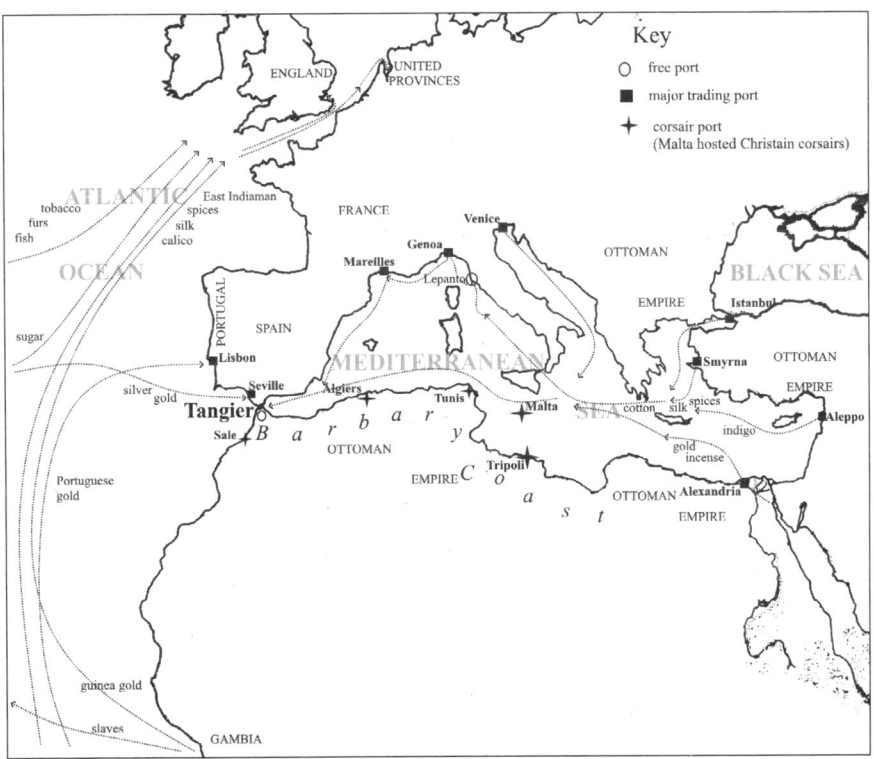

Tangier at the centre of seventeenth-century trade routes. (Author)

TANGIER: THE EARLIEST BATTLE HONOUR

Although every section of Tangier society contained a thorough mix of all British nationalities there was no such thing as 'British' at this time. However, the city's funding and governance were down to the English sovereign, it was known as English Tangier and as far as the Moors were concerned it was occupied by the English. For narrative convenience I sometimes refer to the army as 'the English' despite the fact is was frequently recruited in Ireland and Scotland.

I have tried to avoid common errors which have gained credibility through repetition, particularly on the internet. The timeline and almost all the incidents in the book follow the historical record closely as verified through original documents - the exceptions are a few of the more personal incidents which are fiction.

Tangier as a battle honour is the earliest battle shown on any British regimental colours. The actual award of the honours was not made until 1910.

Two regiments were awarded 'Tangier 1662–1680', both having been present for the whole of the period of fighting in Tangier:

> The Queen's descended from the 1st Tangier, and the
> Royal Dragoons, who can trace their origins to the Tangier Horse.

Three regiments trace their beginnings to regiments sent as reinforcements during the period known as the Siege of Tangier during 1680 and they were awarded the battle honour of 'Tangier 1680'.

> Coldstream Guards,
> Grenadier Guards, and the
> Royal Scots, previously Dumbartons Scots.

INTRODUCTION

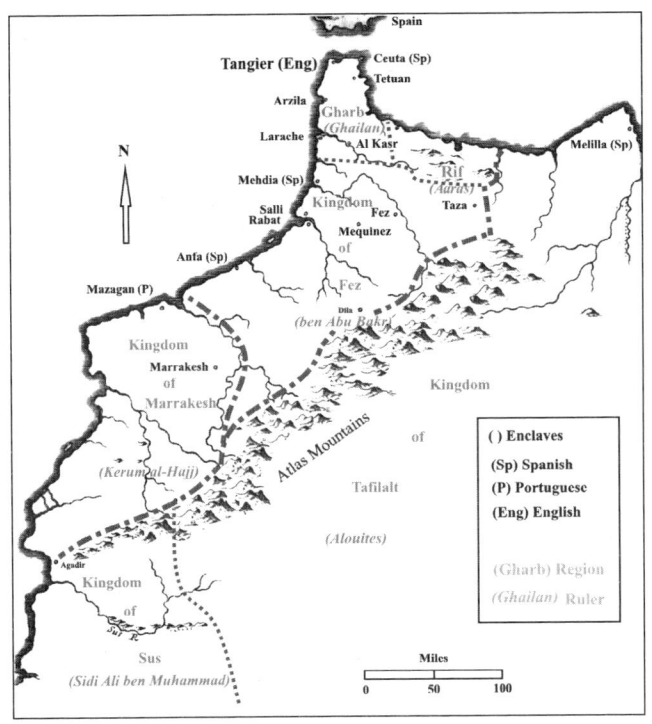

Morocco, 1660.
(Author)

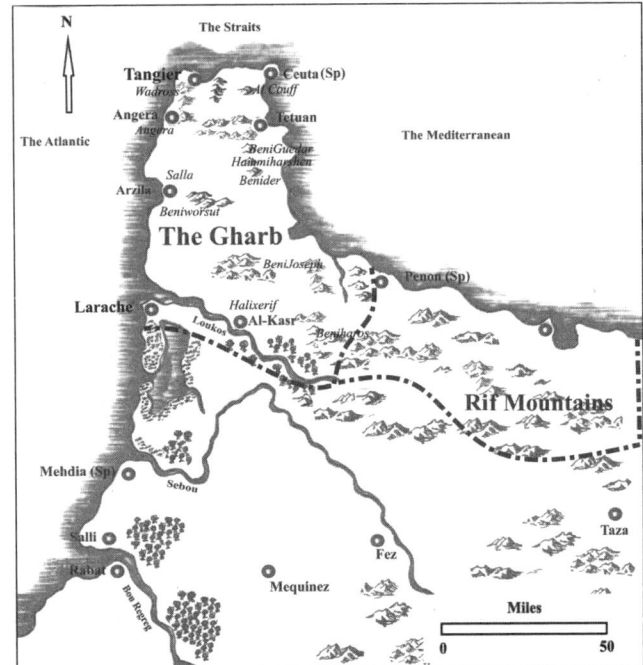

North Fez.
(Author)

TANGIER: THE EARLIEST BATTLE HONOUR

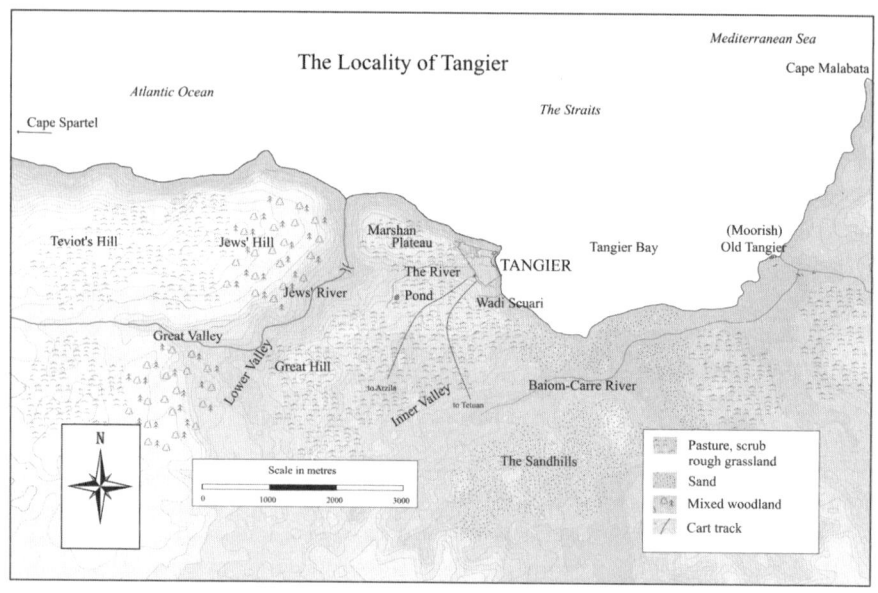

The locality of Tangier. (Author)

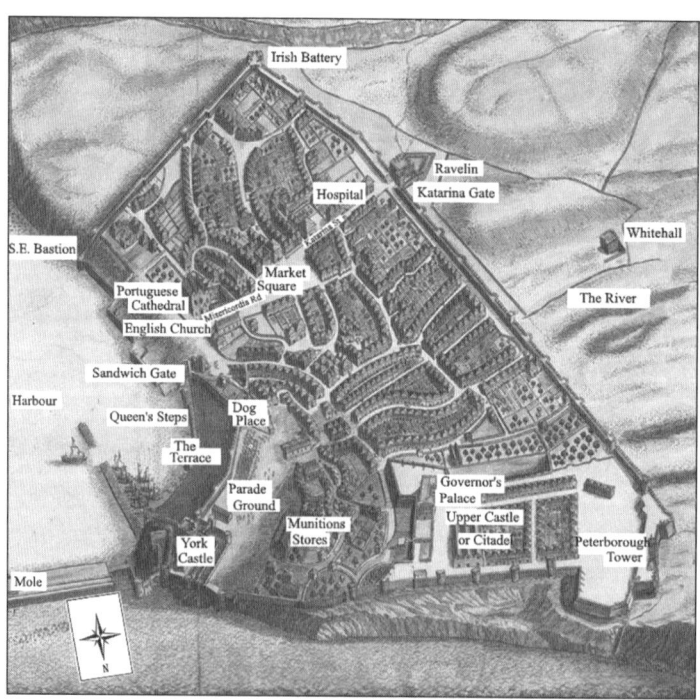

Tangier city locations. (Author's labels on 'The City of Tanger' (a section of map) John Ogilby, 1670; New York Public Library: Public Domain)

Prequel

14 January 1662

Tangier, Morocco

He deflected the first lance from his smart blue jacket with a sweep of his fancy cutlass and the second with the polished barrel of his expensive pistol; he swayed away from the third as it thrust towards his face, but the round shot from the harquebusier found its mark and forced a neat hole in his forehead on its way to his brain. A freshly sharpened shamshir scimitar wielded by a sun-tanned Moor sliced through his neck under the strap of his helmet, severing head from body before he hit the ground. The rash Aidill, commander of the Portuguese cavalry, had paid the ultimate price.

Why he had decided to take his troop out on a raid to steal cattle and abduct Moorish women was beyond comprehension. The English Earl had already offered to assume control of the town. The Portuguese had but a few weeks to wait, idling the time away secure within the city walls until the new garrison arrived, after which they could sail home to Lisbon and allow Tangier to become a series of anecdotes to amuse admirers at an endless round of dinner parties.

The raiding party was an aberration. Perhaps he was trying to impress the Earl of Sandwich riding at anchor in the bay. Maybe he sought more beef for the farewell ox roast, or more slave girls for his estate in the Portuguese countryside. Perhaps he wanted one more story to set the court ladies' hearts throbbing.

The Moorish lookout had seen him ride out of Katarina Gate; watched him lead the troop of blue coats alongside the dry moat outside the city walls; seen the breastplates glittering in the morning sun as they turned to ride along the bank of the bubbling river. He had counted a hundred and forty black hats with fluttering white feathers cross the ford. They were heading towards the besieging Moors encamped on the hills beyond Jews' River. The Portuguese must have seen Qaid Ghailan ride off with most of his men and thought to catch the depleted camp by surprise.

The lookout leapt onto his horse and set off to give warning. But when he turned to check the progress of the Portuguese cavalry he saw they had not crossed the bridge, they were following Jews' River up through the Great Valley. They were going inland towards the villages. They were after cattle.

As a Berber Hamut knew he could ride circles around the ponderous Portuguese cavalry. He had plenty of time to gather enough men to make these unbelievers regret their temerity in leaving the safety of their city to challenge the local men on their own ground. He galloped off to find the other pickets and make preparations.

Some hours later the Aidill and his troop reappeared on the grassy plateau at the head of the valley, corralling a herd of three or four hundred cattle, leading half a dozen strings of camels and driving several groups of wailing women in black shawls. It was a clear sunny winter day and after a successful foray they were almost within sight of Tangier. Less than an hour down the grassy valley and across the hillocks a relaxing evening of eating, drinking and telling tales awaited them.

A hundred Moorish lancers were also anticipating an evening of feasting and telling stories. Swathed in white, scarlet turbites covered with white scarves, camouflaged in the long silver grass, they laid beside their horses, perfectly still, muskets loaded and ready. Enraged by the insult of the raid, infuriated by the capture of their women, the warriors were desperate to exact revenge. They would take no prisoners, and they would kill the Aidill first.

They waited.

The Portuguese were spread over a wide area. Totally absorbed in controlling the animals, they had no idea they were riding in the midst of their enemy.

The Aidill was trying to hurry a string of reluctant veiled females along. Tied together, pleading to be released, they were stumbling over the rough ground. When the commander had unwittingly progressed to the middle of a small group of lancers and there was no chance of escape, the Moorish leader sprang up and gave an eagle cry.

PREQUEL

The half-dozen tribesmen around the Aidill roused their horses, swung themselves up into the saddle, raised their lances and struck. Instantly the whole plain seemed to erupt with screaming lancers.

Stunned by the sudden attack from all directions the Portuguese troopers were paralysed. Then, seeing the Aidill hacked to death and their colleagues being toppled, they panicked, abandoned the spoil and their comrades and kicked their steeds into headlong flight.

They offered no resistance as they rode for their lives. The triumphant Moors whooped and screamed, dug their spurs, fired their muskets and wielded lance or scimitar to attack the defenceless fleeing men.

17 January 1662

Something dragged at Edward Barlow's sleeve.

He flicked his wrist, drew his hand across his chest ready for a dismissive swipe and glared down.

Huge brown eyes crinkled up at him. A small hand offered a white blossom of welcome.

Edward looked at a young woman, head-to-toe in black, holding the child back by his shirt. She nodded. He accepted the sprig of aromatic flowers. He stroked the flies from the child's face, touched his cheek and smiled. A tear welled in the boy's eye.

'Su padre murió ayer,' the woman whispered.

'His father was killed by the Moors,' his companion said flatly. 'Now she's looking for a replacement. Move on Barlow, you're holding us up!'

'Us' was him and his mate – they were the last two of the cohort of more than a hundred seaman sweating their way up the steep slope of Rua de Misericordia. Edward Barlow, at nineteen years of age, was a young man of inexhaustible curiosity and infinite independence. On being told to 'hurry up' his natural inclination was to stop and look around. Gazing down over the waste ground to the city wall and the bay, he saw Admiral Sandwich's fleet, the five 'big ships' moored both ends to keep their guns facing the shore. At a single command Sandwich could send a broadside of near two hundred cannon balls thundering their way over the city into the Moors' camp, carrying a clear and deadly message that the English had arrived.

The admiral's offer of sending men ashore to strengthen the Portuguese garrison had originally been turned down, but the Governor's cavalry had suffered a defeat and he had now asked for assistance.

TANGIER: THE EARLIEST BATTLE HONOUR

Earlier that afternoon the ten volunteers from Barlow's ship had stepped from the longboat onto the dock in front of Tangier's medieval city walls. An immaculately uniformed Portuguese lieutenant had taken the list of names from the officer and without even bothering to count them sent the new recruits off with a weary-looking ensign in a tattered uniform. Their escort's smile was as bright as his buttons, but his hollow eyes, the cuts to his jacket and the tears in his breeches told of a recent fierce battle.

The little group of seamen had dumped their bags in a sheltered corner of the ruined castle's grounds and assembled to receive their weapons. As soon as they had donned their apostles of powder and shot, buckled their sword belts and grabbed their muskets, they were mustered with men from other ships and marched off through the town by their newly appointed colonel.

Now, walking up the main thoroughfare it seemed every single inhabitant of Tangier had turned out to welcome the English, or their guns, to be more accurate.

Edward smiled at the woman, shrugged and continued on his way past the solid red brickwork of the tall, typically rectangular Portuguese cathedral and into the market place full of waving, cheering people with beaming olivine faces. The city was built of brick and stone; the roofs were Spanish-style terracotta tiles; there was a convent, several chapels and a large cross in the market square. It was clearly a Mediterranean, Christian city, not a Barbary town of Muslims. Nonetheless, it seemed somehow a sad place, a neglected city, a city awaiting a saviour.

Only three years in the navy and here he was, hero come to save a city full of good Christian people from rape and pillage by Muslims. It was obvious from the state of the place that Tangier needed a new patron, not a Portugal in decline but a country in the ascendancy. England. But he wanted to see the faraway places spoken of by the old hands; his future was in exploring the world. He could not stay here, but others would.

18 January 1662

The whole city was in turmoil.

The young whore was one of three thousand Portuguese busily packing their belongings to leave Tangier. She checked the poignard in her boot, put all her savings into her money belt, tied her clothes and writing box in

PREQUEL

her bedding and dumped the bundle on the cart waiting in the street. She followed the slow procession through the alleyways to Misericordia.

The fleet in the bay would soon be sailing to Lisbon and Admiral Sandwich had offered free passage to Portugal. Governor Don Luis had been appointed specifically to hand the city over to the English, a task so distasteful to any self-respecting Portuguese that the previous Governor, whose family had been Governors of Tangier for three generations, had refused to do it. Being born and raised in the city, the young woman shared Don Luis' reluctance. He had been well bribed by the Queen Regent, but that made it no easier and he was determined not to relinquish Portuguese authority any earlier than the treaty mandated.

Unfortunately for him, most of his infantry had been shipped off to repel the Spanish invasion of their homeland and the remaining defenders, largely composed of several troops of cavalry, had paid dearly when they tried to steal cattle from the Moors. With the Aidill's death and half the Horse wiped out, the city was virtually defenceless, leaving the Don Luis no choice but to belatedly accept the English offer of reinforcements. The city's stubbornly closed gates had been thrown open for the townspeople to welcome the English sailors.

They might recognise the need for the invasion but with most of the Portuguese soldiers already gone, widows feared for their safety and Portuguese merchants, jealous of their wives and daughters, were determined to save them from the infamously debauched English. All the Portuguese were leaving at the first opportunity.

The quay was packed with people jostling to get into the boats ferrying people to the ships. Most of them gave the young woman a wide berth, considering her unclean in some way, but she held her head high. Her mother had died in childbirth; her father was dead or enslaved, her husband had been hacked to death by the Moors, but she did not rely on alms, she earned her own money. They failed to recognise the service she provided. She had given support and comfort to more poor suffering men than all of them put together.

She surveyed the women and children. What would they all do back in Portugal? The widows could look forward to a life of poverty and exclusion, and she was a widow. A boatload of sailors pulled up to the quay. She stood and stared at the fresh-faced boys leaping out of the cutter and lining up on the quay and they stared back at her. Amongst a crowd of women dressed in all-enclosing black, her red dress, revealing an eye-catching area of white bosom, stood out like a beacon.

TANGIER: THE EARLIEST BATTLE HONOUR

The brawny longshoreman leered at her, picked up her bundle and threw it into the rowboat of refugees.

The young sailors were wide-eyed and so young and virile. They would have money burning a hole in their pockets, money she would be happy to take off them. Money that would help her honour the vow she had made in the cathedral. The vow that seemed impossible to fulfil if she left Tangier.

She was going to Portugal to become a drudge to some poor labourer of a husband. What was she doing? She loved the freedom of life in Tangier.

The longshoreman spat on his hands and bent down to scoop her up.

She backed away. She looked up. The city walls enclosed maybe five hundred houses with a couple of thousand people crammed in; less than half an hour's walk all the way round. It was full of English sailors now the Portuguese had left. Soon there would be thousands of English soldiers and the merchants would return because there was good profit to be made. The surrounding country was fertile and – when they were not forced into war – the local villages were quite content to trade their cattle, corn and dates for fabrics and spices from European traders. There was even gold and silver from beyond the desert. She could earn well and live well.

There was a wild plot with a broken down house over by the city wall. Four hundred pieces of eight would buy the land and pay for the house to be rebuilt. As a home-owner she would soon find a suitable husband and spend her later years in modest comfort.

The longshoreman huffed.

She thought Tangier had a bright future under Portuguese rule, why should it not prosper equally under the English? The Tangier garrison had been a ready source of customers. Her rooms were decent and her Portuguese landlord occupied the rest of the house and watched over her, keeping roughnecks away. He charged only one piece of eight a month, or one English shilling a week, and took the rest in kind when his wife was out. With extra cash from selling information to the Governor, she had lived comfortably. Was there any reason the English would not value her hospitality services and the intelligence she could provide? The Jews, her go-betweens, were locals; the convent would remain, the Catholic priests had been granted permission to stay. Her physical and spiritual needs were well catered for in Tangier, what was to gain by leaving?

'We ain't got all day,' the longshoreman complained.

PREQUEL

No! She must continue her quest. She pointed to her possessions. He shrugged, and heaved her bundle back onto the jetty. Everyone around stared as if she were crazy.

She smiled and waved for a mule man to carry her worldly goods back to her lodging. She fought her way up the Queen's Steps against the flow of refugees.

She would stay and enjoy the freedom of Tangier.

19 January 1662

London, England

In the garret of his ten-room house at the palatial Navy Office terrace in Seething Lane, Samuel Pepys, Clerk of the Acts of the Navy, settled back in his chair to attend to his physical needs, holding the crystal goblet to the candle to admire the colour of the ruby liquid.

He splashed wine into his glass. Not yet thirty years of age and his career was progressing nicely. His acquaintance with two men of opposing dispositions – Downing, the ruthless political intriguer and Admiral Earl Sandwich, the honourable and influential military man and diplomat – was paying dividends, figuratively and literally.

Ah! The navy. The King was a keen yachtsman and saw the need for a strong navy. The Duke of York had been Lord High Admiral since the age of three and was dedicated to ensuring the English out-gunned the Dutch and ruled the waves. A large fleet to back up the forays of men like Sandwich, Robert Holmes and George Cocke would help guarantee the success of York's venture. As Pepys had told fellow diarist John Evelyn, 'Whoever controlled the oceans possessed the keys to the world itself.' Pepys' responsibilities would increase hugely and his ability to profit from his post as teller for the navy would make him a wealthy man.

Admiral Earl Sandwich had been at anchor in Tangier Bay for months patiently waiting to be relieved by Peterborough's army. Now, in January 1662, after so many delays the Tangier garrison of more than three thousand soldiers was on the high seas. Sandwich's man of business had informed him that Peterborough's great expedition – assembled at such cost – was finally on its way to Africa.

He swirled the liquid around and watched how it clung to the side of the glass. He spat the tobacco wad into the spittoon and took a first mouthful

TANGIER: THE EARLIEST BATTLE HONOUR

of his newly purchased wine to dispel the noxious taste; then spat that out. Pepys savoured the second mouthful of Malaga wine whilst considering the implications of the news.

King Charles' wedding arrangements (encouraged by the King of France to weaken Spain, and by the Duke of York to strengthen the Royal African Company) presented more opportunities for increasing Pepys' wealth. The acquisition of Tangier and Bombay as part of the dowry would require an enlarged navy to protect commerce and supply routes. The gold portion of the dowry of the Portuguese princess, Catherine of Braganza, and the promise of free trade with Brazil would greatly improve His Majesty's finances.

One look at his copy of his *Orbis Terrarum* map of the world told how important Tangier would be. Located on the Atlantic coast of North Africa and on the narrow Straits at the entrance to the Mediterranean, it was at the crossroads of all the major trade routes. Spanish galleons from South America, Dutch East Indiamen, Levantine traders in silks and spices; all sailed past Tangier. Whoever held Tangier controlled access to the Straits and would be the envy of France, Spain and the United Provinces.

Mediterranean trade was constricted by the damned ubiquitous corsairs. The frequently agreed peace treaties with Barbary States could never last because piracy was their main source of wealth and they could not afford to be at peace with more than one or two European countries at a time. It was purely a matter of which country maintained the most effective naval strength in the area at any given moment. Given a base amidst the corsairs of Barbary and the murderous Moriscos of Salli, the English navy could rid the seas of those predatory Muslim pirates who stole valuable cargoes and made slaves of thousands of innocent Christians!

Pepys was already well pleased with his decision to invest £200 in the Duke of York's Royal African Company. The group of adventurers held the monopoly on trade with Africa from Salli to the Cape of Good Hope; five thousand miles of the African west coast known to be awash with gold there for the taking. Fine profit could also be made from hides, redwood and ivory, and the vast continent might even prove a good source of slaves. He poured another drink.

Holmes had completed a successful voyage to the Gambia. The man was good for the African business and Pepys was glad for that. He had taken forts from the Dutch and, according to Captain Cocke, he had made such a good friendship with the King of Gambia that he had been given the choice

PREQUEL

of his hundred concubines to lie with. He had come back with ships full of Guinea gold and ivory – even if he had denied it and refused to declare anything for taxation! Holmes' friendship with the Duke of York made him above the law of the land, and Pepys had to accept the fact. The Duke of York was as ruthless as he was acquisitive and would ensure the Company turned a good profit for himself and the King. At the same time, he would be making a healthy return for Pepys.

Still, the man Holmes was a hothead, a more than competent fighter, rather inclined to criticise and too eager to resort to force, whether a personal duel or a full-scale battle. He would get himself into trouble before long, and Pepys would pretend sympathy, but be glad for it all the same, for he'd seen Holmes making eyes at his wife. He laughed to himself, picked up his lute and examined it; perchance the likeness of himself painted on the neck was not so bad as he first thought. He strummed at it absent-mindedly and thought of Tangier.

The King had great ambitions for the city. One James Wilson had ignited York's imagination with the thought of settling the whole countryside from Tangier to Gambia. Consequently, Governor Peterborough had been given a wide-ranging remit to conquer any locals who threatened the city and to continue the conquest throughout Fez and Marrakesh. Unfortunately, he had been granted a smaller military force than he had requested, in particular fewer Horse. Wisdom had it the terrain around Tangier was unsuitable for cavalry, and horses were expensive to maintain. As Tangier was a Crown possession, His Majesty would be in sole control without the need for recourse to Parliament. Oversight of such a venture would need a person of meticulous ways like himself. Pepys would let Sandwich know of his interest in serving on any committees the King might set up to oversee the new colony.

Three or four weeks' sail from England, Tangier would be a remote base for the navy and a convenient entrepôt for merchants to store and sell their goods from Africa, Turkish Levant, the Orient and the New World. Yes, Tangier was a worthy addition to the lands of an aspiring sea power.

Chapter 1

King and Colony

22 January 1662

Tangier, Morocco

The smartly presented Portuguese gun captain in fashionable sky blue coat and spotless black beaver hat put a hand on the fretted hilt of his cutlass and moved closer to the heavy culverin cannon.

His cheek twitching involuntarily, he watched a dozen scruffy sailors in worn slops and knitted woollen Monmouth caps take up position by the other guns in the battery. His one gun crew could only man one cannon; there was nothing to be done about the other four now in English hands.

The colonel had ordered Edward's cohort to the Torre Principal of the citadel to forestall any resistance to the takeover, and in similar scenes all around the city walls the English had quietly assumed control of almost all the artillery.

This morning, five days after Edward's coming ashore, the frigate *Norwich* had anchored in the bay bringing news of three thousand Spanish soldiers just across the narrow stretch of water. It seemed Spain was conspiring with the Moors to take Tangier before the long-delayed Governor Peterborough arrived with the English garrison. Lord Sandwich had instructed gunners from the fleet to help the depleted Portuguese garrison man the citadel cannon to repel any attack. Edward peered out across the Straits to Spanish Gibraltar. He could see no evidence of an army there, but he *had* noticed fully armed men in dull blue English navy slops gathering outside the storehouse and powder cellars in the old castle of Tangier and he could now see a party of his fellow seamen approaching the munitions stores deep under the walls of the citadel.

Word amongst the men was that the Portuguese garrison was unwilling to hand the town over to its new owners and Lord Sandwich had decided to take control of the key defensive positions. He had also ordered the sailors to take good care of all the artillery accoutrements, including the very gun mountings themselves, and watch over the water conduits and fountains.

Lord Sandwich appeared to be a keen supporter of Tangier and, never one to let the grass grow under his feet, already had rows of stables under construction to house the mounts of the hundred Horse they said were on their way from England, and had ordered plans to convert the dilapidated rooms of the Medieval castle into quarters for subalterns and any officers unable to lodge in the citadel housing. Tents had been erected on the wiry grass of the parade ground ready for the seamen, and more would be brought ashore to accommodate the infantry.

Whether there really were three thousand Spaniards poised to cross the Straits and try their luck against an English fleet and a well-positioned citadel Edward doubted. On the other hand, he had seen little evidence of the Portuguese military, despite the protestations of 'no room for the English'. All of the sentries on the walls were English; up until now few of the guns had been manned, the Portuguese cavalry had yet to make an appearance and the reported couple of hundred infantry had confined themselves to their quarters!

He turned to survey the rolling green hills of the countryside. Perfect peace, or so it seemed. It looked like good pasture land and distant hazy blue mountains fed a river running across the meadows and diving under the city wall before running through ancient pipes to feed the wells and conduits of the town and emerge into the bay. There were various stands of trees and even what he took to be orchards. But there were no houses outside the walls, no people taking a stroll in the countryside. The idyllic-looking scene belied the deadly truth. The batteries at the corners of the city walls, and the heavily fortified Katarina Gate with its triangular defensive ravelin, told of frequent attacks by their Moorish neighbours. Were the inhabitants of Tangier prisoners in their own city?

29 January 1662

He could not be certain.

He squinted and turned his head, shut his weaker eye.

He was known for his keen eyesight, often the one sent to the top of the mainmast to espy a corsair sail before it had a chance to make a run for safety. A week of rain had cleared the air for this winter sun, and from high on the Torre do Sino, the highest point of Tangier citadel, Edward could see several miles up the Atlantic coast of Spain towards Cadiz.

The distant dot could be a ship on the horizon or it could be a gull in the near distance coming to sample the eels in the shallows of Tangier Bay.

He brought both eyes to bear again. Were there more dots? He looked away at the clear blue of the Mediterranean, then back. Three, no four dots, and the first was bigger. Edward watched the tiny spots become vertical dashes. They kept formation; there must be a squadron at least.

The relief fleet bringing the new garrison of more than two thousand soldiers had departed the Downs off the south coast of England some weeks ago and, given favourable weather, might well be arriving. A goodly breeze was tugging at his sleeves and extending the red cross of Saint George's flag to its full length. If those ships had the same wind they could be in the Straits within the hour.

He ran down to tell the gun captain to signal the approach of ships with the usual double cannon shot, detailed another of the seamen to ensure the officers in the Medieval castle had heard and knew of the fleet – whether those approaching were friend or foe everyone needed to be on duty to welcome or repel. He stood watching until he was certain the ships were English, then ran along the city walls to Katarina Gate, shouting the news of the fleet's arrival.

Edward knew his time in Tangier was limited. He'd made the most of his two weeks to satisfy his curiosity about the place.

When named in a detail to scull out for supplies, he had looked back at the houses spread out on its hillside. The city was dominated by the old Medieval castle perched on the high rocky bluff at the north-west headland of the bay. From its square tower two castellated medieval walls spread out like arms to fold the city into their safe embrace. The nearer wall came down the hill to the sea, whence it curved around the bay for half a mile until it reached the round eastern tower. The farther wall stretched about a mile along the top of the ridge to Irish Battery before turning down to the sea as the east wall, meeting the first at the water's edge eastern tower.

Outside the east wall the green slope quickly turned to more broken terrain with scrub and sand dunes that somehow allowed a small river to reach the sea. Further on, the Moorish village of Old Tangier lay between a wider river and a high green hill, and beyond that the bay curved round to complete the semicircle.

TANGIER: THE EARLIEST BATTLE HONOUR

He had strolled around the whole circuit of the city walls in less than an hour, admiring the views from each tower. He had explored every street, wandered through the Jewish Quarter, poked his head into every one of the nine chapels and surveyed the convent. He had tried talking to the locals, but the few Portuguese women were jealously guarded by their men, who prevented any conversation. He had sampled the market produce; the bread was tasty, the grilled fish fresh and crispy. Poor though he was, he had sampled the beer at many of the drinking houses on Tavernos Street.

But it was not beer on his mind now. From Katarina Gate it was only a few minutes to the only accessible female in Tangier. In an alleyway off Bye Street, a beguiling Portuguese woman sat at a window. Red and yellow feathers in her hair with auburn ringlets cascading down over wide open sleeves bedecked with silken ribbons, the young woman's embroidered corsage overflowed with the most delightful alabaster bosom. She was as handsome as any of the young ladies he had seen in Lisbon. He walked that alleyway whenever he could, and every time he passed she invited him to share a jug of wine and spend time in her company. He had promised himself he would spend his winnings at dice on discovering whether she was as welcoming as she seemed.

Now it came to it he was full of doubts. Some of his crewmates had the pox and the treatment seemed as bad as the disease. It may be better to forgo the pleasure and be certain of avoiding judgement from above. But his mate said she was clean and he was experienced in these matters. He said she was worth the money as well. If he didn't take this chance he might never experience the pleasure. He loitered at the end of her street, trying to decide. This could well be his last chance.

***

She had seen lust in the eyes of the young English seaman.

He passed her window several times every day. She was certain he wanted to sample her delights, and she needed all the customers she could get since the Portuguese army had left, but no words of encouragement had succeeding in enticing him into her boudoir.

Until today.

Today she had worn her lucky black bodice, embroidered with bright red flowers. She stroked it. It was so soft. She could never have afforded to buy such a beautiful garment – it probably cost three or four pieces of eight

– but a ship's captain had given it her in payment. Pulled tight with scarlet laces, the shiny silk showed her figure off to its best advantage. Men could not resist those beautiful breasts.

The young seaman was obviously inexperienced and had paid top price. He would have become a regular but she knew he would be shipped off as soon as the new garrison arrived. Unless, maybe, she mused, she might persuade him to jump ship and join the army.

Her thoughts were interrupted by the gentle scrape of paper slipped under her door. Three rapid knocks on the shutters were followed by another three. She put a knife in the fire, then loosened her corset to allow her bosom to resume its natural position, breathed a sigh of relief, disentangled the last of the feathers from her hair and went to fetch the letter.

She slid the hot knife under the seal and unfolded the parchment. She picked up the candlestick and went upstairs to her tiny garret room, swung the shelf out on its hinge and positioned the support. Then she placed the tallow candle and the letter on the makeshift desk. She pulled the small hair box from under the bed, lifted the lid and took out the inkpot and quill. Reaching up onto the canopy of the four-poster, she grasped a sheet of paper, pulled the stool over and read the letter in the flickering light.

She had first contacted the Jews, well-known as go-betweens, a year ago when her cavalryman father had failed to return from a raid. They had agreed to make enquiries of her father's fate if she gathered information from her customers and became a contact in their network of spies. If her father were alive the Redemption Fathers might buy his release. The Spanish religious Order of Mercedarians had not been welcome in Portuguese Tangier and would be no more welcomed by the English but they had ransomed thousands of Europeans from Morocco over the years. The Jews told her that by Islamic law a slave should be sold for the original price paid by the owner, but in practice slaves fetched whatever price the owner considered their worth. They said they thought her father might fetch a hundred pieces of eight. It was a lot of money but she had vowed to dedicate her life to discovering her father's fate and buying his freedom if he were alive. She had negotiated an arrangement to sell intelligence to the Portuguese Governor's secretary, keeping the Jews sweet and making a small extra income. She was not sure it was right to now provide the English with intelligence; many Portuguese would consider it treason.

Rumour was Don Luis' wife was saying Portugal could not afford to maintain Tangier whilst trying to defend itself against the Spanish. She said giving up Tangier would clear the way for Queen Regent Luisa Maria to marry off her daughter, Catherine of Braganza, to the King of England, giving Portugal great influence in the court of England. If the queen of Portugal saw the English as friends, so be it; it was not her decision; surely the English Governor would be prepared to pay for intelligence about the activities of Ghailan, the Moorish warlord. It would be no more dangerous to supply information to the English Governor than to the Portuguese, and her arrangement with the Jews would continue. After a few moments' thought she flipped the inkwell lid, dipped the nib and started writing. Half an hour later she signed the letter 'James Wilson', dusted it with pounce, folded it over and sealed it as always, with a drop of red wax impressed with her fingerprint.

She threw on a shawl, slipped her poignard into her boot and stepped out into the darkness. The streets were busy with English soldiers wandering about, smoking and drinking, but there were plenty of Portuguese still preparing to leave and she felt safe enough. Jews' Lane was quiet and she quickly walked to the house with the large vine hanging over black shutters. She made sure there was no one about and slipped the note under the peeling blue door.

The next day Nathaniel Luke, secretary to Lord Peterborough, was reading a note from 'James Wilson' informing him of Ghailan's absence with most of the elite Moorish Horse and thousands of Moorish lancers on campaign against nearby Tetuan, which was resisting his call to arms. Tetuan would rather trade with Tangier than fight. Ghailan would offer Tangier peace only if the Governor agreed to cease trading with Tetuan. Ghailan's part-time warriors had no cannon and no siege equipment and stood little chance of defeating the city state.

'Wilson' proposed 'an arrangement' for the 'supply of future intelligence regarding your enemy.'

30 January 1662

The next day Edward Barlow stood on the crumbling battlements of the Medieval castle watching the ceremony and musing on life. The window woman had been all he had hoped for and he was well satisfied with his lot. He had made a good choice in volunteering to come ashore, but he was feeling a little sad for the Portuguese residents of the township. The woman had told him most of them had been in the city for many years and they did not wish to leave, but neither did they want to stay under the English. She was patient with him and she seemed to really like him. He might jump ship and stay to see her again, but she said everyone was going, except the priests, and of course the Jews who, he was learning through his travels, were able to adapt to any governance.

The regiments assembled below numbered more soldiers than Edward had ever seen in one place. They had marched up into the city and across to the fort with the casual efficiency of experienced troops, before dressing into four regiments. These were not callow recruits or pressed men, they were professional soldiers who wore their uniforms with careless formality and bore their weapons with the ease of familiarity. These were veterans, men to be feared.

A regiment of about a thousand stood behind a green flag, wearing red coats with breeches and hat ribbons of green. The second regiment, numbering somewhat more than the first, had blue linings and wore Monmouth caps. The other two regiments were about half the size of the first and he heard broad Irish accents floating up from them before they were brought to order. What an impressive sight!

***

Captain Palmes Fairborne of the Governor's Regiment of Tangier stood at the front of his company on the parade ground of the dilapidated old castle.

The three months since muster on Putney Heath had crept by at snail's pace. His brief courtship of Marjory and their hastily arranged marriage had helped pass the time, but the seemingly endless delays in sailing for Tangier were a constant irritation. It had been almost as if Peterborough did not want to take up his governorship. Palmes was desperate to assume his responsibilities, train his men and engage the enemy.

He was a soldier, and a soldier's job was to be as efficient as possible in confronting and defeating the foe. He had fought at Candia, earning the praise of his colonel, and been promoted to captain. His burning ambition now was to prove himself against the Moors and gain further promotions. His new Commander-in-chief, Governor Peterborough, had marched them up to this parade ground to stand in the midday sun whilst he received the trappings of power. The ceremony was necessary, but in truth they should have landed the day before.

TANGIER: THE EARLIEST BATTLE HONOUR

The fool of a Portuguese Governor, Don Luis, all in silk and feathers like a character from a court play, was presenting Peterborough with a beautiful horse with a richly tooled saddle, a jewelled scimitar, finely crafted silver spurs and a ferocious-looking lance. Palmes shifted his weight from one foot to the other. He had seen no evidence that Peterborough could ride a horse in anger, let alone wield a lance at the same time! He knew the Earl had managed to get himself wounded and defeated at least twice, but was unaware of any successful battles. Hopefully he could at least manage the huge iron keys of the town handed over with a great flourish to end the ceremony.

Apparently there was little accommodation in the town and Admiral Sandwich had arranged for the medieval Castelo Novo to be renamed York Castle and prepared for the new garrison. It was as well someone was competent at organising; just a pity Peterborough was Governor rather than Sandwich. At least they were ashore now and hopefully they could pack the Portuguese off and find decent accommodation for him and his wife and billets for his company.

Palmes was apprehensive about how three thousand men of different religious convictions, differing nationalities and opposing views on sovereignty and parliamentary rights, who not so long ago had fought on opposite sides of fierce conflicts, would manage to live together cheek by jowl. The thousand men of the Governor's Regiment were largely veterans disbanded from Cromwell's fiercely Protestant New Model Army and Harley's Regiment had been part of Cromwell's expeditionary force sent to help eject the Spanish from the Low Countries, whilst the two Irish regiments, largely composed of Catholics, had been part of Charles II's Royalist Army fighting alongside the Spaniards.

Four regiments totalling three thousand men who, if they were not busy fighting a common enemy would be cutting each other's throats. Here they were in English Tangier with a hundred Horse, troopers of higher breeding who considered themselves superior to any other military men, and eighty-odd Portuguese cavalry not yet assembled.

Palmes' major had told him Sandwich had already purchased several houses and suggested they should all be thinking of something similar. As soon as the parade had been dismissed, Palmes settled his men in their temporary quarters before finding a Portuguese cavalry officer to walk him round the town. The officer related how a few days earlier their Aidill had led them out on a suicidal raid that had resulted in the loss of a dozen men of quality and more than fifty experienced troopers. He thought a few of the heavy cavalry unit might be prepared to stay on and work with the English, but most would want to leave the scene of such a shocking defeat.

Outside the castle grounds they were immediately immersed in Babel. The whole place was a seething mass of women enshrouded head to toe in black, desperately emptying their houses onto handcarts whilst chattering to their neighbours and shouting at the excited flock of children rampaging everywhere. The street was stacked with furniture; chests were being stuffed with drapes and curtains, boxes overflowed with cooking utensils and all manner of household objects. Lord Sandwich had announced free passage to Lisbon and the merchants and their families were already loaded onto the English ships.

The frantic widows hastily packing did not trust the English sailors. Now a Portuguese merchantman had offered passage to the first two hundred evacuees to present themselves on the quay with their belongings, so this chaos was to be expected, but what was not expected was refugees prising window frames from their houses and taking the doors off their hinges. Those leaving were clearly determined to take everything that was not nailed down, and a good deal of that which was.

Weaving through the melee, Palmes and his escort walked up the steep cobbled roadway past the cathedral to the market square, thronging with people, even busier than the streets through which they had struggled. From there they could see all the way up Katarina Street to the tower of Katarina Gate, but they took a left turn and walked towards what appeared to be another gateway in the south wall. On closer inspection Palmes saw the archway was walled up. The officer explained the Portuguese tradition that gates through which a general led his troops to defeat were permanently sealed. As they followed the city wall to a secluded area with large houses and extensive gardens, Palmes wondered how many gates would be walled up by the English.

All the commissioned officers were commandeering houses for purchase or rent and in this corner of Tangier away from the bustle of the crowded streets Palmes had discovered the ideal location for his family house.

London, England

Extended families were a godsend; Pepys' cousin, Lord Sandwich, had given him priceless advice, helped him acquire his place in the Admiralty and continued to sponsor him.

TANGIER: THE EARLIEST BATTLE HONOUR

Charles II had depended upon *his* cousin, Louis XIV of France, for many years in exile. Unfortunately, ten years living off other people's goodwill had left their mark on the King and his brother, His Highness the Duke of York. Now, with little warning, they had wealth beyond dreams; but they did not seem to realise that they had obligations to match.

Whilst the King appeared content to devise ways to squander his income creating pleasurable opportunities for his own enjoyment, the Duke of York seemed more inclined to invest his time and gold in trading companies for his own profit.

A group of merchants had proposed an independent Morocco Company, which would build its own forts and arm its own ships, but luckily the Duke of York was keen to keep the trade and the navy under his own control and he and Sandwich had persuaded His Majesty to fund a Crown colony. Sandwich had shown Pepys a copy of the King's Commission for Peterborough, which began:

> We intend forthwith to settle and secure our City Of Tangers and the territories and Dominions adjacent in or near the Coasts of Barbary or the Kingdoms of Sus, Fez, and Morocco, some or one of them in the continent of Africa. And for that purpose have resolved by and with the advice of our Privy Councell forthwith to raise, drawe forth and Transport thither such forces of Horse and Foot as we shall judge necessary ... We appoint you the said Henry Earl of Peterburgh Governor-General of all forces, both Horse and Foot ... which are or shall remain or be drawn into our city of tangier or any other of our Dominions or territories in or near the said kingdoms of Sus, Fez, and Morocco, and all forts Cities or castles or other partes and places whatsoever which by your conduct and successes shall be reduced to our obedience and subjection.

Peterborough was empowered to arm, train, conduct and lead out the natives and other inhabitants 'to defend our said city of Tangier ... and then to fight, kill, slay and subdue to our obedience and to invade surprize and reduce such towns forts castles and countries as shall declare or maintain any hostility against us ... and to possess and strengthen them with forts and garrisons ...'

KING AND COLONY

To 'settle and secure our City Of Tangers and the territories and Dominions' was a huge undertaking and the military establishment of Tangier had been set at two regiments of a thousand men raised in England, and two regiments of five hundred shipped from Dunkirk.

Getting these hardened soldiers far away from England was a worthy end in itself, but whether His Majesty had the financial means to maintain them was uncertain. If the city were, as declared, a free city little would be raised from taxes and the anticipated 'confiscations, prizes, goods and merchandises condemned by a Court of Admiralty' would have to materialise quickly, along with burgeoning trade to generate income from mooring fees and storage charges, or Treasurer Povey would be hard pressed to find the cash to maintain such a garrison.

Given these wide-ranging expectations, Pepys had privately expressed concern to Sandwich that Peterborough might not be the best candidate for Governor. He was a royalist to the last drop of blood and it was clear the Duke of York wished to reward that loyalty, but he had not proved himself a successful soldier, nor was he a man of great imagination or energy. He did not appear the sort of person to follow through on the King's declared intent 'to fight, kill, slay'.

Chapter 2

King and Warlord

February 1662

Tangier, Morocco

Palmes, still awaiting his first taste of action against the enemy, had been summoned to yet another meeting. All the commissioned officers were gathered in what he took to be the ballroom of the Governor's Palace, holding their wine glasses ready for a loyal toast. At length Peterborough stood on the dais, held up His Majesty's Declaration so all could witness the King's seal and solemnly read it out to the assembled gentlemen.

His Majesty's commission gave Peterborough permission to make unremitting war on anyone who threatened the city, and to occupy and annex any towns or lands necessary for the security of Tangier. In short, the army was there to defeat anyone who threatened them, it mattered not whether Turk, corsair or Spaniard; and to conquer lands. Just as English settlers were colonising Virginia and Pennsylvania in the New World, so they would colonise Africa. Palmes nodded in agreement.

Given such a free hand, it seemed strange for Peterborough to be sending gifts to the petty chiefs of each of the neighbouring towns, and even more so to Ghailan, warlord of a few tribes of Moors, who was trying to impress by displaying hordes of ill-disciplined horsemen riding the bounds outside the city walls. A few rounds of grapeshot would soon teach them who was in charge.

Palmes had learned something of Muslim fighting ways in Candia. If a Christian occupier gave gifts to a Muslim overlord, Islam translated it as payment for occupying Muslim territory. It made it acceptable for the Christian to be there, but he was acknowledging the overlord's right to set terms and eject the Christian whenever he wished. It could be a pragmatic way for the Muslim to accept Christian occupation, but it did make the whole arrangement somewhat fragile. Either way, it was done and the occupation was a fact.

For Palmes, as for many of the officers and soldiers, it was a new beginning. Not quite a Promised Land of milk and honey, but a fertile land full of the King's promise.

At last a favourable wind had permitted Sandwich to head for Lisbon to transport Catherine of Braganza, future Queen of England, to meet Charles II, her promised husband and the promised saviour of her father's country. Before he had left, the admiral had overseen the evacuation of almost all three thousand Portuguese, mainly women and children, the menfolk having been buried there or departed before the English arrival. Unfortunately, those leaving had taken everything except the stone walls and roof tiles. No wood remained anywhere, no cooking utensils, no beds or straw. The new arrivals were at the mercy of the environment. They would have to make do with what they could forage locally or buy from the Moroccans, or the Spanish across the Straits. This was not an auspicious start to their new life.

Luckily Palmes' wife Marjory had come with a small settlement, and he had some savings. He was not wealthy, but he had enough to negotiate credit with one of the merchants collecting orders for a trip to Cadiz, and could contract for enough timber to refit the house with joists and floors, windows and doors. His wife was a practical woman who would be able to oversee the work whilst Palmes was exercising his men.

Sandwich was a wise man and *he* was investing in the future of Tangier. It was a new dawn; Tangier was a city about to be reborn under English rule. It was a God-given opportunity for Palmes to make his fortune by buying property in Tangier and doing all he could to enthuse the troops and defeat the Moors.

May 1662

From the hillside a Moorish Almocaden brushed a fly away and narrowed his eyes to study Tangier. Sensing its rider's impatience, his horse shifted its stance.

Hamut had helped the Almocaden plan this encounter. Hamut knew the Christian invaders had orders to conquer anyone who challenged their occupation of Tangier. As if the Moroccans could be subjugated by a few pork-eating men in fancy red coats and pig-leather shoes! He would teach

TANGIER: THE EARLIEST BATTLE HONOUR

these interlopers to stay behind their crumbling walls until the united armies of Allah deigned to eject them from their enclave and expunge the insult to Islam.

Ghailan was a religious leader, a warrior of Allah, following Muhammad. He had called the tribes to unite against the Nazarani Christians. Ben Abu Bakr had led Fez in its revolt against faraway Marrakesh, but he was a blind old Holy man living in a monastery, incapable of holding what he had won.

The tribes in the north of Fez, in the mountains of Rif and the hills of the Gharb, were fiercely independent. Every city had its own Qaid governor, every cavila district had its Almocaden; they had asserted their autonomy by refusing to pay taxes. Ghailan did not demand high taxes; he did not oppress the people. He had killed Ben Abu Bakr's local governor, married into the families of Al-Kasr, Arzila and Angera. He trained his army of more than ten thousand well and led them courageously; he had proved himself an able warrior of the one true God and his men would willingly die for their cause.

The thirty cavilas had won their freedom but anarchy did not have the strength that came from uniting in Allah. The Portuguese, the Spanish and now the English had invaded their land; places that had been Muslim for centuries were overrun by Christians. One tribe, one city, one cavila at a time Ghailan was uniting the Gharb. Tetuan would be next – a large cavila with ten thousand fighting men, it had refused to send men to join Ghailan. He had gone to persuade it. With warlord Ghailan two days' journey away besieging Tetuan, the Moors remaining at Tangier were determined to keep the English busy.

Here under the cloudless sky outside Tangier, hundreds of Moorish skirmishers had advanced along the lush valleys and down the green hillsides, from bush to bush, rock to rock, gully to gully, until they were within range. At the signal from their leader they had broken cover and fired at the city walls, waved their weapons, shouted insults and taunted the sentinels. Now they kept up sporadic fire and awaited a response.

The English were becoming bolder by the day. They regularly foraged beyond the agreed limits and it was time they were taught to respect the terms of the ceasefire. They had shown their impulsive nature a few weeks earlier. One of their sergeants had taken a small group of men reconnoitring beyond cannon range without Horse for support. Courageous they called him. With his whole group lying dead in the grass, 'foolish' might be a better description. They had even named a hill after him, 'Baker's Folly'. If he could be so easily ambushed, perhaps his brothers in arms were equally naive.

Today the Almocaden would try to trick the English with the oldest of all strategies.

They did not have long to wait.

The Tangier city gates opened and a line of redcoats emerged. Hamut counted five hundred musketeers as they emerged from the gate and lined up in ranks. With the blue of their breeches and stockings matching their battle flag, they looked an imposing sight.

As soon as the men were in position, the lieutenant ordered a first volley, quickly followed by a second. The drummers beat the advance and the captains urged their companies forward. Despite fierce fire from the Moorish skirmishers, the Englishmen made good ground before forming up again, presenting arms and firing more volleys. Under such orderly and sustained firepower, the Moors broke and ran into a shallow valley. Harley's Regiment cheered and charged after them.

The general of the Moorish lancers sent Hamut to monitor the English advance.

Almost invisible, riding below the ridges, keeping to the shrubs with their fresh green leaves of spring, Hamut tracked the skirmishers' retreat. Every hundred paces the Moors took cover. The crackle of muskets and puffs of smoke brought the English to a halt and they formed up under the merciless African sun to return fire. The tribesmen scrambled off again; the redcoats cheered and the pursuit resumed; there was no doubt the skirmishers were in retreat.

Before long they were some way up the valley, out of sight of the city guns. The heat of the day and the rising ground were beginning to take their toll and the redcoat advance was losing its momentum, but their obvious success reinforced their enthusiasm and they continued forward, oblivious to the ebbing of their strength. At last, far from the city, with his men at the limit of their endurance and running short of ammunition, the lieutenant gave the order for the drums to beat the retreat and the exhausted soldiers began the trek back to Tangier.

With a smile of satisfaction, Hamut dug his spurs into his horse's flank, sped to the hilltop and fired his English musketoon. The Moorish general's call of 'Allahu Akbar' echoed around the hills. Waving his lance high over his head, he charged down to join his men in the attack.

The retreating infantrymen heard the familiar sound of the Muslim battle cry 'God is great!' Their stomachs tightened. They had been tricked into

TANGIER: THE EARLIEST BATTLE HONOUR

an ambush. A swarm of Moorish riders appeared on the valley slopes and swooped down to encircle them. The attackers had become the attacked.

Trying to face their men in all directions at once, the captains did their best to organise an orderly withdrawal, but with few pikemen and little ammunition they had to rely on sporadic musket-fire to keep the whooping Moorish lancers at a distance.

The retreat was long and slow, a far cry from their victorious advance. The continuous harassment of the riders, and the musket-fire from skirmishers they had previously been pursuing, took their toll. It was impossible to carry their injured comrades whilst defending themselves and anyone who could not walk was left on the battlefield to be carried off into slavery by the triumphant horsemen.

Step by step, the redcoats fought their way back to the desperately needed cover of cannon fire from Katarina Gate and the Irish Battery.

By the time the Moorish general called his men off, Hamut had personally shot two non-believers and skewered another with his lance. The simplest of all ambushes, attack and run away, had seen three hundred redcoats killed or captured.

***

Palmes shook his head, yanked the brim of his hat down to hide his disgust and stomped down the tower of Katarina Gate. The bedraggled men dribbling in the gate were thoroughly drained and utterly beaten. But more than anything, they were angry.

Palmes followed them to the hospital. In truth it was a house, chosen for its thick stone walls and small windows that kept the heat out, but made for a depressingly dark place to be avoided if at all possible. He passed the least seriously injured – men with minor cuts and lead shot in their extremities – and entered the room for urgent cases. These men had been hacked by scimitars and suffered severed limbs or head and torso wounds – men waiting patiently despite their pain and fear. He had walked past more than a hundred wounded, suffering men before he came to the most serious cases. Half a dozen Catholic Dominicans were holding rosaries and offering alternative ministrations to the Protestant chaplains moving amongst those whose wounds were likely to prove mortal as they waited for their turn on the operating table. Palmes' reflection on the tragedy of men suffering for the stupidity of their officer was interrupted by the uncontrollable scream of agony as a surgeon sawed through a leg without anaesthetic. Palmes picked the wooden peg from the floor and replaced it between the man's teeth, held his hand and looked into his eyes. The mutilated man clamped his jaws onto the peg, gave a watery smile and breathed his last.

Back in his house, Palmes slammed the door behind him, jammed his hat onto the peg, kicked a chair round and slumped into the seat. Marjory came running into the room and Palmes poured out his anger.

How *anyone* could fall for such a well-known ploy was beyond knowing.

Despite the ceasefire agreement, the Moors had irritated Peterborough by sending skirmishers against those who ventured far outside the city walls. The Governor had responded by regularly marching a large force beyond the agreed lines, but only after careful reconnaissance.

A few weeks earlier, Baker's inexperience and blind faith in the treaty with the Moors had got his men killed at Baker's Folly. It was immediately clear that Ghailan thought Peterborough had broken the treaty. Since Baker's murder everyone was aware they were in a state of undeclared war, if not outright warfare. It was apparent Ghailan had agreed peace only to gain breathing space to decamp with his main army to subdue other towns, without accepting the right of armed Christians to occupy Muslim land.

Major Fiennes was a hothead. He had not listened to the wisdom of the Portuguese cavalrymen. They knew it was suicide for infantry to venture beyond direct cannon range of the walls. They would never have sent companies of Foot out without sufficient pikemen to ward off an attack, and a troop of Horse within shouting distance to see the enemy lancers off. Major indeed! Peterborough should court martial him for losing three hundred irreplaceable veterans.

And what was Peterborough's reaction? Was he going to send out a proper army to punish Ghailan? Was he looking to give the enemy a beating and restore the morale of his fighting men? Not at all! He was holed up in his citadel on the top of the hill. When Palmes had asked him what they were going to do he had ordered everyone to remain in the city and rely on supplies coming in by sea.

How were they to colonise Africa if they sat on their arses and played cards all day, hoping Ghailan would not attack?

Peterborough was an incompetent. They said he was a favourite of the Duke of York, a closet follower of the Roman faith. Palmes could see no other reason why he would be tolerated. He should be replaced immediately. Put Sandwich in. He was not one to be bullied and played for a fool!

TANGIER: THE EARLIEST BATTLE HONOUR

It was rumoured the King had written to Ghailan in the belief he was some sort of sovereign, because Peterborough had told him as much. It was common knowledge the Moor was a warlord, leader of a few small cavilas or counties with an army of ten thousand part-time militiamen. He was merely a tribal leader forever squabbling with other tribes. The garrison should be taking the attack to *him* – demanding their own terms, establishing territorial boundaries and offering lucrative trade to the nearby villages and townships.

What were they doing? Cowering behind the city walls?

Luckily it was also rumoured that Peterborough was about to escape to England.

June 1662

Tangier, Morocco

It was several weeks since half her customers had gone missing after that fool Fiennes had led his disastrous attack. Even she could have warned him it was a trap. Ghailan had used the same tactics against the Portuguese; secrete your Foot and Lancers in the grass and bushes, send a few skirmishers to attack and run away, ambush the soldiers who advanced too far. Simple! How stupid could the English be?

Her Portuguese officer customers used to say Ghailan's ambition was not to take Tangier, he wanted the foreigners to buy peace with weapons and powder he could use to extend his territory beyond the Gharb. His dream was to be King of the whole of Fez, the most fertile half of Morocco north of the Atlas Mountains.

At least her most frequent customer was still here, the one who had christened her Dover 'in honour of her two white cliffs' he said. The English name had stuck and that was how she was known, so much more respectful than 'the whore'.

But even through the noisy activities of the enthusiastic captain she thought she had heard … she turned her head on the pillow and strained to listen …. yes, there again, another three rapid knocks.

A while later she smoothed her favourite pink underskirt and left him to get dressed. Downstairs she scooped up the letter and hid it behind the painting of Saint Katarina. Then, carrying two glasses of Malbec, returned to help him with his buttons. She was careful not to show her impatience, paying him the same attention as usual and not stinting his time.

KING AND WARLORD

Within minutes of him leaving she was at her desk carefully transcribing the note she had received.

Her informant said since Tangier had ceased trade with Tetuan that cavila had agreed peace terms with Ghailan without being defeated. Ghailan was now off to attack Salli, 'which he hath in his imagination swallowed already' as her informant wrote, but 'did not adventure to take possession until he had secured peace with Tangier.'

She had already enlisted a friend of the Governor's secretary as a customer and had heard about the English King writing to Ghailan thinking the Moor was a King. She would do her best to persuade the governor that Ghailan was merely warlord of a few cavilas, fully occupied in trying to keep them under control. In Ghailan's absence her Jewish contacts could establish communication with the Anglophile Governor of Tetuan.

Before the next hour had struck on the town clock she had slipped 'JW's' latest missive under the blue door in Jew's Lane, confident her contact would deliver it to Nathaniel Luke that night, and the secretary would forward it to the Governor, who had agreed to pay two pieces of eight for every letter.

On the way back she saw a group of Spanish merchants in animated conversation drinking outside the Boar Tavern. Hoping to attract a customer, she sat at a nearby table and ordered a glass of wine. She overheard the men complaining about the Duke of Medina's new decree banning trade between Spain and Tangier, and discussing ways of avoiding his enforcers whilst continuing to sail their produce across the Straits in their small 'barca longa' sailboats.

Dover sensed an opportunity. If Spain were upset with the English occupation of Tangier, this Duke might be willing to pay for information about smugglers. On the other hand, she would not want to stop cheap wine and food coming across from Spain. Intelligence about the garrison would be more valuable, but it would be dangerous, and she would not want to betray Tangier. Pity, she could do with the money. She drank the wine down.

Meandering through the streets, memories came flooding back of her father playing hide and seek amongst the vines. She hoped he was not suffering too badly. It would be wonderful if only she could bring him back. She needed more pieces of eight.

As soon as she got home she set to work scribing an account of Lord Sandwich busily wading on the seashore rocks and rowing about in the bay with a pole and sounding lead. She wrote that she had seen people wielding surveying equipment and sighting glasses busily walking the city walls and even venturing outside the city with a man in a dark blue velvet outfit. The man had a slight limp and carried scars on his face, but he seemed to be a man of some importance. Some said he was from Sweden, others declared he was from Dunkirk in a country called Flanders. She added that she would endeavour to discover more of what was going on, but needed a supply of pieces of eight to buy beer and wine to loosen men's tongues. She checked there was no one downstairs, then signed it JW, addressed it simply to 'Medina', sealed it and slipped her shoe off to imprint the black wax with her big toe.

She replaced her shoe, threw on a shawl and walked back to Rua de Tavernos, where she came to an arrangement with the Spanish merchants to carry letters across the Straits.

July 1662

London, England

The Tangier garrison was only six months into its occupation and already Peterborough was back in England complaining to Pepys and the commissioners that he did not have enough men.

Settled comfortably in his office at the Navy Office off Tower Hill in London, Pepys was pleased with his foresight in having the ceiling-high window included in the area partitioned for his own use. Despite looking out on tall apartments, the light was good and on a warm summer day such as this he could open the top to enjoy a breath of fresh air.

The month he had spent arranging the bookcases and organising the shelves and cupboards had been well spent. Since he had given up wine and the theatre he had spent more time at work, more time carving out a career. He would make this disputed role of Clerk of the Acts to the Navy all it should be. He had begun by drilling a small hole in the panel behind his seat in his private office so he could observe everyone in the main office and have oversight of every order, contract and warrant, every letter, order and command from the Lord High Admiral and the Admiralty commissioners. He would discover how the navy worked and he would learn multiplication and accounting procedures. He would make himself indispensable.

In closest confidence, Sandwich had told Pepys of the King's desire to sell Dunkirk to France. Charles wanted to save the £120,000 a year expense of maintaining the garrison and thought he could gain as much as £500,000 for the sale as well as ensuring a friendly relationship with Louis XIV. Abandoning Dunkirk would not be popular with Protestants, but Sandwich believed they would be better served by a solvent England with a strong navy rather than a bankrupt country with no resources.

At the same time, Pepys had learned something of Tangier. The Portuguese Queen Regent may have been too clever for the gullible Charles; offloading two liabilities – a princess with few prospects and a vulnerable city – while gaining England as a powerful ally against Spain.

Her ambassador had approached His Majesty through General Monck. He held considerable sway as the person who had enabled Charles to return as King. Monck had been persuaded that Tangier was the key to Mediterranean trade and, with Bombay and the offer of free trade with Brazil and the East Indies, would enrich the country and His Majesty. The addition of half a million in gold was the lure that would catch the King's eye.

The clause in the marriage agreement obliging the King to send troops to defend Portugal against Spain provided an opportunity to be rid of thousands of New Model Army veterans of dubious loyalty to the Crown, whilst having their wages paid by a foreign country.

The King would have his Catholic princess, gain territories abroad and rid himself of an unwanted army. The deal had been done and English Tangier was a reality. Now the King had to give Peterborough a backbone and send him back to Tangier as soon as possible to get on with his job. The Portuguese had held it with far fewer than Peterborough's current garrison.

November 1662

Tangier, Morocco

Charles' acquisition of Tangier had come at the perfect time for Palmes. He had fought the Turks in Candia and was confident he could prove himself in Barbary.

Even in defence Palmes knew soldiers should not be confined to garrison duties; an army needed opportunities to go on the offensive, to take the attack to the enemy.

He was pleased Sandwich had sent his trusted fire-master, who had set to work swiftly and proved himself a worthy engineer. In his signature blue velvet coat, Beckman, the Swedish military engineer and fire-master, proudly displayed his maps, which covered the huge oak table in the meeting room of the Governor's Palace. He had surveyed the land around Tangier and drawn up plans to strengthen the city walls to provide more gun platforms and – most encouraging to Palmes – a ring of forts to secure an outer perimeter of wide, deep ditches, or entrenchments, enclosing sufficient land to feed cattle and provide fodder for the horses.

Peterborough had left for England a second time; ten months in post and already three of those spent in England! Hopefully this was a sign he did not intend to remain as Governor. At least while he was in England he might persuade His Majesty to pay for the extensive works Beckman had planned.

November 1662

London, England

Pepys would not want *his* finances controlled by the King.

He had left the Admiralty early and walked to the Globe to celebrate news of his appointment to the Committee for the Affairs of Tangier. He poured a glass of Bordeaux and sat eyeing the serving maid and contemplating what the future might bring.

It was true a King should be able to appear splendid and reflect the glory of his country, but Charles was proving incapable of disposing of his revenues wisely. Six months into his marriage and nearly a year into his tenure of Tangier he was allocating vast amounts of money to his family and mistresses, rewarding his supporters and generally gifting money for no useful purpose. Unfortunately he was also proving to be a poor deal-maker; impetuous and disinterested, but at last he had done what Sandwich had been pressing on him and set up a committee to deal with Tangier.

Lord Sandwich, Pepys' sponsor, had promised to get him appointed to the new committee; he would be small fry in the presence of His Highness the Duke of York and the other worthies, but he would listen carefully and hope to impress.

The King's marriage settlement promised a dowry of two million Portuguese crowns, worth nearly two years of Royal household expenditure, and he had agreed the sale of Dunkirk to France for £400,000, bringing him nearly as much again. Getting rid of Dunkirk would save him £120,000 a year on garrison costs. Even if Tangier cost £70,000 a year, his net savings would be £40,000 or £50,000.

Unfortunately, the King's dowry, which had been expected in money, jewels, sugars or other merchandises, had not materialised. The Conde da Ponte had been sent to the Earl of Sandwich with Bills of Exchange in place of gold, and even those were for only a fraction of the promised amount. Three weeks of haggling proved fruitless and Sandwich had eventually accepted what was being offered.

Now the Portuguese Queen Regent was calling on His Majesty to honour the wedding settlement clause obliging the King to pay for raising, equipping and transporting 3,000 men to assist Portugal in their struggle for independence from Spain. In addition the Portuguese were asking Charles to declare war on Spain, meaning England would continue to pay those English regiments. Add the cost of garrisoning Tangier and Bombay and what had appeared a healthy windfall for the Crown would be spent within a year in maintaining the obligations he had assumed as part of the nuptial agreement.

It was an open secret that the King was displeased with Peterborough's performance as Governor of Tangier and intended to replace him with Rutherford, an aggressive and competent commander from Dunkirk, but Sandwich said the King intended to grant Peterborough a life pension out of the Tangier budget. If he continued giving money away at this rate Tangier would be a millstone around His Majesty's neck, putting him at the mercy of Parliament should it choose to withhold funds.

Pepys guessed His Majesty had finally set up this Committee for the Affairs of Tangier to relieve himself of direct responsibility for Tangier's finances. He had placed Monck on the committee, his reward no doubt for persuading the King it would be a valuable acquisition. Others were the Duke of York, always at the forefront of money-spinning schemes; Sandwich, another keen advocate of the city; Peterborough as Governor; and several more including Povey as Treasurer for Tangier. Pepys was invited at Lord Sandwich's suggestion. He leapt at the opportunity to be close to the heart of the action and hopefully in a position to make a profit from the Committee.

One of the first acts of the Committee would be to summons the Scot Lord Rutherford fresh from completing the English withdrawal from

TANGIER: THE EARLIEST BATTLE HONOUR

Dunkirk to discuss the King's intention of making him Lord Teviot and appointing him Governor of Tangier. A Catholic replacing a Protestant was not to Pepys' liking, but it could have been worse; at least the Duke of York had not gained approval for the Irish Catholic John Fitzgerald to be promoted from Lieutenant Governor.

Chapter 3

Bastions and Redoubts

April 1663

London, England

What to write of this encounter?

Pepys dropped into his chair, opened his diary and sat looking at the page.

He did not want his writing to be read in his lifetime, that was why he wrote in a mixture of languages and some encoded, but he did want posterity to judge him kindly, with understanding, and acknowledge his difficulties and achievements. He could write of his clever plan to make profit from Tangier. Ten pence in the shilling of soldiers' pay would be spent with victuallers in England, and the assigning of contracts would be a profitable business for which he would volunteer. Should he write of his misgivings about Teviot?

Tangier was a most considerable place and he was forever grateful to Lord Sandwich for getting him on the Tangier Committee. But Teviot was a problem. The man was believed to have made too much profit from his governorship of Dunkirk and it appeared he designed to make even greater profit from Tangier.

It was not clear why the authority and instructions the commissioners had given Teviot had displeased him but the new Governor of Tangier had stormed off in high dudgeon without taking his leave, which had upset everyone. Clearly the man would be difficult to control and may prove ill for the garrison. Nonetheless, Pepys thought him a worthy soldier, careful, crafty and ruthless, and he could turn out to be a fortuitous appointment by the King. The man would be in Tangier in a few weeks and they would soon know what sort of governor he would make.

TANGIER: THE EARLIEST BATTLE HONOUR

Yes, he would tell his diary of his concern about Teviot, but not of his own plans for generating revenue. It would be easy to keep the income from such activities secret, shrouded in the mist that crept up the Thames and wrapped itself around his house.

June 1663

Tangier, Morocco

It was a good omen, the best possible weather for their task.

Palmes, high on the fort over Katarina Gate, had been watching as one by one the ships at anchor in the bay were blotted out by the white clouds silently rolling in from the Straits. They crept over the sea walls to cover the lower town, then climbed relentlessly up the hill street by street. His men were at ease assembled in the newly enlarged Katarina bastion, impatient to get out of the town, to face the enemy; to see the fire-master's plans into action. They knew an advanced fort was essential to help defend the vulnerable land facing the gate.

Teviot, the new governor, had arrived in May and had not yet been in Tangier a month, but already he was proving a canny soldier. He had detailed Palmes' company to spread a carpet of six thousand caltrops – small iron tripods with a fourth leg sticking up, so whichever way it sat one sharp tip would point up to cause painful injury to anyone standing on it – at a distance from the new construction to deter horses, and numerous grenades with matchlock matches to make the enemy believe the ground was likely to explode beneath their very feet and make the infantry wary of advancing.

Behind the ranks of pikemen, musketeers and grenadiers stood a large cohort of men with adzes to level the ground, six hundred men in fatigues and Monmouth caps ready to hoist baskets of stone and lime onto their backs, and a group of masons to build a new fort. It was midsummer, but those who had lived many years in Tangier had predicted the sea mist, and Engineer Beckman had seized the opportunity to get his redoubt started, sending men out, like ghosts in the pale moonlight, to mark out the land ready.

In the early morning as the mist had enclosed them all in its cold blanket, Palmes descended to lead his company out into the trenches and around the hillside. They could hear the boots of the construction parties following the marked track up to the work site at the top of the hill.

BASTIONS AND REDOUBTS

Beckman was everywhere, rattling off instructions, encouraging, cajoling, berating, advising and using every means he knew to speed the construction. His tireless enthusiasm and infectious conviction that the fort would save the men's lives in battles to come inspired the sappers to pour their energy into their work.

As the summer sun climbed higher in the sky its heat began to disperse the mist; the protective veil of whiteness thinned, revealing the mass of men furiously working on the walls of the fort. The Moors would see what was happening and launch an attack to interrupt the building work. Palmes signalled his defenders to keep quiet and listen for an enemy advance. Straining their ears, almost forgetting to breathe, they checked and rechecked their weapons and peered into the last swirling vestiges of mist. All they could hear was the sound of stone landing on stone as basket-loads of rock were delivered, and wooden mallets on masonry as the blocks were levelled. Before long the walls of grey marl were standing three feet tall.

Ghailan must be able to hear and see what was happening. Palmes was certain he would not allow work to continue without interference. He was sure to attack.

But the day continued, the fatigue party dumped more rocks, the masons chipped the stone into shape and the labourers worked the pulleys on the makeshift cranes to heave them into place. Block by back-breaking block the walls grew and by the time the relief company arrived at sunset the masonry stood four feet high. The captain of the night watch told Palmes that Teviot had received intelligence of Ghailan's severe displeasure at the building of the fort and plans to attack the hill with four thousand Horse and two thousand Foot.

Palmes' men retired as far as the ravelin, and huddled together for warmth, sleeping under the stars in their uniforms with their weapons to hand.

***

Cannon fire! Palmes leapt to his feet, table knife in hand, his platter of beef jumping across the table. Teviot sprang up, tearing his napkin from his neck and reaching for his sword. The sound of gunfire, shouts and screams streamed in through the wide open windows and echoed round the dining room.

Teviot was incensed. The Moors were attacking – at lunchtime!

TANGIER: THE EARLIEST BATTLE HONOUR

Palmes knew immediately they had left insufficient men to defend the trench beyond the fort.

The night had passed without incident and the morning had seen the fort grow in height and strength. The men in the trenches had fallen to idle chatting, playing dice or catnapping. Lunchtime arrived and in the scorching heat of the midday sun the officers had retired to their makeshift mess in the tower above Katarina Gate.

Palmes, Norwood and the other officers around the table grabbed their weapons and ran out to the walls buttoning their uniforms, to be greeted by the horrendous sight of hundreds of whooping horsemen inside the entrenchments. Palmes had not seen this many of the enemy at one time. Moorish Horse were streaming round Pole Fort, waving muskets and calling on Allah. The lead Moor, black cheich headscarf wrapped round his face leaving only his piercing eyes visible, riding a horse bedecked with red and green silks, planted a huge black battle standard beside the paved road leading from Katarina Gate to Pole. Someone pointed out Ghailan all in black with gold embroidered symbols shimmering on his djellaba and horse clothes, wielding an iron lance in one hand, waving a petronel pistol-cum-musketoon in the other, directing his Black Corps to surround the fort. He was a solid-looking individual; it would take a good lance thrust to dislodge him from the saddle.

Where were all the defenders?

To the left Fitzharris' Regiment of four hundred was already lined up in good order with pikes bristling like a hedgehog ready to receive the charge of five hundred lance-hefting, musket-aiming enemy Horse in red and white. Off to the right, Lieutenant Colonel Knightly had run to a small rise and drawn up a solid line of pikes to intercept the enemy's Violet Corps. He was commanding volleys of musket-fire and sporadic showers of deadly splinters from exploding grenades, to prevent several hundred whooping horsemen joining the attack on the redoubt.

From the top of the ten foot high Pole Fort the single cannon was raining grapeshot on the attacking hordes as fast as the gunners could reload: a far cry from their earlier duty of firing an early morning shot to confirm the defenders were in their entrenchments! The musket fire from the low walls was incessant, and grenades exploded, panicking horses and creating chaos as the Moors struggled to prevent their wide-eyed, bucking steeds from bolting. Major Rudyard and his garrison of three dozen doughty men were giving good account of themselves, defending Beckman's Fort.

BASTIONS AND REDOUBTS

The Moorish Horse was leading maybe fifteen hundred Berber lancers, and where the lancers came the infantry would surely follow. Palmes shouted for the drums to beat the Assembly. Within seconds men came tumbling out of houses, grasping weapons, shrugging bandoliers of apostles over their heads and buckling belts.

Moors were already swarming up against the walls of the fort. Lacking ladders, they stood on the saddles of their horses and climbed on each other's backs in their eagerness to scale the low walls. The defenders frantically thrust pikes at the assailants and clubbed them away from the ramparts with musket butts. It seemed the defenders could only hold on a few more minutes. Palmes had to get his men out there quickly.

He ran down the steps shouting for action, calling his officers by name. Within seconds his company was lined up. They were still loading muskets and lighting slow matches as Palmes quick-marched them, following Norwood's Company through Katarina Gate and out of the new ravelin. The group of fifty soldiers left in the trenches over lunchtime, who had fled the attack, reappeared to join the reinforcements.

The enemy Black Corps attacking the rear of Pole Fort now saw several hundred men lining up behind them, pikes and muskets forward. The horsemen would be under attack from the fort at the front and this new battalion behind. Uncertain whether to press their assault on the fort or turn to face the fresh threat, they turned one way then the other. Some riders edged towards the redcoats, others rode towards the fort; most looked around waiting for orders.

At the blast of a trumpet, a spectacular figure in crimson velvet and gold mounted on a white horse emerged from the melee. Waving his silver-inlaid musket above his bright white turban and crimson fez, the Moorish chieftain urged the flag bearer forward, rallied the hesitating men and directed the wavering general of the Black Corps to charge the infantry battalion.

Palmes saw Fitzharris to his left struggling to keep the Red and White Corps back, and Knightly suffering a battering from the continued assaults of the Violet Corps. He could leave Norwood's company to manage on its own and reinforce Knightly or outflank the Moors attacking Fitzharris; but the Black Corps seemed to be the greater threat. Perhaps he should extend Norwood's line and try to relieve Pole, but then it could be too late for Fitzharris.

The harsh metallic blare of more trumpets rent the sky. An ear-splitting chorus of cavalry screams ripped the fractured air. The pounding of hooves

TANGIER: THE EARLIEST BATTLE HONOUR

seemed to shake the ground. Palmes' men turned as one to see Colonel Bridges charging full pelt out of Katarina Gate, breastplate flashing sunlight, green sash flying, holding his musketoon on high. The cornet, Queen's-green guidon streaming, sabre pointed towards the enemy, was trying to keep up with his captain. The thundering hooves of a hundred heavy horses following their leader could not drown out the spine-tingling screaming of the troop attacking at full gallop.

Such was the magnificent, irresistible charge of the Tangier Horse.

The brave general of the Black Corps changed direction away from Norwood to meet the looming cavalry. His followers lowered their lances and prepared to meet the onslaught head-on. As the cavalry closed, the disparity in size between the huge long-tailed English horses and the lightweight Barb hill ponies became obvious. The manoeuvrability of the smaller horses was of no use now; with the entrenchments, the fort and the ranks of redcoats there was no room for manoeuvre, nowhere to hide. The wedge of heavyweights bore down on the mass of lightweights.

The sheer size and momentum of the brawny horses made for a devastating impact. The first volley of musketoon fire was deadly; the subsequent pistol-fire toppled a hundred Moors; the heavy sabres descending in irresistible arcs from high above sliced through insubstantial antelope hide adarga shields – designed to deflect glancing blows from lances – and mutilated the bodies of hundreds of brave Moors. The lancers turned tail and galloped off looking for support from the muskets of their skirmishers.

Bridges' valiant charge had provided the impetus the British attack needed. Norwood, keen to redeem himself for leaving his post, led a ferocious attack to regain the trenches around the fort. A couple of musket volleys forced the skirmishers to keep their heads down, exploding grenades blasted shrapnel through the thin woollen clothes of the defenders and the charge of pikemen followed by sword-wielding musketeers forced any remaining able-bodied Moors to abandon the trenches and retreat as fast as they could. Needham pressed forward around the other side of Pole, shouting to his men to force home the advantage won by the cavalry.

Palmes' men advanced in good order, firing volleys one rank at a time, reloading and pushing the enemy back step by step. With the Moors faltering, Major Rudyard of the Pole garrison took up his hangar sword and led his small garrison out of the redoubt to clear the walls. A Moorish horseman, seeing his chance to impale a man of obvious importance, spurred his steed in the direction of the major. Palmes cried out a warning, but his shout was lost in the clamour of battle. He watched the rider drop the point of his lance and aim for the centre of Rudyard's back. The deadly blade was within inches of its mark when a subaltern pushed Rudyard out of harm's way. The lance pierced the major's coat and ripped through the fabric as he fell. The saviour swung his musket stock and knocked the assailant from his horse, then smashed the butt down on his skull. Undaunted, the major scrambled to his feet and resumed his charge.

At last the Moors were faltering. Palmes jumped into the trench, scrambled over bodies and followed Needham and Norwood out of the far side of the ditch to wave the men forward. The breeze moved the curtain of gunpowder smoke aside, revealing the crimson-robed Moorish general rallying his men. Seeing the three officers facing him, the Moor raised his musket towards Needham. Norwood shouted. Needham raised his pistol and fired. Two simultaneous shots, a puff of white powder smoke from the general's musket and one from Needham's pistol. Needham fell back clutching his arm; the Moor's body jerked, his hand went to his chest and he dropped to the ground lifeless.

Ghailan's black figure appeared behind the fallen leader. Palmes was close enough to see the warlord's broad olivine face and large blonde moustache as he let out a loud wail, called to his men to retreat, turned his horse away and galloped off. The Moorish lancers retrieved the body of their fallen general without interference from the English.

A while later, walking through the hospital offering a few words to each injured man, Palmes knew, despite the losses, the day had been a signal success. It was good to see Lord Teviot taking firm action. He would not allow Ghailan's hit-and-run tactics to keep them cooped up in the city, as had Peterborough. The settlers needed supplies from the surrounding countryside and cattle needed grazing. It was the garrison's task to enclose land and protect it, and ensure the population was well provisioned. Teviot had been quick to set his defences and begin work on additional strongholds outside the city walls. The garrison had repelled the Moors decisively, causing them more pain than it was worth. Today had been a significant victory and a turning point. It would make Ghailan think twice before attacking the city's defences in future.

Beckman was a competent engineer and a worthy soldier as well, earning his pay as captain of a hundred fighting men. Hopefully the new man Moore would design a solid breakwater or mole to protect the harbour and, more importantly, persuade the King to fund it.

TANGIER: THE EARLIEST BATTLE HONOUR

June 1663

Ghailan's tented city outside Tangier, Morocco

The sombre mood was deepened by Ghailan's frown as the little group studied the warlord ensconced on luxurious silk cushions on the deeply carpeted floor.

Hamut had led the Jewish messengers through the town of cloth. They walked between the countless small tents of the Moorish lancers, past the larger communal tents of the skirmishers with muskets stacked outside; skirted the stacks of hay and straw outside the stables; threaded their way through the artisans and artificers, already working to make good damaged weapons and horse furniture, and the steamy kitchen tents. They stared at the glittering spherical suns and crescent moons on the tent poles of the colourful marquees of the nobles and finally came to the huge green and gold square pavilion of Ghailan, leader of twenty cavilas. They walked on silk carpets, mouths open, staring at the animal skins, silk ribbons and gold lace adorning the warlord's mobile palace.

Ghailan's attempt to punish the new governor for his temerity in building yet another fort outside the city walls had ended in the tragic demise of one of his most valued men, the General of Horse, and the calamity of chaotic retreat with the loss of hundreds of good fighting men. Since his latest victories over Ben Abu Bakr, Ghailan could call on twenty thousand men but even so he could not afford to lose so many in one futile attack.

There were few signs of mourning, but the bountiful feast on the low table would not make up for a disastrous day. Hamut was fearful of what might be in the note from the English Governor Teviot. Messengers were often blamed for the message, and he had seen men eviscerated for carrying unwanted words. Ghailan was a dignified man who lived by the honourable rules of his religion but Hamut was not keen to test the warlord's character.

He tentatively ushered the Jews forward.

Ghailan read the note.

The warlord shifted on his cushion, clearly annoyed by the reminder of his rashness in attacking so close to the city walls as to allow a surprise counter by the hated English heavy cavalry. Ghailan frowned. A flick of his hand dismissed the Jews, whose repeated bows as they backed away expressed their relief. The attendant chieftains sat motionless, leaving the bounteous repast untouched.

BASTIONS AND REDOUBTS

Ghailan addressed his guests, telling them that God willing it was his mission to drive the Christians from the land of Islam. Today Allah had *not* been willing and had chosen to take his friend and ally from them. On the very day of this loss, Teviot had sent these two Jews with a rebuke for attacking during his midday repast. Was it possible Allah agreed and had caused the attack to fail for this reason; Teviot had also held out the olive branch, offering to return the Muslim dead.

Hamut breathed a sigh of relief.

After some thought, Ghailan summoned the Spanish envoy and dictated a reply in Arabic for him to scribe in Spanish:

> To Lord Teviot etc, I received your Excellencie's of the 14th current in which you seem to complain that I did not bid you welcome; whereas on the contrary it belongs to me to do so: Persons of your quality being accustomed in these parts to give notice of their arrival and not to dispose of anything as your Excellencie had done in my lands. Notwithstanding I gave my order to my subjects that, on occasion presenting itself they should give good quarter to your Excellencies, as they did with the Centinel which they took the other day, whom I charged them to use well. As to the correspondence it is well-known how punctual I am in it, of which you may be informed. I did not expect less from your Excellencie's courtesie than you have used to the dead, for which I am infinitely obliged to you, but my men were but dust when alive, and now dead are no more, therefore to dust let them return. God keep your Excellencie many years, so I desire.

Ghailan took the Spaniard's quill and signed with a flourish in flowing Arabic script 'Cidi Hamet Hader Ben Ali Ghailan Mulai West Barbary, Arzila, Al-Kasr, Tetuan, Sala, & etc', and dismissed the envoy.

He smiled. He called the Spaniard back and added a postscript in Arabic lettering. 'If your Excellencie please to send any person or persons from you, you may do it, and this shall secure him which goes with my servant.'

Hamut was pleased. Good relations were a prerequisite for an honourable war. Good relations demanded open lines of communication. Good communication might lead to a treaty and profitable trade. His family had dates to sell and wished for a market in Tangier to gain warm English cloth for the winter. Expelling the unbelievers could wait.

July 1663

Tangier, Morocco

It was summer, the night wind from the mountains was ruffling the water and playing with the red and white pennant on the main mast, but it could not stir the huge red ensign at the stern of the English man-of-war.

Dover drew her dark cloak a little tighter across her bosom, shrank into the shadows of the cathedral and peeled the orange she had plucked from a neighbour's tree. When she had been awoken by the salute from the city walls she had dressed, thrown on her dark grey cloak and hurried here. This was an ideal place from which to observe the activities in the harbour, with a view all the way from the ground in front of the old castle – now renamed York Castle – along the wharf, across the harbour with its growing number of merchant ships and round to the Sandhills and Old Tangier.

As the man-of-war glided into harbour, Dover had counted more than twenty guns on one side. She waited for the ship to swing round in the current and read the name *Reserve*, confirming her suspicion. This was the infamous Captain Holmes bringing a new Lieutenant Colonel, the man rumoured to be in line to displace Fitzgerald as Lieutenant Governor, and maybe Governor before long. The governorship of this city changed every time the wind blew from a different direction. Governor Teviot had only been in Tangier a few months before he had negotiated this six-month truce with Ghailan and sailed off to England, leaving Colonel Fitzgerald in charge. Now this Norwood was arriving. By the time he got his feet under the table no doubt Teviot would be back, but she desperately wanted to see what this Norwood was like and whether she thought him fit to lead her city.

The sun was still below the horizon as the three men strode up Misericordia and the cold air was so clear she could see the Spanish houses across the Straits.

She recognised the moustachioed Colonel Fitzgerald accompanying two very lively middle-aged men, both clean shaven and expensively garbed and both enjoying themselves; talking and laughing. The elder of the two newcomers, a greying man, must be Norwood – she had seen him before!

BASTIONS AND REDOUBTS

He had fought in the battle for Pole earlier in the year, but she had not known his name. He had a reputation as a valiant soldier and a wily man; he might make a good governor, but perhaps not a suitable Deputy. The younger, shorter, stocky man – equally lively, with an accent a bit like some of the Irish soldiers – must be Holmes, reputedly a fiery individual of impulsive nature, but good judgement. She quite liked the look of his cheekily cocked hat, his orange taffeta sleeves and the way his mouth turned up at the ends, as if just waiting to break into a smile.

She had heard tell the two of them had caused some sort of diplomatic incident in Lisbon whilst viewing the Portuguese King's bulls and she could well believe it watching them chattering and roaring with laughter. They must have had an entertaining voyage together; even now they were totally absorbed in each other's company and it was easy for her to walk close behind and eavesdrop on their conversation about Holmes' voyage to the Gambia, where he attacked the Dutch merchants and set up a monopoly of African trade in Guinea gold, ivory and slaves for the Duke of York's Royal African Company. Holmes was saying the Duke of York was keen to push out from Tangier and colonise the continent, and Tangier was to provide a staging post entrepôt with warehousing, and a safe haven for ships travelling to and from Gambia.

The men paused at the lofty Catholic cathedral and discussed the architectural detail in the brickwork whilst they puffed and panted from the steep ascent. The calls of sellers and good-natured haggling of buyers betrayed the market taking place nearby, and they continued into the square to be confronted by a colourful confusion of people and stalls. Dover turned her shawl to show the red and yellow pattern, unfastened the top three buttons of her dress and followed the three men.

The smell of meat attracted them to Butchers Row, where a sun-tanned Moor offered them cubes of freshly killed boar to taste. They discussed the possibility of hunting their own and promised to return to the stall once they had eaten breakfast.

They followed the scent of brewing coffee to find an olive-skinned Portuguese matron wafting an Arabic coffee pot above her head and pouring hot black liquid into a copper cup on a small silver tray. The spreading cloud of steam exuded the inviting smell, and the table was spread with hot crispy baklava. As Fitzgerald proffered tuppence in place of the half real requested for three cups, Dover let her cloak fall open and put a hand out for one of the Greek delicacies, brushing her arm against Holmes. He looked down

TANGIER: THE EARLIEST BATTLE HONOUR

into her ebony eyes and deep cleavage and she gave him one of her special smiles.

He nodded an apology and she inclined her head in a query. He seemed to hesitate a second, then tilted his head towards his friend. She shrugged, smiled again and moved off slowly with a provocative roll of her hips. When she looked back both Holmes and Norwood were watching her. She already knew Norwood was not married; now she had learned he had an eye for an available woman.

Smiling villagers unloaded baskets from their camels and professed poverty whilst haggling over prices and bartering for goods, all the while praising Allah for peace and the opportunity to do business with the housewives and merchants milling about the square. Dover wandered round the tables overhung with cloth of indigo blue, pomegranate gold and alkanet purple, examining the fruit and absorbing the festive mood. As she moved from stall to stall she heard Portuguese, French, Dutch and even Spanish. Merchants were beginning to see opportunities in Tangier; ships from different countries were coming into the harbour and using the newly extended warehouses. People were bemoaning how the cost of renting a house was rising. Everyone knew the army officers had commandeered all the best houses, some had two or three, often leaving them empty, but today all that was forgotten and it seemed everyone was cheerful, full of new-found optimism and looking forward to a bright future.

Carcasses of boar and venison hung from butchers' hooks to be sold whole for the entertaining tables of commissioned officers and dignitaries or carved in pieces for merchants, subalterns and craftsmen. Rabbit, beef and mutton were on sale in small portions, complete with accompanying flies, for anyone who had been paid recently or could obtain credit. Dover eyed the cages of squawking birds. She was paid in meat by one of her slaughterhouse customers but had not tasted game in many months. The man in blue velvet was poking his finger, choosing a brace of guinea fowl – he must be entertaining this evening – those tasty birds and pheasant commanded the highest prices and were reserved for the wealthy.

He may be wealthy but he did not look happy. Since his return to Tangier she had discovered he was Captain Beckman, the engineer in charge of military building. He strode about the town carrying sheaves of paper, always in a hurry, always followed by other army officers and men with surveying equipment. He had built the extra ravelin walls in front of Katarina Gate, made the watchtower higher, and built Pole Fort and other redoubts. She treated him to her sunbeam smile, and he could not help himself grin in response. She raised her eyebrows, but he seemed too embarrassed to carry on in public. She chose a cheaper bird, a partridge, and paid for it to be wrung and plucked.

She may not be having too much success this morning, but almost overnight with the peace treaty her customers had become less morose, more talkative and more generous. Life had gone from being a miserable, barely tolerable existence to a pleasant round of walking the lanes and beach front in the warm morning, relaxing indoors during the heat of the day and eating and drinking outdoors in the cool morning and warm evenings. Officers were rowed about the bay and reportedly rode out of Katarina Gate to hunt wild boar.

She chose a bunch of Midol dates and paid for okra to add to her usual greens and fruit. She smiled to herself to think there was to be a market day every week whilst Teviot's six-month truce lasted.

A table of colourfully decorated earthenware caught her eye and she flirted with the seller to get a good deal on an egg-shaped candle-holder in bright red and green to replace the broken one she stood in the window to show her night-time callers she was available. She moved on to a small stall with writing materials. The soldiers' pay was always in arrears, and she had to keep a list for each one to make his mark. She was paying for a few sheets of cheap paper to bind into a small book for a record of her customers' debts, and some good-quality ink for her letters, when a quiet voice spoke a few words near her ear. Another letter, urgent it seemed.

Dover meandered to the wild plot, pushed some orange pips into the soil and walked back to her lodging. She locked the door behind her before bending to pick up the letter. She opened it with a heated knife as always and took it upstairs to her desk. Sitting in the clear crisp sunlight, the warmth of the coffee turned cold in her stomach.

Tangier was about to be betrayed.

She knew Beckman, her man in velvet, had been in Spain. No longer 'Captain' Beckman, he had been sacked when Harley's Regiment had been absorbed by Teviot's to save money and his captaincy had ceased to exist. This note told her Beckman had been feeling aggrieved because the ever-grasping Teviot had not given him notice of the termination, nor paid him his salary to date, only handed him letters of credit with two Dutch merchants. Spreading word of his disenchantment with the English, Beckman had been negotiating with the Duke of Medina to help the Spanish and Ghailan take

TANGIER: THE EARLIEST BATTLE HONOUR

Tangier. He had secured an offer of one hundred thousand ducats to advise them how to take the city, and a regiment of soldiers to lead into the attack. Dover had just seen Beckman in the market – he must be here to prepare for a Spanish attack.

The Spanish held several enclaves in North Africa and could be expected to resent the English incursion into their backyard. They were known to be constantly plotting with Ghailan to attack Tangier, but Teviot's freshly signed peace treaty had lulled the governor into a false sense of security and he had left for England. His absence offered the perfect opportunity for Ghailan to surprise the garrison.

Her informant was travelling with the Spanish envoy Don Diego in the great train of people journeying from Spanish Ceuta to meet Ghailan, and would keep her informed.

Dover retrieved her writing implements and began a letter to Nathaniel Luke, the governor's secretary. Beckman had to be apprehended and Don Diego's embassy thwarted.

As soon as she had finished the one letter she began another. She had to maintain the impression of keeping the Duke of Medina informed, and had plenty to write about Norwood and Holmes.

Some days later she knew her letter had been received. Lieutenant Governor Fitzgerald had asked the friendly Qaid of Tetuan to receive Addison, the chaplain to the Tangier Regiment, as a guest and provide him with an introduction to influential people in Ghailan's retinue. Addison's mission was to discover the true purpose of the Spanish envoy's visit. Some supposed it was to seek more favourable terms for the Spanish enclaves in Morocco, whilst others thought it was to offer Spanish assistance in toppling Tangier. No one knew why Ghailan was entertaining the visit; whether he truly wanted peace and trade with Tangier or the Spanish or was merely playing one off against the other to gain powder and weapons.

At church the next Sunday she said a prayer for the chaplain and wished him 'God speed'.

Chapter 4

Broken Treaty

September 1663

A plain outside Tetuan, Morocco

A dozen shrieking Moroccan horsemen bore down on the English chaplain at full gallop in line abreast.

Hamut had watched such spectacles many times, but on this occasion the line of Moors wrapped in white linen, waving muskets, had added the shout of 'Death to infidels' to the usual ululating.

The magnificence of the occasion seemed lost on Addison, who looked distinctly uncomfortable but tried to appear calm, knowing bravery was prized above all by nomadic tribes. At the last possible moment the Moors raised both hands over their heads to discharge their firearms into the air with a bright flash and a puff of white smoke. Expecting to be trampled by horses whose riders were precariously perched on the saddle with no visible means of control, the chaplain appeared greatly relieved when the powder play riders managed to bring their steeds to a halt without crashing into him or the nearby dignitaries. The cloud of dust gradually cleared, revealing a great spectacle. The proud warriors of the royal squadron formed up in line showing off their beautifully presented horses decked out in highly embroidered collars of gold or silver, studded with glistening pearls and sparkling jewels. The riders wore brightly coloured pantaloons and jackets with gaudy silk sashes of every colour and held their silver and mother-of-pearl-encrusted muskets high with both hands.

This remission was short-lived, however. As soon as the first wave of horsemen veered away, a second appeared through the swirling dust, this time holding lances horizontally, each aimed at one of the guests' hearts. On they came, scarves streaming back, spittle flying from the horses' open mouths, raising their lances for the coup de grâce, so close that

TANGIER: THE EARLIEST BATTLE HONOUR

Addison shrank back into the knees of the spectator behind him. At the precise moment the chaplain crossed himself to commend his soul to God and started to raise his hands in self-defence, the charging men dropped down the flanks of their mounts, stabbed their lances into flags lying on the ground and steered their horses away, raising their flagged lances on high and kicking sand into the faces of the audience.

The huge circle of spectators gathered in the summer sun on the dry plain outside Tetuan cheered and clapped their approval. Don Diego looked as though his heart could not stand much more of this entertainment and was no doubt relieved to see musicians running into the makeshift arena and striking up with trumpets, drums and maracas to announce the entry of a large group of black-skinned dancers.

The women spread out around the arena, the men carried long staffs and each one stomped his way around his female partner showing off his indigo and kola-orange pants and leggings covered in ostrich feathers, whilst she shook her hips and rustled her ankle-length skirt of countless strings of amber beads, and shimmied her shoulders, making her multi-layered ivory necklace flash in the sunlight. Not used to the subtleties of the music and the dance, he might find it monotonously repetitive but at least Don Diego was not threatened with being trampled or skewered.

The Tangier governor had been absent for several months and Hamut knew Ghailan was busily trying to extract guns and powder from the Spanish on the promise of a joint attack on Tangier. The Duke of Medina had held talks in Spanish Ceuta and sent Don Diego to meet Ghailan. On his journey he was being shown every courtesy but no audience with the warlord-cum-priest. For that prize he would be obliged to travel the eighty miles to Arzila via Tetuan to give the maximum number of people the chance to see the envoy of the great King of Spain coming to pay his respects to the Moorish overlord.

The dancers were followed by an acrobatic team, who, true to their militaristic heritage carried lances but the fast drum beat accompanying their entrance and the incessant shaking of their shoulders and bending of their knees in time to the music made it clear they were entertainers not soldiers. Addison had seen enough; he retired to his tent to pen a letter informing his contact in Tangier what he had so far discovered of Don Diego's designs.

Hamut had been detailed to ensure Addison's letters were delivered swiftly. He quickly took the scroll to his own tent and read it. The letter said Ghailan was giving Don Diego a welcome to impress him with the warlord's power rather than rolling out a purple carpet and showing deference; that even though the Spaniard was bringing a gift reputed to be worth forty thousand pieces of eight, equivalent to £10,000, he was clearly being treated as a supplicant. Addison had learned Don Diego had been asking questions about the Tangier defences, the size of the garrison, the disposition of sentinels, the height and strength of the walls and the position and type of cannon and wished to dress in Moorish clothes and ride with Ghailan to view the city himself. Don Diego had confessed that the Spanish held an evil eye on the 'Immortal Teviot' for the harm he had wreaked on their interests when fighting for France in the Low Countries, and he had been demeaning Teviot in letters to Ghailan at every opportunity.

Evidence of Addison's spying might help Hamut gain Ghailan's favour. He copied the letter, resealed it and handed it to one of the royal Tetuan couriers for delivery to Tangier.

November 1663

Tangier, Morocco

Everyone was shouting. Such a thing had never been seen. Ghailan was at Katarina Gate calling for Lieutenant Governor Fitzgerald to ride out on a hawking party.

Dover ran up the steps, her loosely bound bust bouncing nicely, past one of her clients. Fittingly, it was the one who had first called her 'Dover'. Looking down from the top of Katarina Gate, true enough, there below was the squat figure of Ghailan, hawk on arm, at the head of a party of fifty men of obvious rank. Girded in expensively coloured djellaba, smiling moustachioed face, his resonant voice called on the Lieutenant Governor Fitzgerald to join him on an excursion. It was clear the warlord's intelligence had told him of Teviot's continuing absence in England.

A short while later the gate opened and Fitzgerald emerged with an escort of a dozen officers in smart grey coats with sashes of red, yellow or blue and matching shoulder ribbons and lace elbow ruffs. Peering down at the band of handsome Moors, Dover thought she recognised one of the warlord's group. It looked like the Spaniard Don Diego, but before she could get a good sight of him he had turned away.

TANGIER: THE EARLIEST BATTLE HONOUR

She had been informed Don Diego was still with Ghailan more than three months after leaving Ceuta on his mission – he had apparently promised to remain with the warlord until they had carried out a joint attack on Tangier. It was as well she had warned Fitzgerald of the Don's request to survey Tangier in the company of Ghailan. As cover for his visit to the city the warlord had brought a letter for King Charles, which he delivered before the party rode off round the city walls, probably to give the Spaniard a chance to count the cannon real and fake mounted for his visit, and then ventured out into the hinterland.

Back in her house after a pleasant walk around the city, Dover found she had three notes.

The first was a copy of the letter Ghailan had delivered personally:

> Sacred Royal Majesty having been advertised by His Excellencie the earl of Teviot of his sudden occasion to visit these parts, I could not forbear this address in respect of the peace and good intelligence we have lately effected in your Majestie's Name. And having found His Excellencie a Cavalier of great valour and honour and of so noble a mind I could not choose but desire to correspond with him by my letters to signify my inclination of compliance in all things that concern the service of your Majestie and which formerly I have forborn to do for want of so fit a juncture to enable me …
>
> If in any part of our dominions there is anything that offers itself for your Majesties service, the signification of your commands shall be esteemed the greatest favour that can be expressed. God keep your Majesty and give you all manner of felicity.

The second informed her Colonel Fitzgerald had extended the truce with Ghailan despite hearing of Spanish plans to send 2,000 infantry to help the Moors mount a stealthy night attack on Tangier. Dover knew nothing of such plans; perhaps it was a ploy by the Colonel to ensure Teviot brought reinforcements when he returned from England. Even so she could feed intelligence to the Duke of Medina that might forestall such a plan were it in his mind - she would advise him a new secret night-watch had been instituted with a hundred infantrymen patrolling the shoreline twixt nightfall and dawn, to set a trap for unsuspecting Spanish forces. She smiled to herself, and she would add the expected imminent arrival of Teviot, saying he was reported to be on the high seas.

The third set her pulse racing. The Jews had information her father was alive. His military and secretarial skills made him a valuable commodity and he had been sold on to merchants travelling south to Marrakesh. It was a great relief to know he had survived and being highly regarded would be well provided for. If he were ever traced the price of his freedom would be high.

January 1664

She knew it had been too good to last. It was less than a year since Teviot had arrived as the new governor and started expanding the bounds of Tangier and already the bubble had burst.

Copies of the Declaration had been hung all around the city on Teviot's return, in January, from a six-month sojourn in England. The nice-looking secretary Nathaniel Luke looked so solemn and full of his own importance as he read it out:

> Our City of Tanger is and shall be a port free to all merchants as well as foreigners and others with their ships and vessels, except such ships and vessels which shall come from beyond the Cape of Good Hope and except ships coming from our English plantations for and during such time and upon such terms articles and conditions as are herein after expressed, that is to say first it shall be lawful for all our good subjects and the subjects of other nations in amity with us, except before excepted, to come freely into out port at Tanger, with their ships, vessels and merchandises and to land the same or any part thereof and lay them up in such warehouses and other places as they think fit.
>
> All persons coming into our said port with any ships or merchandises shall enter or cause to be entered in their registry there to be kept for that purpose, all the goods, wares, merchandises and commodities by them landed and shall pay or cause to be paid for every hundred pounds worth of goods landed according to the rates and values of merchandises set down in the book of rates established in England, five shillings for the entry thereof and no other duty or payment whatsoever.
>
> It shall be lawful for all persons to export or sell upon the place the goods imported at his and their will and pleasure without paying any further or other imposition of duty whatsoever.

TANGIER: THE EARLIEST BATTLE HONOUR

All persons exporting any goods from our said port and City of Tanger into any part of our Kingdom of England or Ireland shall be obliged to export the same in English shipping and with English mariners.

This liberty and freedom of our port at Tanger shall continue from the nine and twentieth day of September 1662 for and during the full time and term of five years from thenceforth next coming. In all which time there shall be no further or greater improvement of our customs within the said port. And we do also declare that when the whole five years shall be elapsed we shall not make any new or greater imposition upon the trade of that port, without first giving public notice thereof after the expiration of five years by the space of two years before any such new or greater imposition shall take effect.

So there it was. English plans to conquer Moroccan cities, to expand this enclave into a colony, to bring Christendom to North Africa as Portugal had once done, all were forgotten. Now Tangier was to be a free-trade port, nothing more. She'd shrugged. That was not so bad. If the Governor ceased his personal taxation of merchants, there might be more trades, more sailors, more wealthy merchants, more customers for her. More than that, more spices from the east, more fabrics from the Indies, more sugar from the English colonies.

Only a few weeks ago a talkative captain had told her an English agent named Beckman had given King Charles of England letters from the Duke of Medina offering Beckman 100,000 ducats to betray Tangier and lead an attack by Ghailan's men. Apparently His Majesty was greatly upset and had instructed Governor Teviot to refuse to honour the condition in the extended truce that prevented more forts being built. Having been sent copies of the letters, Teviot concluded he urgently needed to start building new forts to keep Ghailan and the Spanish cannon far from the city walls.

Ghailan, already annoyed at not receiving the tribute of fifty barrels of gunpowder he had been promised under the first treaty, was furious to see preparations for the building of new forts, contrary to their agreement, and sent a note chastising Teviot, telling him he would resume hostilities under the same gentlemanly rules of conduct as previously.

Knowing of Ghailan's duplicity, Teviot had taken exception to the warlord's message and to the Moroccan Jews who had brought it. The hot-headed Governor said he had brought four hundred reinforcements and was not afraid of Ghailan; he had shouted out 'Bon chat, bon rat, we are not jelly!' and replied in extremely terse terms he would not only continue to build forts, he would have war 'without quarter' and had ordered the Jews thrown out of Tangier.

At the words 'without quarter' Dover shivered involuntarily. She had seen the results of all-out war, and it had cost her a husband in extremely unpleasant circumstances she could not bear to bring to mind. It was one thing for honourable enemies to fight hard and true, it was quite another for hatred to determine the treatment of enemies and prisoners.

Further, the Jews were excellent financiers and merchant go-betweens, and had been seen as neutral messengers and mediators between the Christians and the Muslims. Must they leave? Their loss would be felt by everyone in Tangier, more so by Dover because she would lose her own informants and messenger and it would take time to find others.

The King of England was half a world away; he could never know what was happening in Tangier. Why did this fire-breathing Scot Teviot not act as any good diplomat would? Was he not married? Did he not know how to deal with tricky people? He could have an easy life, dissemble in both directions, procrastinate, smooth ruffled feathers and let everyone ply their trade and make money. Ghailan could save face, the King could make great profit from an entrepôt, and Teviot could run his city on a small budget and pocket his share of the garrison salaries (as all commanders did), take bribes from the merchants (as all governors did), and live a life of luxury enjoying the pleasures offered by a trading centre in a beautiful climate.

Declaring war was no way to attract merchants and business. Tangier would be a city in a permanent state of siege. She crossed herself. May God save us all!

January 1664

Palmes took a mouthful of the Governor's fresh supply of Bordeaux and leaned over the maps Teviot's new military engineer had spread on the table.

He was pleased Teviot was back. Lieutenant Governor John Fitzgerald was a very difficult man to work with. He issued orders without any explanation, organising things for the benefit of his own regiment at the cost of everyone else. Food for the men became poor quality and in short supply, leading to frequent illness through malnutrition and it was said some even died of starvation. Taking money out of the soldiers' provisions was not unusual of course, but there were limits.

TANGIER: THE EARLIEST BATTLE HONOUR

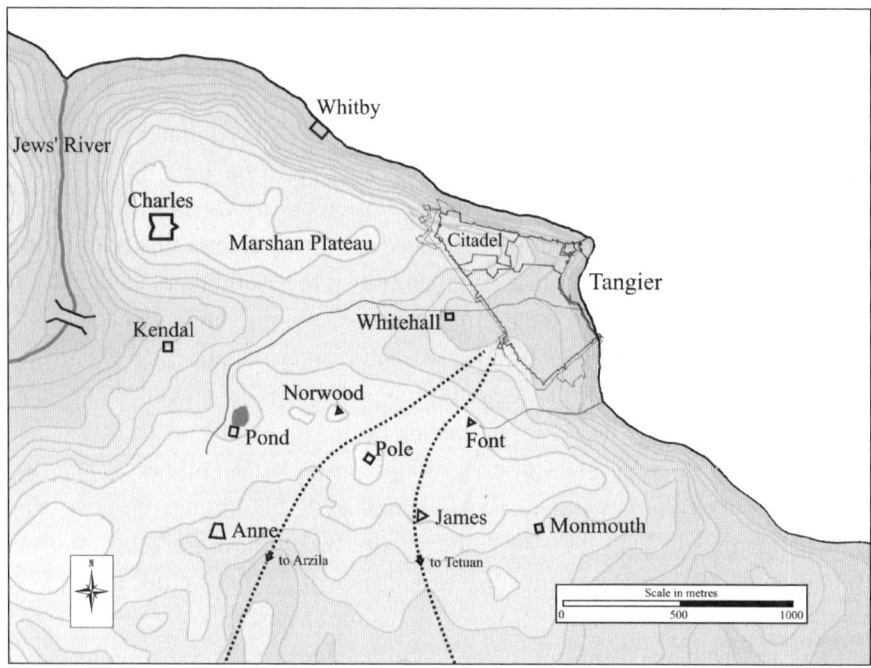

Forts 1663–1664. (Author)

Teviot's return to Tangier brought an air of optimism and a feeling that anything could be achieved. He too made money at every opportunity, but at least he made a show of consulting his officers and had good military reasons for his decisions and orders. The four hundred men he had recruited in Scotland brought the garrison back up to nearly two thousand, but he saw the need for more cavalry and had amalgamated the four infantry regiments into two and used the savings on officers to add two troops of Horse.

Palmes was pleased de Gomme had been chosen as the new military engineer. He had been considering asking for a reassignment to Bombay, the other Portuguese territory acquired by the King, hearing it might be a profitable posting. But by sending a man who had been favoured by Charles I, the King was signalling the importance of Tangier.

Palmes examined the maps more closely. The forts were of no real interest; they were standard construction. What did take his attention was their positioning. The fort labelled 'Charles' was positioned to defend the upper castle, the citadel – an obvious need – but instead of being placed on the nearest hill it was located at the far end of Marshan Plateau, overlooking

Jews' River. Next was Kendal Fort, guarding a pass but again positioned further away than one would expect, and Fort Anne was far beyond Pole Fort.

Palmes was all for aggression and taking the fight to Ghailan, but these new forts would be at the limits of accurate fire from the cannon on the city walls. They could house a company of men but forts had to be manned twenty-four hours a day, and it would be difficult to defend this many forts spread over such an area from a garrison of two thousand men, especially if they could not rely on supporting fire from the city or even from each other. When Palmes got the chance to question de Gomme he got a blank look and was informed the engineer had given the Governor what he had requested.

Palmes knew he should try to persuade Teviot to bring the new forts closer so they could be defended by cannon-fire from Tangier city walls, reduce the length of boundary, and make them smaller to be garrisoned by fewer men. On the other hand, the cost of these large forts would allow Teviot to take a sizable cut for himself, which might explain the maps. It would not be wise to question Teviot's decisions, especially as Palmes relied on the Governor for promotion. He would have to tread carefully.

On top of all this there was to be a new civil authority! The pen-pushers in England had decided the army officers could not run a city successfully. The Portuguese priests had been complaining to the Queen about their chapels being requisitioned for essential use as soldiers' quarters and storage. The merchants were moaning of fees imposed by the Governors contrary to the 'free city' designation of Tangier. Some people were demanding a civil jurisdiction, a mayor, a corporation, civil courts. Whatever next? The last thing Tangier needed was busybodies meddling in the everyday affairs, wanting a say in everything and slowing vital decisions.

Palmes went to bed that night a worried man.

May 1664

Nathaniel Luke was enjoying the ride in the warm spring sun. The beginning of May was the perfect time in Morocco. The chill wind of winter, the long spells of rain and the dull dank days were all forgotten. The sky was clear beautiful blue from the summit of the distant mountains at the head of the valley in the south to the horizon of Spanish hills over the Straits to the north. The heat of summer was still a few weeks away. Spring was a time of rebirth, optimism. Teviot was back and all was well with the world.

TANGIER: THE EARLIEST BATTLE HONOUR

Normally stuck behind the desk, he had asked to accompany the Earl on this expedition with all the best veterans of the garrison. He had donned his Sunday best, booked out a pair of good-quality pistols from the regimental stores and borrowed a cavalry officer's sabre and belt to wear under his elegant best jacket. He turned in his saddle and looked back at Tangier bathed in sunshine – it was an omen of the bright future to come.

Lookouts at the top of Peterborough Tower would be noting their progress, sentries on the walls would be watching out over the fatigue parties toiling on the new forts. The city was looking imperious, they had been through a difficult time, the indecision and disappointment of Peterborough, the self-harm confrontations of Fitzgerald, but they had weathered those early issues. Now was the golden age.

The Moors swore he never slept. He was invincible. 'The Devil', they called him. Up ahead, leading the column of seven companies, more than four hundred men, was Earl Teviot. This canny Scotsman had killed the General of the Algarnes Horse, had captured the prized red battle standard and, to the great chagrin of Ghailan, been responsible for the death of one of the warlord's close relations.

Yes, Teviot had proved himself more than a match for the Moroccans. He always scouted the ground carefully, and posted sentries to protect his men so Nathaniel had been able to report to the commissioners that the new forts were pushing the bounds of Tangier further out. The city was no longer a confining prison, it was the hub of a productive, expanding territory. He could almost hear Ghailan's sighing and the gnashing of the Spanish Duke de Medina's teeth.

Teviot was pleased with his work and had written home requesting permission to take leave once again. Nathaniel glanced back again to catch sight of the city before it disappeared behind the hills. On the plateau ahead Charles, the large fort whose construction Teviot had overseen day by day for months, stood guard. Further down the lower valley the bridge across Jews' River was wide enough to take the column three abreast over the gushing, bubbling water rushing down to the Atlantic. Across the river was the steep hill covered with the trees that were to provide timbers for the new forts, extensions to their houses and additional warehouse storage for the increasing trade.

Teviot had left the cavalry foraging to the south of the river with a sizable contingent of Foot to cover their retreat if the Horse were surprised by

Moorish lancers. Even though intelligence reported the bulk of Ghailan's forces were away fighting Ben Abu Bakr they had reconnoitred far beyond that point and found no enemy lurking in the long grass or among the rocks.

Once across the bridge Teviot divided his column into three and set each unit a separate route to scout before meeting at the top of Jews' Mount.

They had not progressed far into the woods before a crackle of gunfire and round shot came winging out of the undergrowth. Everyone dived for cover. Teviot called an advance and the captains gave the orders. The musketeers crept forward to encourage the skirmishers' fire that would pinpoint their position. The grenadiers crouched low through the bracken, took grenades from their pouches, lit the fuses and tossed them. A series of explosions and screams told them their weapons had done their work. The redcoats moved from tree to tree and the process was repeated. In short time the enemy snipers were put to flight. With a loud cheer, Teviot's men careered on through the woods to the top of the hill.

They emerged from the darkness of the wood into the bright sun to see the enemy in full flight down the grassy slope to the next hill. Nathaniel's chest swelled. This was his first taste of battle; his heart beat quickly. The excitement of the chase was in his blood. He leapt onto his mount, drew his cutlass, yelled like so many others, and kicked his horse forward.

Seeing a chance for a decisive victory that would give the garrison control of this hill, almost three miles beyond the city walls, Teviot and his men pursued the fleeing Moors halfway up the next hill.

There was a trumpeting in the distance. It was answered by the blast of horns nearby.

Nathaniel's blood ran cold. He knew at once. They had fallen into the same trap as so many before. Men seemed to grow up from the grass. A host of men in white appeared all around.

The terrifying sight and sound of hundreds of Moorish Foot firing muskets at them.

Teviot shouted orders, relayed by the captains. The men and officers, chosen by Teviot for their experience and skill, fell into practised ranks. Nathaniel dismounted and pulled his pistol. Successive volleys from rows of superior snaphaunce muskets felled many of the Moors and kept the rest at a distance.

Nathaniel began to feel more confident. The withdrawal was orderly and controlled and before long the veteran band of redcoats had almost made

TANGIER: THE EARLIEST BATTLE HONOUR

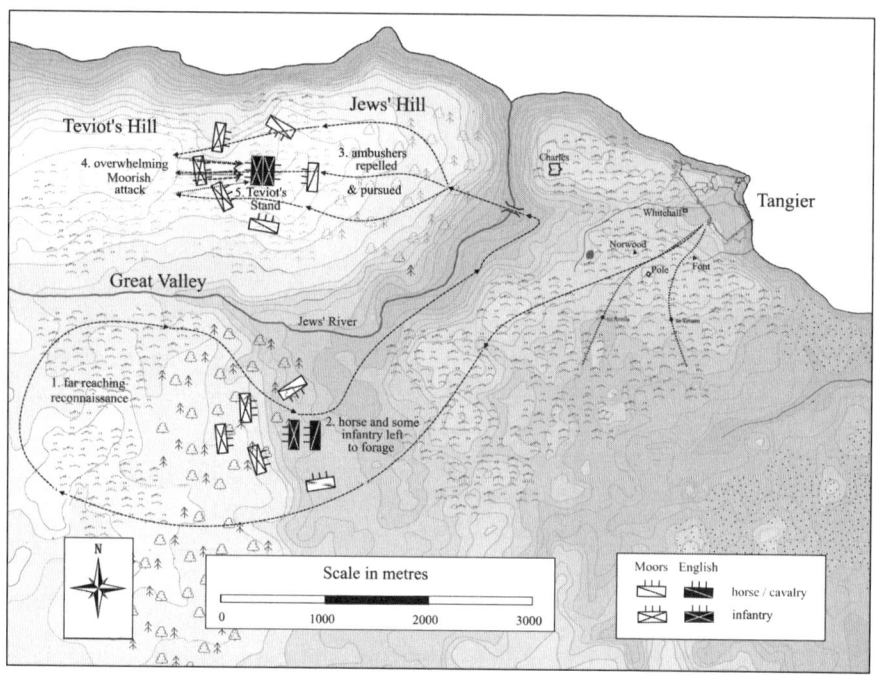

Teviot's stand, May 1664. (Author)

it down the slope ready to retreat back to the top of Jews' Mount with the advantage of high ground and the enclosing safety of the trees.

The blare of trumpets and thunder of hoof-beats was followed by what seemed like thousands of richly decked Moorish Horse wielding scimitars and musketoons charging at them, circling them, cutting them off from the wood. His optimism was replaced by dread.

The captains barked orders and the men formed squares, the pikemen presented their thirteen-foot poles facing all directions. The musketeers primed their weapons, loaded, and waited for the Moors to come close enough to be sure of a hit with every musket ball. They had to make their ammunition last until their own heavy cavalry came to the rescue.

But Nathaniel knew in his heart the first trumpeting he had heard was the enemy charge on the cavalry foraging down in the valley beyond the river. They were fighting for their lives at the same time as Teviot's men were trying to repel the furious attacks from this countless horde. Nathaniel knew that his first taste of action was to be his last. He fired at the nearest rider and reloaded, then checked his sabre, determined to sell his life dearly.

BROKEN TREATY

The grenadiers had used most of their grenades in their advance through the woods, and the remainder in their retreat to Jews' Mount. Now at their hour of most need they had none left to repel the enemy horsemen. The lancers came in close, fired their muskets and rode off to reload, taking their toll on the immobile targets of British musketeers.

Already many hundreds of Moors had fallen, but for every one shot down another took his place. One by one the defenders fell with no one to replace them. As their ranks were depleted by the continued attacks, the defensive fire became less effective; the enemy came closer and their fire grew more intense. At length the small groups of soldiers ran out of ammunition. They drew their swords for the last desperate hand-to-hand fight. The riders juggled their lances and closed in for the final kill.

With no ammunition left Nathaniel threw his useless pistol aside, drew his sabre and clambered over dead and dying to meet the circling lancers.

***

The small band of retainers hiding in the woods were aghast. They didn't want to believe their eyes. They had watched the impossible. The invincible Earl Teviot had just been killed. Not only that – the cream of the garrison had died with him. None taken prisoner; Teviot had told Ghailan he wanted war without quarter and this was the result. The garrison had given no quarter and asked none. They had committed a great slaughter of the elite Moorish Horse, and to a man had died fighting.

Many hundreds of the enemy skirmishers and lancers covered the ground, dead and dying. The remaining, victorious Moors were walking among the English bodies, finishing off the wounded. Some sought revenge for comrades by mutilating the dead redcoat soldiers; most contented themselves with stripping anything of value.

There was no cheering and little by way of celebration. Ghailan all in black dismounted and walked over to Teviot's body to confirm it was indeed his feared enemy, then got on his horse and slowly rode away, knowing it was a battle won at too high a cost. It would take years to recover from such a great loss of skilled Moorish warriors, and this almost certainly spelled the end of his ambitions against Tangier or any other enemy of note.

To the great relief of the nine survivors of Teviot's expedition the Moors did not search the woods; a few rode on down the hill towards Tangier, most followed Ghailan back to their camp.

TANGIER: THE EARLIEST BATTLE HONOUR

Long after the last horseman had ridden out of sight the little group abandoned the logs they had been gathering and made their sorry way down through the bracken. Crouched in the bushes at the bottom of the wood, seeing a ship flying English flags coming up Jews' River, they broke cover and waved and shouted heedless of the danger of any lurking enemy, but the easterly breeze that carried their voices towards the ship, meant she could not make headway up the river. Deflated, they watched the vessel carefully go about and sail back to the sea and started the walk along the shoreline to Whitby.

June 1664

London, England

Some weeks later Pepys threw the report onto his office desk.

The other members of the Commission were quick to find fault with Teviot, and it was true he was an impulsive creature. On the other hand, all previous reports of his military actions described how he sent the cavalry out to ascertain the disposition of the enemy, and indeed on this occasion the eyewitness testified to the same care. Only in the final action of the battle had he been unable to control his men in their headlong pursuit of a fleeing enemy.

It was His Majesty who had ordered Teviot to be more aggressive and continue building additional forts, despite Fitzgerald agreeing peace terms expressly forbidding them. In this respect Teviot's death could be laid at the King's door.

It was not all bad news. The report from the Colonel of Horse, Tobias Bridges, seemed to indicate the Moors had suffered great loss, an assessment borne out by the lack of serious follow-up attacks. Even though Ghailan had refused to agree a ceasefire, and had fortified nearby Old Tangier on the other side of Tangier Bay with the assistance of the Spanish, he had not pressed home a supposed advantage.

Whatever the truth, no amount of complaining would change the situation. Pepys would support the sending of five hundred reinforcements. The garrison would still number less than two thousand, nearly a thousand fewer than its original establishment, saving at least £15,000 a year. Awarding medals would raise the men's spirits. Bridges' actions in the absence of Lieutenant Governor Fitzgerald certainly deserved one, he had often led the

Horse in effective actions and even in the face of the shock massacre of the cream of the garrison he had kept everyone working together building new forts. Pay was more than six months in arrears and supplies were short but Bridges had kept morale high and Tangier was apparently flourishing.

The only possible cloud on the horizon was a report that France was preparing to invade Jejil in Algiers. A French naval presence in North Africa, not far from Tangier, might challenge English superiority, and require a response.

April 1665

Tangier, Morocco

The woman alongside the immaculately attired man was casting her eyes over one particular slave.

Hamut tightened his stomach muscles, aware his slim frame covered with perfectly smooth olive skin was attractive to ladies of higher rank. How fortunes had changed in the twelve months since he had watched Teviot's army slaughtered! Luckily of all the captives lined up for sale on the quayside, Allah had blessed him with a twinkle in his rich brown eyes. That, along with jet black hair and a lithe body, gave him an advantage in catching women's attention. Flirtations with his tutor's wife had taught him to make the most of his looks.

Here he was being appraised by the new Governor; he knew this would be his only chance, and was thankful that despite the deprivations suffered since his unfortunate capture he had kept himself fit and clean.

So he stood tall, shoulders back, assumed an admiring smile and gave the lady a look that he hoped was a confident invitation; then dropped his eyes before looking at her briefly again. As the wealthy man drew alongside, Hamut stepped slightly forward, bent down on one knee and addressed him in French, offering himself as a practised mathematician and scribe.

Having spent his early life being groomed for high office, living in comfort and being educated in Islam, mathematics and the sciences, Hamut was fluent in French and English as well as Arabic and Berber. His tutor's wife had taught him much in her husband's absence and he had learned Allah favoured those who threw themselves on his mercy while doing what they could to help themselves.

Hamut had fought alongside Ghailan's commanders and watched the warlord's negotiations. He had seen slaves at the market, in the prisons, in the galleys and labouring and knew once you were passed by in the first sale you had little chance of recovering. A captive had to make an impression while still fit and healthy for he had little chance once starved and beaten.

The woman returned Hamut's hint of a smile with sparkling eyes and agreed with her husband's suggestion of the usefulness of a slave or two. Feigning lack of interest, she agreed he would do as well as any other.

A while later Hamut was presented to the new Governor as a gift from the merchants of Tangier. They hoped the Lord Belasyse would look favourably upon their endeavours to make the city a foremost trading post.

April displayed Tangier at her very best and Belasyse declared himself impressed by the clear spring air, the comfortable temperature, the scent of orange blossom pervading the city and the green pastures seeming to stretch from the city walls to the blue mountains in the distance; he acknowledged Tangier as a city of 'Nobleness of Situation'.

Hamut kept his eyes on the ground as the great Lord gave instructions to his secretary to get him scrubbed up and fitted with suitable clothes. He had thought himself unlucky when their brigantine had been captured by an English privateer. Spies had reported the English fleet had been ordered home to join the war against their Dutch competitors and he judged his journey safe enough, but his lone ship had been surprised by Tangier pirates. Merchants of the city had apparently obtained a privateers' licence and sent out a squadron of well-armed ships to challenge the Barbary corsairs in their own seas.

Now he was beginning to think maybe Allah had a plan for him. If he could learn quickly and work efficiently to become indispensable to his new master and find ways to please Christian ladies he might yet be able to serve in the jihad against the infidel.

May 1665

Tangier, Morocco

Palmes had arranged with Cholmley, the chief contractor for the mole, to inspect his work in the cool clear light of early morning to avoid the punishing heat of the midsummer sun. Swagger stick tucked under his arm, he watched the mole-men and slaves already hard at work.

BROKEN TREATY

Teviot's death had not been in vain, bringing Palmes' own promotion to major. The late governor had obviously commended Palmes to the commissioners, proving the wisdom of not questioning Teviot about the positioning of the forts.

The last twelve months had seen great developments in Tangier. Tobias Bridge's enthusiasm and energy had drawn everyone together and they had achieved more than Palmes would have thought possible in raising morale and giving the city a sense of purpose. The temporary governor had initially seconded many of Cholmley's mole labourers to guard duties, and later, with the arrival of the fleet to help bolster the defences, he had diverted men and materials to complete Charles and Anne Forts and begin another, Monmouth. On his return Lieutenant Governor Fitzgerald had brought five hundred recruits to replace those lost on Teviot's Hill, and continued building new forts at pace.

Talking to Cholmley, it seemed the breakwater was a different matter. The engineer confessed his early optimism had evaporated. He had

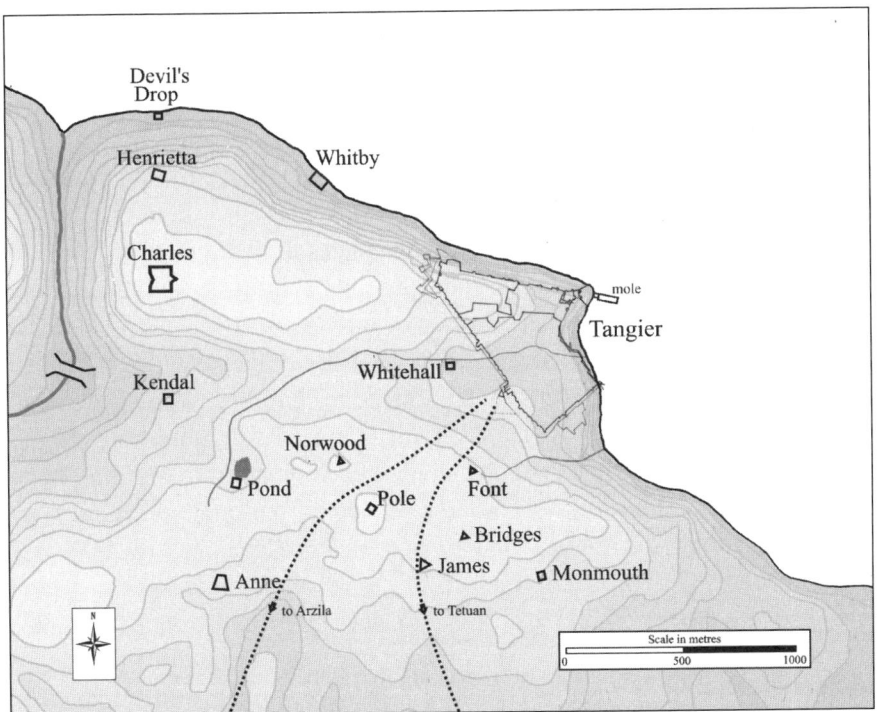

Forts in December 1664. (Author)

TANGIER: THE EARLIEST BATTLE HONOUR

expected the exciting project to make him famous – the 'constructor of the most ambitious maritime project ever attempted'. The Bay of Tangier was no Portsmouth, it provided no natural shelter. There was no great river to sail up to escape the high sea, like the Severn at Bristol. If Tangier were to become a safe refuge from Atlantic storms it needed a mighty harbour wall. Sandwich knew it and his very first action had been to survey the bay, plumb the depths and record the extent of the natural reef. Cholmley had won the contract and would be responsible for England's first entrepôt, a port to rival Venice, Livorno and Genoa.

Unfortunately it had been difficult from the very beginning. The reputation of Tangier as a place of hardship had made it difficult to recruit the masons and miners he needed; he had personally travelled to his home county of Yorkshire, to Whitby, where he had persuaded forty skilled workers to pack their tools and travel to Africa with him. His assistant, Shere, was a capable man but he would be of more use if he spent less time courting every woman in sight. Palmes should take care his wife was not on Shere's list. They had been there well over a year now and he would have expected greater progress on the mole.

They had built a jetty, but he had not realised the Levant wind blew as often and as hard. On too many days it had proved impossible to sail the rock from the quarry to the bay. His workmen had cut a road around the point to the harbour. He had organised the building of carts and the procurement of draft horses from Spain and stables for a hundred horses, along with magazines for stores. He had cottages built at the quarry and all the facilities needed for the mole-men and their families – a village in fact that he named Whitby after their home town.

In the midst of all this hard work the fool Teviot had got himself killed along with five hundred of his men and Bridges had been ordered to send a detachment of his Irish soldiers to reinforce the Portuguese Brigade. As a consequence, Cholmley's quarrymen had been diverted to building huge forts; then they had built Devil's Drop to defend the quarry, followed by Henrietta Redoubt to command the top of Marshan Plateau between Charles Fort and Devil's Drop. All this caused severe delays to the mole.

It had only been possible to get back to work on the mole once the winter storms had abated. Cholmley was pleased Charles' war against the Dutch would at least ensure the new Governor Belasyse would prioritise the mole to build a battery to repel enemy ships.

BROKEN TREATY

Still Palmes had his promotion, even if it was dead man's shoes, but chances of further advancement were minimal since the garrison establishment had been cut permanently to two regiments to save money. Military ability was no longer enough, preferment came from sponsors. He would have to gain favour with Secretary of State Bennet. He must learn to compose succinct, interesting letters and write often. He would speak to Belasyse's secretary.

The loss of Teviot had been a huge blow to the morale of the city, but Palmes could see the hero's death might be the sacrifice that would speed the building of forts and the mole and guarantee Tangier's development as an entrepreneurial centre of English excellence in Africa; that is if the Dutch did not flatten the city before the mole became effective.

Chapter 5

The Navy Distracted

May 1665

Tangier, Morocco

There was nowhere to hide.

Dover had secreted the letter she had been opening, it would have to wait, pulled on her wedge-heeled shoes that gave good shape to her legs and carefully tied the ribbons into large bows before hurrying out to see what the noise was all about.

For her, as for all the other citizens, watching ships fight it out was part of the regular entertainment. People stood on rooftops, crowded the high ground in the town, found a place on the city walls or sometimes you could even see from the shore. Usually it was a lone plodding European merchant running before the wind trying to reach the enclosing arms of Tangier to evade slavery at the hands of a speedy Maghreb corsair, often a Turk running from a Maltese and a life of rowing the infamous Knights' galleys, or maybe an Englishman bristling with guns blasting broadsides at a tricky pirate before he could escape to a safe harbour.

Given a light wind or variable weather the contest might offer hours of entertainment. Sometimes a frigate in the bay would weigh anchor to defend a friendly flag, or, even better, to pursue a rich prize. Several ships had been equipped as privateers with lateen sails, oars and light brass guns. Rowed by the enslaved crewmen of captured Barbary corsairs, they were fast gaining a fearsome reputation matching that of the Turks. The prize money helped make good the garrison pay that so often either failed to arrive or was pocketed by the Governor or other administrators. The plunder from captured merchant ships helped provision the city.

But the ships today were not fighting a running battle. This was not a spectator sport. This was serious. This fleet would not be exchanging broadsides of red

THE NAVY DISTRACTED

hot cannon balls with English ships-of-the-line. These ships, nearly twenty of them, had in mind the destruction of Tangier. It was not enough that they blockaded the city and prevented pay and rations reaching the garrison – now they planned a massive bombardment, sending death-dealing cannonballs and shrapnel to smash the Tangerines' houses and shred their bodies.

Flying red, white and blue horizontal stripes, these were Dutch men-of-war thinking to make war on the helpless inhabitants of English Tangier. They intended to flatten the defences and allow the Moors to walk in unopposed, to help the Spanish achieve their long-held ambition of taking over this outpost of Stuart impertinence.

Lord Belasyse had been a welcome sight, bringing long-awaited pay for the soldiers and three hundred recruits for the depleted garrison. Dover had been busy ensuring her customers paid her their owings before wasting it on beer and tobacco.

Belasyse himself not been idle in his first six weeks of governorship. He was reportedly from the north of England, where they were said to breed them tough. He had fought his way through the King's War in England, and was a man of considerable military exprience who believed in being prepared. Already he had personally overseen the building of a new fort at the end of the mole, and had it fitted with heavy cannon. The noise of those cannon echoing around the bay at all times of day and night had borne witness to the training of gunners, ready for just such an occasion as this. The guns of the citadel, the mole and the two frigates in the bay were all ready to respond to any attack.

The population of Tangier could not feel comfortable with their army reduced to half its original strength when fifteen Dutch warships sat waiting to attack, but they did know that their governor had prepared their city's defence as well as he could, and that many men from the United Provinces would die in any attempt on their city.

The attackers could see Tangier was better defended than they had expected. The wind would need to be fresh enough to enable them to manoeuvre into position – and move to advantage – to avoid presenting themselves as sitting targets to the defenders and their privateers, but the weather had been inconsistent and the Dutch admiral had waited patiently.

The defenders prayed. Was God for the Dutch, or was he an English god? Should the wind not change perhaps the Dutch would be recalled to fight battles in defence of the United Provinces rather than assaulting cities far from home.

TANGIER: THE EARLIEST BATTLE HONOUR

There was a change in the air. Everyone held their breath.

The red cross of Saint George on the end of the mole started to flutter. The swirling breeze would not declare itself. The flag swung one way, then the other. Would it bring the attacking fleet in close with the assurance of an easy assault, or was it the prayed-for Levantine easterly to blow the ships back into the Atlantic whence they had come?

The standard lifted, flapped listlessly, sank, lifted again, fluttered, then began to fly, stiffened, flew to the west. It was the Levant wind picking up strength. Channelled through the Straits of Gibraltar, it was blowing fiercely now. Everyone watching cheered to encourage the warm reassuring, rescuing wind of their pleas.

The Dutch fleet could make no headway against the easterly wind, and could wait no longer for a westerly. A thousand watching Tangerines threw hats in the air and congratulated each other as the admiral's ship raised the signal flags for withdrawal, went about and sailed westward through the fleet. The guns of Tangier fired a mock salute and the church bells rang out calling the faithful to thank God for their deliverance. Within the hour all Dutch ships were out of sight and the widows' drinking houses of Tangier were full of people celebrating with a two-penny quart of beer or a silver-groat flagon of Spanish wine.

Dover walked to her wild plot and was pleased to find two of her orange seeds had sprouted into spindly seedlings. She made a mental note to return with twigs to protect them, and hurried back to her rooms, impatient to read the letter. The recently introduced postal service from Tangier to Spain, Portugal and England was a blessing; it made it so much easier to keep in touch with her network of informers.

But what she read was the most spine-chilling news she had ever received. The Arab Sultan Al-Rashid of Tafilalt had overcome all his challengers, amalgamated the southern Kingdoms of Tafilalt and Marrakesh and created a great army to conquer wealthy Fez and its breakaway areas of Rif and the Gharb. This new Sultan was sweeping all before him, torturing and massacring thousands who resisted him, and utterly destroying any cities that refused his terms. Some of Ghailan's cavilas had already been terrified into submission, more were under siege.

She pulled out a sheet of parchment and set to work scraping it for reuse. The promised expulsion of the Jews had not been rigorously pursued and her contacts remained in Tangier. Nonetheless she knew she was unlikely to hear any news of her father whilst the chaos of internecine warfare continued.

October 1665

Hamut dived under his desk.

Seconds later he emerged sheepishly, hoping no one had seen his reaction to the cannon-fire from the citadel battery. His six months in Tangier had been more successful than he could have dreamed. He had worked hard to become a trusted member of the Belasyse household. The Governor relied on him as interpreter and a source of information about the ways of the Moors, their customs and habits, their religion and methods of warfare, and even a scribe of correspondence. Most recently he had been given the task of agreeing with Cholmley how the engineer was going to pay Belasyse the £2,000 fee for the Governor's co-operation in speeding the construction of mole. In the Governor's Palace he was at the heart of everything that was happening in Tangier.

He ran to the window to see the cause of the cannon-fire. There were masts on the horizon beyond Cape Spartel and the fierce westerly stretching the flags would bring the ships to Tangier in short time. Soldiers straggled onto the walls of York Castle. People were emerging from their houses, chatting in the autumn sun as they strolled to the usual assembly places to greet the ships.

Belasyse called. Hamut closed the lid on the inkwell, wiped the nib of his quill and blotted the letter he had been writing. In his hurry he almost ran into the Governor, who was striding along the corridor issuing instructions to officers, pulling on his coat and anxiously looking out of the windows as he went. Belasyse ordered him to fetch wine and goblets to the viewing gallery and to tell the cook to prepare refreshments.

A few minutes later, glass in hand and one eye to the large mounted spyglass, the Governor was listing the ships he could see; an English frigate, a Dutch man-of-war, another Dutch warship, an English merchantman, another merchant. The Dutch were attacking an English convoy. He rattled off a new series of orders and men hurried to do his bidding.

The trumpeter's call to arms blaring from the top of Peterborough Tower brought the whole city to life. Gunners appeared at the batteries on the city walls; soldiers swarmed all over York Castle, running up the steps to the battlements, assembling on the parade ground. Men in green breeches and stockings ran along the mole, donning long red waistcoats, or leather jerkins and aprons, and within minutes were pulling the heavy guns from their shelters, rolling out barrels of powder and stacking cannonballs

TANGIER: THE EARLIEST BATTLE HONOUR

nearby. Others were carrying long staffs with rammers or ladles. All were under the control of the battery commander, carrying his mace of office and ranging quadrant. People were pouring out of their houses, hurrying to vantage points to get the best view. Sailors appeared on the decks of the frigates, privateers and merchantmen in the harbour. The organisation and efficiency of these Tangerines was most impressive, everyone seemed to know where to go and what to do.

Supply convoys were becoming less frequent as the war with the United Provinces proceeded and the plague spread. Following news of the overwhelming English victory against the Dutch at the Battle of Lowestoft, Belasyse had been hoping for relief from the blockade and arrival of much-needed supplies of food, pay for the soldiers and new recruits. Sadly all he had received was news of a solitary supply ship being captured by the Dutch who were still patrolling the waters around the Iberian Peninsula. Now another disaster seemed to be unfolding, this time within their view.

Lord Belasyse frequently complained Tangier was a forgotten outpost, and that despite protestations of high regard for Tangier the King seemed always occupied with other matters. The great Lord was becoming disillusioned with his appointment and told his friends the increasing shortage of men and supplies meant he had to reduce the number of troops of Horse from three to one to maintain his Foot regiments. He had even formed a militia of all the citizens of fighting age to help defend the city walls.

With insufficient Foot and fewer cavalry to ride to the rescue of any troops in jeopardy it was useless and dangerous to venture out of the city, and impossible to properly control the tract of land enclosed within the line of forts. Belasyse often spoke of his frustration at the lack of resources and his intention to seek a return to England. Hamut was afraid a new governor might not show him the same favour, but Europeans often took their slaves back to England with them, Hamut was working on Lady Belasyse, but he had to avoid antagonising His Lordship.

The rising chatter from the officers' wives brought his attention back to the chaotic gaggle of ships coming ever closer, sails billowing and pennants streaming. Everyone strained their eyes to see the colours of the flags, to determine friend from enemy. Stood on tip-toe, they were asking each other what was happening, which ships were gaining, who was escaping, who was captured. One English frigate was surrounded by Dutch, and despite her yardarms hanging uselessly and her sails flapping was blazing cannon-fire in all directions.

The blast of cannon from the nearby citadel battery and the whistle of cannonballs told them a Dutch ship was within range. Belasyse announced the nearest vessel was an English merchant trying to outrun a Dutch frigate.

The attacking ship was much the quicker but the crew of the merchant were working hard to squeeze every knot of speed from the straining canvas; heeled over, she appeared near to capsizing. Fountains of white water around the frigate showed the cannonballs were close to their mark. The Dutchman altered course but was still closing. She fired a warning shot across the merchantman's bow, but the doughty crew opened fire with its own guns, and a cheer went up from the spectators as the frigate's foremast buckled and fell forward into the sea. The pursuer slewed to one side and slowed. The merchant ship drew away from the frigate, but within a few minutes the offending sail had been cut away and the Dutchman resumed the chase.

Another volley from the citadel guns, this time a series of splashes around the hull of the pursuing ship, but still it kept coming. By now the two ships were close enough for all onshore to see what was happening and close enough for the batteries on the mole to get in on the action. Cholmley had not been idle during the summer; the mole now boasted twenty cannon facing seaward and another ten looking over the bay. A concerted broadside from the mole resulting in a hail of more than a dozen cannonballs on and around the frigate was enough to convince the Dutchman to abandon that particular quest and go about to try another. A great cheer rose from the Tangier crowds, followed by a faint echo from the merchantman as it sailed past the point to the relative safety of the Straits. Within minutes the thankful crew released its sails one by one to round the mole and cruise into the quiet waters of the harbour.

More and more ships were coming closer. The observers' attention shifted to two of the King's frigates seeming to be leading the escape rather than trying to protect the merchantmen. What were they thinking to leave the helpless supply convoy behind? Once they had reached the protection of the citadel batteries, their captains took heart and, to the jeers of the crowd and the boos of the children, turned their broadsides to face the enemy. Now the noise of continuous cannon-fire deafened the watchers, making conversation impossible, and the wind-borne clouds of smoke drifted across the city, making observation of the ferocious battle at sea difficult, but all the more engaging.

A dozen English ships were crowding into the entrance to the Straits harried by as many Dutch men-of-war. Another merchantman limped to safety with a broken mast, bringing more cheers; the enemy strategy shifted from trying to capture prizes to heading them off or destroying them. At last the English frigates, ably assisted by the shore batteries, were getting the upper hand and the Dutch men-of-war had to turn away before they were trapped in the Straits under fire from all quarters.

Belasyse ordered extra flags raised all along the city walls and hurried off to meet the arriving crews.

The citizens of Tangier hung out bunting and crowded the shoreline waving, cheering and welcoming the crews of the arriving ships as they rowed ashore to greet the waiting Governor and the line of assembled merchants eager to receive their cargoes.

Tangier was celebrating. Belasyse said it had proved its worth as a refuge not only from corsairs, who would generally avoid an opponent with more than half a dozen small guns, but from the well-armed ships of a European fleet. At the reception these merchantmen said they had escaped the Dutch thanks to the sheer bravery of the captain and crew of an English frigate *Merlyn*, now in enemy hands, but it was thanks to Tangier they had found safe haven.

Hamut took another glass of wine to Lady Belasyse.

January 1666

Dover was a worried woman.

It was a cold winter day; the southerly wind had been blowing strong from the snow-covered mountains.

Ten months since the English war against the Dutch had begun. Ten months since her soldiers had been paid. The officers always seemed to have money but the men had to live on credit. They had no money to buy fresh food; they lived on salt pork, biscuit, peas and bread. They could not afford local fruit or vegetables; it was no wonder that living in the healthiest climate imaginable, even though the quarantine rules had kept the plague out of the city, the soldiers suffered from every other possible illness and the dismal hospital was always full.

THE NAVY DISTRACTED

Six months since the mole cannon had seen off the Dutch fleet there had been little action from them or the Moors. Nonetheless, in Tangier change was coming. Dover had received news she could hardly believe, that even while the Sultan Al-Rashid was invading Fez and the Gharb, and the plague threatened the whole country, Ghailan had recklessly attacked his erstwhile allies in Spanish Ceuta and suffered a terrible defeat. So much for his supposed alliance with Spain. His depleted army had retreated to winter in Al-Kasr. Belasyse was reportedly off to England, whether he would return seemed uncertain, and she could not discover who was likely to be the next Governor.

Dover composed a letter to Belasyse's secretary advising him of Ghailan's defeat and suggesting the Governor, Lieutenant Governor, Commander, or whoever might be in charge should consider an alliance with Tetuan and Salli for mutual defence against Al-Rashid's invasion.

Chapter 6

Waning Warlord

June 1666

Arzila, Morocco

The sparkling sea reflected the unrelenting sun in beams sharp enough to pierce Hamut's eyes.

Midday in the height of summer, civilised people should be lying on their mattress being fanned by slaves, or slouching in the shade preserving energy. But today there was no time for relaxing. Hamut had been keen to sail the thirty miles to Arzila as the interpreter between Ghailan and the English. Once here he had encouraged the warlord to appeal to Norwood and was now on the quayside helping the workers load Ghailan's valuables.

The blinkered horse, silk blanket coated in dust, sweat and blood was blissfully unaware of any danger; the camel, dribbling spittle as always, was being stubborn and the young lioness was playfully cute. Ghailan's most precious items were being loaded onto the English ship to be taken to Tangier for safe-keeping. Hamut certainly did not want to be here when Al-Rashid arrived with his triumphant army, and must be away shortly even if they had to tow their ship out of the harbour with a longboat.

Ghailan was visibly shaken. The impregnable fortresses guarding the mountain passes from Taza had not so much fallen as stepped aside. Ghailan's position at Al-Kasr had been untenable. Nobody knew which cities would support him and which would fold.

Ghailan had made a major error of judgement. His spies had told him the Spanish troops at Ceuta were below strength, many having been withdrawn for a final attack on Portugal, those remaining were poorly trained, with low morale; this was the perfect time to attack and regain the respect of the Almocaden.

Ghailan had believed the intelligence, but his attack was not well prepared and his light horsemen had been massacred by the by-no-means

WANING WARLORD

under-strength Spanish heavy cavalry. He had retreated across the mountains to his stronghold of Al-Kasr. Word of the defeat had been reported to Sultan Al-Rashid, who knew the governor of the mountain pass cavila of Beniharos, Lasin el Phut, was upset with Ghailan for being left out of peace negotiations with Tangier. The Sultan saw the opportunity to make a decisive move against a weakened Ghailan. Phut advised Al-Rashid when and where to attack, and withdrew his troops from defending the pass.

The Sultan's men had taken Ghailan's second line of defenders by surprise and swept down on his reserves, putting them to flight. Ghailan gathered men from Al-Kasr and sped to intercept Al-Rashid. They met in a desperate battle, but five more of Ghailan's generals had been bribed by el Phut and deserted the warlord. Ghailan fought ferociously to rally his fleeing men, and for a while the outcome was in doubt, but Ghailan was wounded three times in the body and twice in the face and his supporters persuaded him to escape to fight another day.

Ghailan saw he did not have the manpower to defend Al-Kasr, and kept riding until he reached Arzila.

Now he was holed up here with just the slimmest of chance of surviving; he was hanging by a spider's thread of hope in the English at Tangier almost thirty miles away. Knowing the English dreaded an attack from the Spanish, the wily fox had negotiated a mutual support treaty whereby he would support Tangier if it were attacked by any Christian power, and the English would come to Ghailan's aid if he were threatened by a Muslim power.

That treaty was about to be put to the test.

Ghailan wrote:

Excellent Sir,

All places are overspread with Disasters and events of our war. The ill success at this time befaln me hath been by the design of my enemy, the Xerif of Tefilete, who, falling in with his army, surprised my careless outguards and broke and rooted the whole body. Upon notice whereof I got on horseback at Al-Kasr but found my people running away in so great disorder that it exceeded my power to raly them till I came to Arzila. Whence I am now necessitated to crave your Excellencies assistance upon the account of that peace and friendship solemnly contracted betwixt us and therefore I desire that you would send me a boat of good bigness that I should be put to any straight I might send to you for succour which I doubt not but your Excellency will please to send me upon honourable terms. Also I desire your Exellency that in case any of my Guards of what quality whatsoever do retire to your Citty with cattle or otherwise, that you would vouchsafe to favour them with your protection and supply their necessities. I crave your excellencies commands which I am ready to perform with great willingness.

The bearers your mariners promise to return, by whom I entreat you to send large embarkation.

>May God keep your Excellency

None of Ghailan's allies believed the English would honour the treaty, not when Ghailan had killed hundreds of their soldiers.

Hamut had been annoyed when Belasyse had not taken him to England but perhaps Allah had left him in Tangier for a purpose. Norwood had proved he was prepared to take Ghailan in and risk Al-Rashid's anger. Hamut was here to reassure Ghailan, bring him succour and help Norwood fulfil the treaty.

February 1667

Palmes let out a shout of triumph.

He burrowed among the jumble of trunks and fabrics, held a walnut box on high and shouted in triumph. Apothecary Robert put down the bottle he was examining and looked at the handsome chest the major was proudly displaying. It appeared to be exactly what they were seeking.

This warehouse contained the cargo from a Turkish galley Palmes had seen tied up among several prize ships on the wharf. Hewn from rare Lebanon cedar, the beautiful ship was clearly something special used for transporting dignitaries, so its medicine chest was likely to hold what they needed. He had collected his friends, Surgeon White and Apothecary Robert and hurried to the record office to determine where the plunder from the Turk was stored, awaiting auction.

Since his wife had given birth to their first child – a son – she had been weak and suffered from fainting fits. The surgeon and the apothecary had examined her and after consulting their handbooks a lengthy discussion had decided her condition could best be improved by a potion. The apothecary had all the ingredients for that cure except one. He had no mummy powder.

Palmes had seen a bottle labelled 'ground mummy dust' in the apothecary's own medicine chest, but the doctor had admitted it was not the genuine article; the powder had been manufactured by dipping pork meat in alcohol and hanging it over a smoky fire of wet oak. He could not prescribe that for Fairborne's wife, she had to have the genuine article; he smiled as he said he did not want to risk a duel with her fiery husband.

Palmes pulled at the lid, but the apothecary's chest was locked with a large brass clasp. He reached for his knife, but Robert lifted the box from his grasp. He explained there would be a key in a hidden compartment; if he could find it he would save the beautiful chest for his own use.

He held it to the meagre light emerging from the narrow slit of a window. He grunted, pulled a surgical probe from an inside pocket and pushed it into a tiny hole in the brass plate. A small drawer sprang out from the mother of pearl pattern on the side of the box. Lying in the drawer was a silver key. The apothecary held it up, then like a conjuror performing his climactic trick he inserted the key into the padlock. It clicked open.

Three heads met over the casket, gazing down eagerly to see what it contained. The ornate tops of two dozen bottles and jars were held in a yoke to prevent them falling or jostling each other. The apothecary gently laid the box on top of a large chest, removed the yoke and began lifting the jars, reading the labels and shaking his head.

Palmes was becoming more deflated with each bottle returned to its place. His shoulders drooped as the penultimate jar emerged, a dull brown Italianate arbarello painted with strange yellow symbols. Not promising. The medical man held it up, pointed a finger to the decorations and smiled broadly, announcing they were Egyptian hieroglyphics. This was it, genuine mummy dust – the magic of a pharaoh's remains.

The apothecary slotted the precious jar back into its place, carefully replaced the yoke, closed the lid, locked the clasp, pocketed the key and clutched the treasure to his bosom. Not wishing to be accused of theft, Palmes signed the book for the medicine chest and tucked his swagger stick under his arm.

On the way up Queen's Steps, Palmes told his friends his letter to Secretary of State Bennet had been answered by Under Secretary Williamson, and asked their opinion on whether he should accede to Williamson's request for regular intelligence regarding Tangier. The surgeon advised him Williamson was known to be an influential sponsor to be cultivated carefully with frequent letters and maybe a gift, such as a silk carpet, an ostrich or a fine Moorish colt.

They had almost reached Palmes' house in the market square when they were accosted by a soldier. Palmes recognised the slightly swaying man as the belligerent Lieutenant James Fitzgerald, who seemed to believe his length of service gave him the right to show disrespect to his superiors. The man demanded to know whether he was down for night duty as in the roster. Palmes consulted his pocket book and confirmed it. The tall lieutenant stepped forward, glared down at Palmes and shouted that he had exchanged duties with another. Refusing to be intimidated Palmes, calmly replaced his notebook and took hold of his swagger stick.

Fitzgerald's face reddened. He bellowed that he should not be down for the duty; he wagged his finger in Palmes' face and accused him of threatening him with his stick. Palmes said had no intention of hitting him, explaining he was holding his stick as always. He called two nearby guards to take the lieutenant under close arrest for insubordination. At that moment Lieutenant Colonel Edward Fitzgerald appeared and in his usual arrogant way accused Palmes of improper treatment of a subordinate. When Palmes denied it the lieutenant colonel said he was calling him a liar and demanded satisfaction. Surgeon White tried to calm him, but he was adamant a duel was the only way to settle the dispute.

Duelling was illegal, and Palmes was sure the incident had been deliberately arranged, but he would not suffer the dishonour of a refusal and he was certainly not afraid to exchange pistol shots with Edward Fitzgerald; the two men nominated seconds, chose swords as weapons and retired to waste ground.

They took guard and Palmes put his sword forward to touch Fitzgerald's as was the usual practice. Fitzgerald lunged hoping to catch Palmes unawares, but the major had seen the trick before and quickly stepped aside, swinging his own sword up under his opponent's with all his might. The surprise was Fitzgerald's as the anticipated strike into Palmes' chest did not materialise, and the upward hit threw his own sword from his grasp. He stood aghast, expecting the worst, but Palmes being a man of strict honour, nodded to his opponent to retrieve his weapon. Fitzgerald grabbed his cutlass from the ground and, still bent double swung round, sword out trying again to surprise Palmes. The major jumped backwards and the blade sliced through the air where he had stood half a second before. At that instant Lieutenant

Governor Norwood strode across the grass and planted himself between the two men.

Norwood held his hand high to stop the fight and declared the garrison was not well-blessed with officers and could certainly not afford for two of the best to kill each other in the middle of a war against Ghailan by land and the Dutch by sea. He ordered them to cease their confrontation and accompany him to his office to make up their differences.

May 1667

London, England

Pepys rocked back in his chair, removed his new green spectacles and closed his eyes to relieve the pain, shut out the mundane study and conjure her face.

It was impossible to get her out of his mind. It must be the warm spring air. She sang, danced and recited at the King's Theatre Company. She was an entertainer, no more, but he found her attractive and witty, the pleasantest company in the whole world. Her husband was a surly fellow who treated her badly and Pepys fancied her for his lover. He had agreed to be godfather to her son, but he had been careless in inviting her to drink at his table when his wife was with him, and in the coach on the way home his wife had called her a whore. Maybe when it came to seeking harmless pleasures Pepys was merely incompetent.

But however incompetent he thought himself, His Majesty could always surprise him with something worse. The mole contractor Cholmley had rightly said Tangier needed a king with healthy finances. Unfortunately they had a king who had returned to his Goldsmith Bankers to continue drawing credit on his future tax income, even when that had been greatly reduced by the dreadful Fire of London the previous year.

His Majesty's complete disregard for the value of money had come home to haunt him. It was not enough that the King had overspent his income by more than £500,000 every year since his coronation, as well as spending the Queen's dowry and all the French silver from selling Dunkirk. He lavished money on his favourites and his mistresses. He had handed over his Post Office income to the Duke of York. He had signed the profits of the beer tax over to his favourite, Barbara Palmer, given her an income of £25,000 a year *and* paid off her frequent enormous gambling debts. She was capable of losing more in one evening than the navy spent in a month!

TANGIER: THE EARLIEST BATTLE HONOUR

When His Majesty had requested an additional £1,500,000 to continue the naval war effort it had become clear how the King had funded a large part of his extravagances; nearly £2,500,000 had gone missing from the navy funds, a sum amounting to twice the King's total annual budget. Parliament refused extra cash without an enquiry into the missing money. Hoping to force Parliament's hand, the King had given orders to lay up the navy – in the midst of a war with the greatest naval power in Europe! Pepys was certain Parliament would not give way; they were not in favour of war against the Protestant Dutch. Lord knows what the Dutch would do if they realised the navy was defenceless – lying at Gravesend protected only by a chain across the harbour mouth. It was like leaving the crown jewels on display for someone to take. In fact some little play-writing whore named Aphra Behn had already predicted the Dutch would attack the Medway.

Pepys was too lowly a minion to lose sleep over the jeopardy of the navy; that was for greater persons than him to consider. However, as treasurer of the Tangier Committee he was expected to balance the books and that city too was outspending its budget, not helped by payment of Lord Peterborough's annual pension of a thousand pounds.

Ever resourceful, he had come up with a plan to save money. When Pepys had told the Duke of York of Belasyse' attempts to sell the governorship of Tangier, he was furious and decided to give the post to the Catholic Lord Middleton. The commissioners did not want a Catholic governor, but they did want to wrest power from the military by dividing authority between the army commander-in-chief and a civil authority – a mayor and corporation. They could delay a new appointment by announcing an inquiry into the governance of the city. By leaving Lieutenant Governor Norwood to run the place they would avoid any conflict over the next appointment at the same time as saving the salary of a governor. The expenses of being English Ambassador to Spain was costing Sandwich enormously and it would be good to repay his patronage and help repair his finances by inviting him to head the inquiry, and together they could delay the findings almost indefinitely.

Even so, the portion of excise tax allocated was insufficient to cover the costs of the commissioners' percentages, the governor's portion, the officers' share and the garrison. In the meantime he would prepare the case for other revenues to be diverted to the city's upkeep. The King would agree, he was sure, if the Duke of York presented it to him. Charles almost always agreed with suggestions from his brother.

Pepys was mighty pleased with his solution to the problem, substantially lowering costs at the same time as reducing the authority of the army officers. Tangier was supposed to be a free city, not a military institution. A mayor would add a much-needed layer of civil authority and control, just as he and the Admiralty provided civil oversight and control over the reckless and headstrong admirals of the fleet.

July 1668

Tangier, Morocco

In Lisbon it might take a public execution or a Royal procession. In Tangier anything new was reason to stop work, make a picnic and gather in a public space, especially in the midsummer heat.

The city was a picture, the fruit trees in bloom, the green grass not yet scorched dry and the sun picking out the orange of the roofs and the saffron, turquoise and emerald doors. Crowds had been gathering for a couple of hours and latecomers unable to secure a place on the terracing were spilling onto the beach, following the retreating sea. Dover could view it all from the battlements of York Castle, where she was the guest of her favourite, most generous, officer. In return for his hospitality she had worn her lightest-weight, most revealing, silk shirt and on their way to the city walls had reached up to one of the saplings on her wild plot to pick a small sprig of orange blossom, giving him a sight of her intimate flesh.

At last the ripple of a broadside salute announced the approach of a ship from the direction of Cape Spartel. The noise of the guns on the tower above her were deafening as they joined with the battery on the ever lengthening mole to return the greeting.

The billowing sails of a xebec rounded the headland. The strong westerly stretched out a long green pennant from one mast-top, the crescent moons of Salli from the other and the huge red and green Moroccan flag flying from the pointed prow. The long-anticipated arrival of this most notorious of warlords was imminent. How he had held Arzila against Al-Rashid for two years after being wounded five times in one battle, supported only by supplies from Tangier, was a mystery to her. The Sultan had pulled off his usual tactic of bribery and found traitors to betray the warlord in his final enclave.

TANGIER: THE EARLIEST BATTLE HONOUR

The salute from the smaller second galley was hardly noticed as everyone's attention was taken by the beautiful lines and rich decoration of the first ship. Although travelling quickly, the xebec left little wake, effortlessly slicing its way through the water and seeming to respond to the helmsman's slightest movement. The crew worked the sails expertly and brought the ship around the impressive three-hundred-yard mole, to tie up beside an equally sleek Venetian galley, the *Salamander*, the Tangier privateer, scourge of Barbary merchant ships and corsairs.

The whole of Tangier watched Ghailan's Xebec disgorge its contents of brightly bedecked dignitaries from the high stern-castle onto the mole.

First to land were Ghailan's own guard wearing white with red fez caps and green sashes and cloaks. Next came Ghailan himself. He was not a tall man, but he had an impressive air about him. The gold embroidery of his emerald green cloak shone in the bright African sunlight, his scarlet waistcoat was held by silver ties and his turquoise trousers almost covered his gold shoes. He strode along the wide pavement followed by a dozen equally gaudily arrayed individuals. The Lieutenant Governor greeted him by removing his hat and nodding his head rather than offering a full bow, but the frown that crossed Ghailan's brow was wiped away by a broad smile occasioned by the apparently spontaneous crackle of small-shot from the Tangier Foot lining the mole – always seen as recognition of military prowess.

Norwood had turned out the whole regiment to impress Ghailan and to keep order, but Tangier's citizens were exceptionally good-natured considering the visitor had been their mortal enemy for more than five years. The townsfolk studied the Moor with intense curiosity, pointing and chattering noisily.

His broad shoulders and thick thighs spoke of hard physical training, his swarthy skin witnessed an outdoor life and his long unkempt hair and sunken eyes attested to recent hardships. His entourage had the appearance of battle-hardened warriors; with flinty visages, scars and eyepatches, they gave the impression of men not to be messed with.

But the individuals of real fascination were Ghailan's women. A bevy of thirty or forty females covered head-to-foot in colourful outfits reminiscent of Turkish carpets issued from the enclosed cabin at the stern of the ship. The patterns on their woollen dresses and head coverings were intricately interwoven shades of red and purple. Their faces were completely covered by black masks sewn with gold or silver edging, with small coins of precious metals hanging from them. Even their eyes were obscured by black gauze, which gave them a mysterious appearance at once enchanting and threatening.

Dover watched the women walk up the Queen's Steps and disappear through Sandwich Gate followed by another three hundred or so of Ghailan's party. By the time the last of the Moors had reached the city gate the head of the procession was crossing Dog Place to enter the castle grounds. As they paraded past the great storehouse she noticed an extra Moor had joined the war chief's retinue. Somewhere during their walk up the narrow street alongside the city wall Hamut, the one-time slave, had smuggled his way into the group of followers. Dover had heard of a strange offer of co-operation received by the Lieutenant Governor and had written a letter warning him to be cautious. Now she saw Hamut secretly joining Ghailan her suspicions were renewed.

Before she could be certain it was Hamut, the leading group had turned the corner of the storehouse into Rua de Sainte Roque to the expensive and lavishly furnished houses and beautiful gardens allotted to the Moors. Lieutenant Governor Norwood had allocated housing within York Castle nominally for Ghailan's security, but it was an open secret that Norwood wanted Ghailan where he could keep him under observation and within easy reach of the Governor's Palace. He wanted Ghailan to have no excuse to explore the defensive weaknesses of the city he had spent much effort and many lives attacking.

Ghailan's visit fulfilled Norwood's promise to honour the terms of their treaty, but in truth it was ill-timed, potentially exposing the poverty of the city due to the privations of the Dutch War: its diminished garrison with its single regiment; unimpressive troop of thirty Horse; and its poor state of repair resulting from lack of cash, to the gaze of the enemy. Norwood had told his officers that giving Ghailan a good impression of the garrison strength might well prevent future battles and a few tired soldiers now was better than many deaths in the future. They were to take extra care in ensuring their companies were smartly turned out, well armed and sober. Every battery would have a sentry on duty at all times, streets would be patrolled regularly and companies put through their training exercises every day except Sunday.

Dover was certain every man watching vowed to discover what was hidden behind the masks of Ghailan's women; she was curious as well and determined to do some investigating of her own.

TANGIER: THE EARLIEST BATTLE HONOUR

August 1668

It was late in the summer of 1668, more than six years since Edward Barlow had last been here, but he instantly recognised the fort at the top of the cliff with the crenulated wall running down to the old castle.

But now the green vegetation of the Atlantic-facing cliff was scarred by the huge patch of rock that signified a landslip, or a quarry. As the *Yarmouth* turned in towards Tangier, Edward caught his first sight of the new resting place of hundreds of tons of stone. The harbour had a new mole. The old groyne had been superseded by a new improved version. Longer, wider, much more substantial and built straight out from the old castle, this breakwater would protect the whole bay – a haven for a large number of ships-of-the-line, not merely a few merchantmen. Tangier would greatly enhance English sea power in the Mediterranean.

Being sent back to Algiers to finish the job he had begun under Lord Sandwich was some small compensation for being pressed into Sir Thomas Allin's fleet. The Algerines had kept the negotiated peace for the duration of the Holland War, but recently they had captured an outward-bound East Indiaman and stolen all of its strongboxes of gold and silver. No one could steal that much money from England without reprisal and Allin had been despatched with a fleet of half a dozen ships plus two fire-ships to destroy all the corsairs in Algiers harbour.

The journey this far had been slowed by uncertain weather and crosswinds and the crew had been on short rations but here they were at last, less one frigate returned to Cadiz for a replacement mast. It was good to see a familiar place that held fond memories, even knowing pressed men like him were not permitted ashore at any port where they might abscond.

Coming into the bay, they ran out their top-deck guns and fired a salute, then brought the frigate round to anchor near the admiral's ship. Allin was already on his way ashore in a longboat, no doubt looking forward to sharing a hearty meal with the owner of the beautifully carved and decorated xebec tied up on the mole, while all Edward's shrinking stomach could expect was some slight increase on his two-thirds rations decreed by their slow progress. But at least with fifty or sixty men allowed shore leave there would be more space for those remaining on the ship.

Once they were anchored and the longboats on their way to the beach Edward fetched his fishing twine and threw the hook and weight over the stern. The water of the bay was clear as day. He could see the sandy seabed and fish glinting in the sunlight as a shoal of a hundred bonito feeding among the flat rocks twisted and turned as one. It would only take one of those to persuade the cook to fill his gnawing stomach.

The next day Edward noticed the xebec was missing and was told the infamous Ghailan who had taken refuge in Tangier had learned of Admiral Allin's mission to Algiers and hastily departed in the moonlit night, his destination unknown. Allin was trying to decide whether to leave while there was a favourable wind or delay until the descending mist cleared and visibility improved.

September 1668

It was a severe disappointment after so much diplomacy on his part.

Although he had been a little disappointed Lady Belasyse had left him in Tangier, he had made a very pleasant life for himself as a secretary to Lieutenant Governor Norwood. He had made it his task to improve relations between the English and Ghailan, passing intelligence to and from his local contacts.

Unfortunately his attempt to anonymously broker the handover of Arzila from Ghailan to Norwood had been met with suspicion, and had failed, reportedly on the advice of someone called JW. He had convinced Ghailan it would prove to his advantage to have England as an ally against Al-Rashid. Ghailan had agreed a mutual defence treaty with Norwood, but no more. His advice had proved worthy when Ghailan had called on Norwood for his surgeon's attentions, copious supplies and, finally, sanctuary in Tangier.

It was unlucky the interfering Portuguese Dominicans had abducted a Portuguese slave girl from Ghailan's harem. The priests had pressed Norwood to have her released, against Hamut's advice and much to Ghailan's displeasure. In addition to taking one of the warlord's concubines Norwood had also stolen a portion of Ghailan's treasury, claiming it was to pay debts he and his followers had run up in Tangier. Hamut had tried to calm Ghailan, but he had sailed off to bad-mouth Norwood to the Divan of Algier and ensure no treaty could be agreed between Admiral Allin and the Dey of Algier.

TANGIER: THE EARLIEST BATTLE HONOUR

January 1669

London, England

Pepys was satisfied.

An exceedingly successful Christmas had rounded off an equally successful year. He had eaten the best fare money could buy, enjoyed wine to excess and had some success dabbling with the maid when his wife was out. He had avoided any retribution from the Dutch destruction of the English laid-up fleet, and in fact the enforced peace following that disaster had saved His Majesty the expense of continued war.

The Admiralty was paying Pepys handsomely and income from Tangier had grown his wealth beyond his imagining. The New Year of 1669 held even greater promise. At the same time the deterioration of his eyesight was causing him great aggravation. Tallow smoke from the candles had always caused him pain, but he had struggled on. Now years of long winter nights in his office and writing his diary in the garret had taken their toll. He could no longer read his music books and even the candlelight at the theatre caused him pain. He feared he would have to abandon his much-loved diary.

Pepys' ruse to save a governor's salary had succeeded admirably, already it was more than two years since Belasyse had returned and they were still awaiting the full results of Sandwich's investigation. Unfortunately the Duke of York could not hold his peace and Lieutenant Governor Norwood had heard rumours of his intention to appoint Middleton as governor. Norwood was becoming agitated and his requests to return to England were becoming too persistent to ignore. It was clear Sandwich would have to go to Tangier shortly, but Pepys would make appropriate recommendations and keep costs down.

It was a pity Norwood had let the city decline into such a condition, and his lack of clear design for making the place profitable was regrettable. His Majesty could not reduce his spending, and the commissioners needed their portion, therefore the city would have to reduce its costs further. The garrison had been reduced to one regiment of about twelve hundred, and half a troop of Horse – even with the end of the Dutch War and the French withdrawal from Algiers it would be difficult to reduce it further.

There was nothing else for it. The city must start to pay its own way, as he had been saying for several years. The disputes between the army officers and the merchants had to cease, trade must be encouraged and the prize moneys must be returned to England as specified in the city charter.

Middleton was a well-chosen successor; he knew he was fortunate to be considered for the job given his penchant for alcohol and would recognise that to continue in the position he would have to do the Commission's bidding. The proposed embassy to the rising Sultan Al-Rashid would be costly, but he seemed to have replaced Ghailan as overlord of the Gharb and if the King's chosen ambassador, Lord Howard, could negotiate a lengthy peace treaty the cost of the garrison could be reduced substantially. Pepys, as treasurer, would expect commission on all Howard's expenses.

The Portuguese war against Spain was coming to a successful conclusion thanks to the English, and with any luck the 'Portuguese Brigade' could be shipped direct to Tangier without setting foot on English soil. They would add some much-needed battle experience to the garrison and the extraordinary rate of attrition would ensure their cost was reduced quickly, perhaps encouraged by the tradition that the colonel of a regiment received a deceased soldier's pay from the time of his death to the next muster.

Yes. Pepys poured himself a congratulatory drink. Since he had begun asserting his authority, Tangier was proving a worthwhile acquisition.

His responsibilities and affairs were in such an orderly state he had earned a rest. He may apply for a leave of absence and take his wife on a tour of Holland and perhaps France. It would do him good, favour his eyes and please Elizabeth at the same time.

March 1669

Near the Straits, Western Mediterranean

The only sound was the gentle slap, slap of water under the bow of the *Yarmouth*.

Edward Barlow knew the coast of Africa held people who could conjure the spirits, and below decks of a night he had heard tales of ghost ships. With fifty guns they were afraid of nothing, but what was coming at them out of the mist was as strange as anything he had ever seen. This one looked to be a sizable ship making its way without sails. He stood on the foredeck transfixed as they approached each other.

TANGIER: THE EARLIEST BATTLE HONOUR

He was not sure whether to hail them or hold his tongue and hope they had not seen him. They drew closer.

The hollow noise of the frigate's flapping sail startled him.

There was no sign of anyone aboard.

There were no masts, no rigging, no sheets, no guns to be seen. He heard moans.

Should he reach for a belaying pin or stand still? Shout for a shipmate or stay quiet.

A shout made him jump. The frigate lurched to the side, sending him careering across the deck to crash into the rail. The steersman cursed Edward for not calling a warning. It was no ghost ship. It was an abandoned hulk wallowing on the long slow swell.

From the shape of the hull and the decoration it was a Spaniard. Everything of value had been stripped. This was the work of corsairs. By now the Spanish crew would be on sale in the Algiers slave market. At least it was not an English ship.

Admiral Allin's visit to Algiers had failed to destroy the pirate ships but they had succeeded in getting English Captain Weslock and his merchantman released and, by making credible threats of death and destruction, persuaded the Dey of Algiers to agree to abide by the treaty in future. What was better for the English was almost sure to be worse for the Spanish.

The weather being calm, the admiral ordered the *Tiger* to take the ship in tow.

***

The oarsmen eagerly pulled for the shore, grateful to be off the ship for a few hours and safely back in Tangier Bay, six months after leaving it, without further incident.

This time Edward had managed to be included in the shore party. The captain knew even pressed men would not jump ship while they were owed pay for the whole voyage and were anyway on the last leg of their journey back to England. If they had sent him ashore with the admiral he could have negotiated a better price for the Spanish hulk than the two score pieces of eight they had obtained; he was sure she could be fitted out and sold as a decent sail. There was no prize money due to the crew out of such a pittance.

They rolled the empty casks up the beach to the waterspout below Sandwich Gate, drinking their fill while the fresh water sparkled its way into the containers.

WANING WARLORD

A vaguely familiar voice spoke softly to him and he looked up to see the smiling face of the whore who had pleased him greatly on his first trip to Tangier many years before. She tilted her head and Edward looked at his fellow sailors. They leered at the full figure of the woman offering herself for their pleasure and nodded their enthusiasm. She took Edward's hand and led him along the beach to the Terrace and lay down under a boxwood bush close to the castle wall.

He was still trying to understand why she had not left for Portugal all those years ago as he gabbled away telling her his total fortune comprised a roll of Spanish tobacco. She laughed and told him to bring three ounces on his return for more water, or failing that, his next visit to Tangier. She could sell the tobacco for two shillings and would not lose on the deal, but he was pleased with her faith in him even though she was a woman of small virtue.

Now it was almost like coming home, and he grinned with anticipation as she held her arms up to receive him.

Chapter 7

Waxing Sultan

July 1669

Tangier, Morocco

Palmes had been expecting this.

He narrowed his eyes and peered into the heat haze over the hills. The slight changes in colour as white shapes shifted over the sun-silvered and bronzed tufts on the sand hills, the occasional telltale movement of the grasses confirmed his suspicions. He spoke to his lieutenant, who shouted for the drummer and trumpeter.

The intelligence of the last eighteen months made it clear Sultan Al-Rashid was intent on expanding his suzerainty. He must have supreme confidence in the ability of his army of African slaves to move against Ghailan in the north while the Dilaites remained a threat a hundred miles to the south. Now he was daring to open a third front against Tangier.

These attacks were probably prompted by Norwood's decision to honour the peace treaty with Ghailan and grant him safe haven last year. Al-Rashid was giving notice that anyone who helped Ghailan would suffer the consequences. At the same time he was doubtless keen to test the city's defences. Before their first attack a month ago his men had reconnoitred the city walls and defences in a show of force, and now, although taking careful cover, the Sultan was moving his men forward in broad daylight.

Whether Al-Rashid was preparing for a full-scale assault or merely seeking the upper hand ready for a negotiated peace, it would do no harm to give him a bloody nose and leave him in no doubt the city was English and not there for the taking.

Many in Tangier thought the establishment of Horse should have been maintained at three troops and the Regiment given full authority to take the attack to Ghailan when at his weakest, to assume control of Arzila. Only a few hours ride away, it was easily defended with a small force as Ghailan had recently proved, and could be supplied by sea. Even now a firm treaty with the warlord could deny Al-Rashid, who would think twice before taking on the combined strength of English Tangier and Ghailan's tribes. Ghailan had advised Palmes that Al-Rashid's army relied on black African foot soldiers and did not have the number of Horse he himself commanded.

The blast of the trumpet jerked Palmes from his reverie. It seemed Al-Rashid was attempting to take James Fort and needed to be taught a lesson. Palmes was the one to do it. He ran down the steps to his waiting battalion. The enemy were visible on the Sandhills beyond Monmouth and James Forts as Palmes led his one hundred and fifty Foot out. He positioned a small group of Horse at front and rear and, drums beating, marched out to meet the enemy.

Palmes had repeatedly warned his men of the likely enemy tactics. He did not march up to their position, but drew his men into line between the two forts, preparing to fight on his own terms. With his wings covered by musket-fire from James and Monmouth, the more distant gap between Monmouth and Cambridge covered by the Irish Battery, and the area beyond James protected by Pole and Anne Forts, Palmes was confident Al-Rashid's men could not surprise him with a flanking move.

Seeing so few men coming against them, the white-clad enemy Foot advanced. Palmes' men took their positions. As Ghailan had predicted, Al-Rashid's Foot – with no experience of fighting Europeans – advanced bravely, shouting their war cries and firing at random. As they came within lethal range, Palmes gave the order. The crackle of musket-fire let go a devastating volley and fifty Africans fell to the ground, but the wave of screaming warriors kept coming. Unperturbed, the second rank of redcoats moved forward, bristling with pikes to discourage a counter-attack by lancers. The second equally destructive volley hit the attackers.

Palmes knew these black African soldiers were bigger and stronger than their Moroccan predecessors, and possibly better armed and more skilful with the musket, but he was told they lacked the religious zeal. They were less foolhardy, more like soldiers and less like fanatics. The third broadside halted the advance. As the scimitar-wielding Africans came to a halt they were now close enough for the grenadiers to see their white eyes and shining black cheeks between the wraps of their headscarves. Close enough for underhand grenades lobbed by men specially chosen for their height and strength. Each of them took a grenade from his bag, pulled the cork with his teeth, inserted a fuse, lit it from a glowing match, waited just long enough to ensure the grenade could not be retrieved and thrown back, and tossed it. They rained down among the unprotected hesitating men, who stood, confused, rooted to the spot. Some of the fizzing globes landed among the ranks, others rolled under the horses of the officer who was screaming at the men to advance.

A series of ear-splitting explosions added to the cacophony and blasted the balls of metal apart; sharp shards ripped through the Africans' thin kaftans, sliced through their flesh and lacerated their organs, tore into the horses' bellies, smashed their legs. The grenades laid low anyone within reach, foot soldier or cavalry officer, spilling out their life's blood to soak into the dry sandy ground.

Anyone left standing ran for cover as more hand grenades landed among the cavalry and any officers who were still trying to rally their men.

A cheer came from the parapet of Monmouth, reinforced by the men watching from James Fort. The company advanced, but Palmes only took them a few yards. He suspected more attackers were hiding behind rocks, laying in the grasses, hanging back ready to pick off any exposed infantrymen who might advance. One such unlucky man was the sergeant, who was too keen to show his valour despite Palmes' order to stay back. Unheeding, he advanced alone and paid the price with a shot in his chest.

Palmes called on the musketmen high on the parapets of the forts. They poured down a steady hail of small arms fire, forcing the Sultan's men to keep their heads down. Under the continuous covering fire men ran forward and dragged the man back to safety, but the surgeon could only make him comfortable for his dying moments.

Grenadiers, who matched the Africans in stature and strength, moved forward, waited for the skirmishers to give their positions away by gunfire, lit the fuses and threw their next load of malicious balls of death. The subsequent explosions almost invariably resulted in the gruesome death of the recipient. If by some miracle the target managed to hang on to life, screaming their final prayers, they did not have long to wait for the coup-de-grace delivered courtesy of a well-honed steel hatchet forged in Sheffield.

The fighting was fierce, but Palmes' men were tried and tested in the heat of battle. His thoughtful strategy and their disciplined performance exacted a severe penalty from their opponents. When they had pushed Al-Rashid's forces back to the limit of the forts' musket fire the light cannon opened up a bombardment. The redcoats saw the enemy general's horse rear up and fall.

The battlefield fell silent for a while and soon after a salute of three salvoes echoed around the hills. A few moments later the enemy withdrew, taking as many dead as they could. Palmes, who had lost only one man, waved his thanks to the garrisons of the forts and took his company back to Katarina Gate in high spirits. This success would be fresh news for Williamson now he had finally acknowledged the generosity of Palmes' gift of the beautiful Moorish colt.

November 1669

Hamut had always been apprehensive of what would happen when the new Governor arrived, but for some reason it had taken three and a half years for the English to replace Belasyse.

This man Middleton was a Scot with a strong accent Hamut found difficult to understand, but he was a man of few words and a heavy drinker and Hamut's instructions usually came from others.

At least he might get this Lord Henry Howard off his backside and out into the country to meet Al-Rashid. The raucous noise coming up from York Castle was testament to Howard's malign influence on the city. He titled himself Ambassador of the King of England. For the three months since his arrival he had proved himself adept at making excuses to avoid ambassadorial duties, idling his time away in pleasure, riding by day, dancing at night, feasting and watching entertainments at all times. It might be amusing to see how the ferocious and terrible Al-Rashid humiliated him, but Hamut was wasting his time here in Tangier.

He felt Middleton distrusted him, and his constant fear was being sent to labour on the mole. He had saved some money and could buy passage in a ship, but he was still a slave and had no standing. He could run away, but if he were caught he would be on the mole as punishment. He had to find a way to get back with Belasyse where he might have some influence.

An untidy pile of papers discarded on a bookshelf caught his eye. Letters from Al-Rashid concerning Howard's mission. He would offer to take those to England and translate them for His Majesty. Middleton and his secretary John Luke would gain credit for an original way to communicate Al-Rashid's thoughts and he would get to England.

By the end of the day Luke had recommended Hamut's mission and Middleton had jumped at the chance to be rid of him.

TANGIER: THE EARLIEST BATTLE HONOUR

Late November 1669

She could not tear her eyes away.

Spell-bound, Dover stared up at the two men on the makeshift stage erected on the Old Parade Ground of the medieval edifice known by the English as York Castle. The noise was deafening. High on the Piso Nobre in front of York Castle tower the refined Noble Lord Howard, surrounded by his courtiers and other members of his delegation, stood cheering louder than anyone.

She had watched wrestling bouts and witnessed duels but she had never seen anything quite so visceral as this. Two hefty men were trying to knock hell out of each other with short, heavy sticks. The first to draw blood from the skull of his opponent above the eyebrow would be the winner of a purse of a silver crown, worth three pieces of eight or two months' pay after stoppages; many in the crowd might win a shilling, a week's pay, if they had chosen the right man, but the idle wealthy who stood high above, screaming and urging the contestants on, were probably shouting for five pounds, more than a private soldier would see in a couple of years.

Each man swung a heavy cudgel in his right hand, but his left fist was wrapped round with a long strap, the other end of which was tied round his knee. By raising his elbow high he could pull the strap tight as a shield to protect his head from the other's blows. Holding their 'guards' in this way, both men were battering each other as hard as they could. One already had a broken nose, scattering blood wherever he went; the other had one eye closed up from a blow to his cheek, his neck black with bruises.

Dover turned away. The whole town had been in turmoil for many weeks now. The lack of pay, more than a year behind, meaning all the soldiers had to live on credit, greatly exacerbated by the lack of provisions since Al-Rashid had imposed a siege, was one thing. The priggish, overbearing Bland, now even more objectionable since being made town mayor, made things much worse; fortunately he had temporarily decided to escape the abuse thrown his way by absenting himself to England, or some said Spain, and good riddance to him. Now there was yet another governor. Everyone in Tangier said Colonel Norwood had been doing a splendid job as governor, he had lived in Tangier, fought the Moors, knew how to handle them. If they had just given him supplies and money to do the job all would have been fine, but His Majesty had sent Lord

Middleton, another of his unknowns her customers said. Rumour had it this one had paid for the privilege of making money from the soldiers' pay, though others said he was sent to Tangier because he was causing trouble in the Scottish Kirk by demanding the return of the bishops.

Despite all that she was very pleased to see her new supply of customers from Portugal, where they had proved their worth in defeating the Spanish and saving her home country from renewed subjugation. In their honour she was braving the cold and leaving her cloak open to reveal her signature embroidered corset with red ribbons and barely contained bosom. They brought pockets full of pay and provided a welcome relief from the destitute garrison.

It was a source of amazement to Dover how a king who purportedly desired a colony, or at least a free port and naval base in the Mediterranean, could treat the city in such a dilatory manner. Money was always short and the brave soldiers were always at the end of the queue when money did arrive. The governors always managed to get their share or more, the merchants got paid, the engineers and contractors were always supplied with gold or silver; it was only the soldiers who were seemingly never paid.

The Mayor and corporation had brought no purpose, no ambition for better times in the city. They spent their time squabbling over money with the military men. Sometimes she surprised herself by staying in this hopeless place – if it weren't for her father she would have given up. She wondered how all the optimistic energy and enthusiasm had drained away so quickly.

It was Lord Howard's useless visit. Dover was convinced he did not want to actually meet the Sultan. He preferred to spend his evenings eating food especially imported from Spain, dancing and dreaming up ways of entertaining his huge retinue during the daytime. He'd even brought an artist, of all things, to sit around and sketch everything in sight, except her. The strange man was not interested in drawing a beautiful woman however much she displayed herself in front of him. He was more interested in Major Fairborne, who he had sketched from all angles posing in his fancy uniform. The major was fine featured, clean shaven, slim, and she would admit quite attractive, but he offered none of the emotional appeal she provided.

It was said the Sultan had first expected Lord Howard to travel to Marrakesh; then modified his invitation to accommodate His Lordship in the much nearer Fez. Safe conduct had been an issue, but was now secured. Now Howard was evidently complaining there were insufficient horses for his retinue to travel to Fez. It would soon be the rainy season and Lord

Howard would certainly not want to travel in the wet. It appeared the Grand Embassy was doomed to failure.

At least Dover's customers assured her Lord Middleton was a professional soldier; maybe that explained his perpetual drunkenness. Hopefully it would also mean they would be safe, even if they could expect to be besieged with no food and no lasting peace with the Sultan.

The City of Tangier was looking bleak indeed, but not yet desperate.

December 1669

He felt the drumming of a horse's hooves rather than heard it. But by the time his exhausted brain had worked out what it was, it was too late ...

***

Christmas Day had withdrawn, taking the storm with it, leaving a beautiful clear sky for the following morning. Palmes' wife had been asking him to ride the lines with her, to work off the excess food and clear the head from the wine of Christmas celebrations, and now the weather had improved they were out in the bright sunshine.

While she had been preparing the children for the maid he had taken his usual brisk walk down to the mole with a couple of fellow officers. Emerging from Sandwich Gate at the top of Queen's Steps, the view over the harbour was magnificent. Scores of ships were riding the short, choppy waves of the dying storm, their proudly painted figureheads nodding at the ultramarine of the water, their colourful flags and banners waving cheerfully at the sky. Some merchantmen waited to offload cargoes from the Levant or rich foods from Spain or Portugal for the wealthier officers, others were preparing to leave and back the stiff breeze to keep them ahead of any corsairs.

But as the worthies turned their gaze towards the mole itself, what a disappointment! It was as if some hungry rock-eating sea monster had taken huge bites out of the pier. They looked further along the structure, the whole thing was starting to succumb to the Atlantic gales and crumble away. It was obvious the mole would not survive the coming winter storms.

Cholmley's small-scale excavation had developed into a massive undertaking employing hundreds of men cutting the rock and transporting it down the cliffs and round the point, by cart and by boat. They had extracted thousands of tons of marl from the cliff and thousands of pounds from the

King's coffers. But, as Palmes never tired of pointing out, the method of construction was wrong. The reef did not provide sufficient protection for loose rocks. The contractors had been lucky up until now. The winters had been kind and the defects in their design had not so far been exposed. They had managed to build several hundred yards of mole and mounted thirty-odd guns on it. That was as well and had deterred the Dutch and the French, but Palmes knew it would take only one full-scale Atlantic storm to wash the whole thing away.

Palmes had read the reports of engineers in Livorno using a cage construction to hold the rocks together. If such a method were needed in the Mediterranean how much more was the need in the Atlantic at Tangier? It was obvious to all. At least it should be, unless one was blinded by the desire to make more profit than was proper. Once again the King was being poorly served. This portion of the King's money had, as was the case with most of the huge fortune that passed through his hands, been wasted.

Hopefully Norwood, who, sadly, was on his way back to London, would be able to talk some sense into the commissioners and divert some of the silver from their own pockets into an improved mole contract. But the truth was His Majesty probably had enough on his mind with the aftermath of the plague, which thankfully had spared Tangier, and now rebuilding the City of London devastated by fire. It was a pity the condition of the place could not provide His Majesty with news to cheer his royal soul. Palmes would speak to Cholmley and write to Arlington in the hopes of getting something worthwhile for His Majesty's gold.

Palmes had been saddened by the recent fall of Candia, where he had served his soldier's apprenticeship. Its surrender after holding out for more than twenty years meant Tangier was even more important in limiting the Turks' influence in the Mediterranean.

After a quick turn around the harbour Palmes had returned home to take his wife for the promised tour of the boundary. He saluted the guard on Katarina Gate, noting they were men who had fought for the Portuguese against Spain. Well used to hardship and lack of appreciation by their hosts, they were equally well-used to decisive victories well-earned through thorough preparation and brave actions. With the crushing Spanish defeat at Montes Claros the Portuguese had only to await a formal peace treaty before deciding they could no longer afford the British soldiers and packed them off. Luckily they were not wanted in England either and had been diverted to Tangier. These were just the sort of men the city needed.

TANGIER: THE EARLIEST BATTLE HONOUR

Palmes and Marjory rode in the warm sunshine, waving to citizens taking advantage of the lovely day for a ride or a walk, and saluting soldiers patrolling the boundaries, always a necessary precaution even though there had been no enemy activity for several weeks with Al-Rashid and Ghailan being diverted by their own quarrel. They had ridden along the palisade to Irish Battery and out to Cambridge Fort for Palmes to show his wife the area of proposed extra fortification, then followed the covered way along the edge of the Sandhills to Monmouth Fort, where they shouted Christmas greetings to the garrison. They were taking it slowly up to James, deep in discussion when the unmistakable sound of musket fire broke out. Palmes left his wife in the care of a group of soldiers and galloped off to the fort.

The musketeers on the ramparts pointed towards the hills and shouted 'Deserter!'

In the distance Palmes could see a figure running towards the Moors' camp. He kicked on and galloped across the loose grasses, his horse's hooves sending up a sandstorm as he went. Not far ahead an enemy sentry was looking his way. A Moor pointed and shouted; others sprang up to join him. They had seen the fugitive. A growing group gathered to watch the spectacle. Some ran towards him, waving their muskets. One or two ran for their horses. This was beginning to look risky, but Palmes was not far from the escaping man. He was committed. He needed just another few strides of his horse. No thought except to catch the miscreant.

***

He had run for all he was worth. He had escaped the musket fire, but he expected one or two of his former mess-mates to be in pursuit. They could earn a reward for catching him. He had bet on being faster than any of them, given the head start he had managed. He had chosen this day to escape because everyone was sleeping off the night's vigil. The Moors' camp fires had burned all night long and the garrison feared a night-time attack. Failing that they expected a dawn raid. Neither had materialised and most of the men were dozing.

Life in Tangier was not worth living. There was plenty of everything for the officers, feasting and dancing, sports and women, luxurious houses and trips home to England. For the common soldier life was desperate. There was little to eat, and even what they had was rotten, their sleeping quarters were cramped, the back streets were filthy and there were not enough men to fulfil all the duty rosters. Pay was a joke, always being many months behind, and when a shipment of silver did come it was swallowed up by debts run up since the previous payday.

Christmas had brought celebrations and parties for the officers and nothing but extra duties for the men. The King may call us his brave lads and say we are in his mind always, but in truth he cares not a jot for those who risk their lives and their all to protect his royal city. As an experienced soldier he had heard he could work for the Sultan and be paid handsomely. Whatever the pay and conditions nothing could be worse than the misery of life in Tangier.

He could see the Moors in their camp not so far away. The sentry was beckoning him on.

…. he looked round. Disaster! He had not bet on an over-zealous major risking life and limb charging after him.

He jumped up onto the bank. The horse's breathing was close. He swerved and changed direction. The snorting was louder. He drew his sword and turned. He saw the swagger-stick swing down towards his forehead …

***

Palmes could see three or four robed riders heading towards him. He knew there would be more close behind. He jumped from his horse, keeping hold of the reins. He reached for the fallen man and lifted him by his coat collar. Talking his stallion round, he threw the unconscious bundle across his neck, shouted and leapt up into the saddle. He could hear the Moors coming for him. He leaned forward and whispered into his horse's ear, urging him on. The lancers scented blood and were riding hard, but his stallion was a mighty beast and was outrunning the Arab mounts. The sound of the pursuers lessened; he patted the horse's neck and allowed him to determine his own speed over the broken ground.

The men watching from the battlements cheered encouragement and unleashed a hail of shot as soon as the Moors came within range. The enemy horsemen veered away, firing their muskets into the air in frustration and admiration.

Palmes dumped the unconscious man at the fort for the men to claim the reward. He could understand the deserter's dissatisfaction. Christmas for the poor wretch had passed with pay eighteen months in arrears and meagre rations of food even the wild jackals would leave untouched. Wealthy persons in England and Tangier were getting rich whilst the soldiers starved.

Even so the punishment decreed for deserting or defecting was death and he had saved this man's life so he could suffer the full penalty to deter others. His wife made him promise if he ever had the chance he would improve the men's lot. Serving in the ranks in Tangier was no way for any person to spend their life.

August 1670

London, England

Sat in the Bear Inn awaiting Lord Sandwich, Pepys had spent some time deciphering Allin's letter. Not that it was in code. His handwriting was an almost illegible spidery scrawl fit only for a man lacking education. Pepys had tried his new spectacles, then a reading glass, and finally resorted to the conical tubes his late wife Elizabeth had bought him before she passed away. The thought of her cruel death from typhoid brought a tear to his eye and he had to pause before he could read on.

Despite his poor hand and paucity of language, the admiral's message was one of good news. Allin was a tarpaulin admiral who knew his business, not a gentleman officer brought up on shore to buy his commission. No lower ship's officer would persuade him to break off an engagement while it was still there to be won. He was a man of great seamanship and of even greater courage. He had been Pepys' choice as Admiral of the Mediterranean fleet, and since he had been in command the number of corsairs captured or disabled had soared, the number of Algerian attacks on English ships had dropped drastically. Tangier was proving a valuable naval base.

Allin had been instructed to warn the Algerines of the consequences if they attacked English ships. They had ignored the warning and as soon as he had returned from his previous tour of duty he had been given the *Resolution* and sent back with a larger fleet to punish the corsairs. In concert with the Dutch he had rescued hundreds of Christians from the oars of galleys, taken several prizes, killed hundreds of Turks and enslaved many more. His latest letter confirmed his continuing success. The Algerines must be ruing the day they had ignored his ultimatum.

Pepys had ordered a bottle of claret in celebration of the good news when Lord Sandwich arrived and blurted out the story of the King's latest extravagances.

A new mistress had arrived fresh from Versailles, a girl named Louise de Kérouialle. The King was smitten and had granted her an income of £15,000 a year. He had mollified Barbara, his previous long-standing or long-lying mistress, by borrowing £8,000 to buy Berkshire House for her, as well as granting her a pension of £30,000 a year and the Post Office revenues of nearly £5,000 a year. The two women, by no means his only mistresses, had been given more than £60,000 this year alone, more than the total allocation for the defence of Tangier. How was it possible for a man to spend so much money on whores?

He also had news the incompetent Lord Howard – who made no end of excuses to avoid doing his job and journeying to treat with Al-Rashid – was on his way back to England. His mission must be one of the most useless expenses His Majesty had ever incurred and the gifts for Al-Rashid costing £4,000 were rotting in a storehouse in Tangier.

It was as well Pepys was working to save His Majesty money in Tangier. His own tough negotiations with contractors must have saved the King many thousands of pounds. It was true he had lined his own pockets very substantially, to the tune of more than three thousand pounds a year, plus payments in kind from grateful merchants. Of course, as was expected, he had denied any additional payments when questioned by the fool Povey who had sold him the post on the understanding any excess payments would be split 50–50 between them. His hard-earned cut of every deal was due to his own diligence and guile; it owed nothing to Povey's incompetence.

Tangier was a gold mine to the governors, who submitted inflated accounts, and to the senior commissioners, who signed them off without query. Why should it not be one of the best flowers in Pepys' garden?

January 1671

Tangier, Morocco

Hamut had been sent back to Tangier; for all the Duke of York's fine words, he was at heart a Christian and a coward.

TANGIER: THE EARLIEST BATTLE HONOUR

He had received Hamut as a gift from Belasyse, given him his freedom, purported to be a friend and allowed him access to court to amuse everyone with tales of the Moors' riding and hunting skills, their feasting; the savage punishments meted out by the Sultans and, most of all, stories of the sexual skills of their concubines. The Duke even gave him his name, James York. But as soon as he suspected Hamut of partaking of the company offered by one of the women who pleasured the Duke, he had shipped him off. A few weeks later he had been sitting off Spain aboard the *Newcastle* awaiting a fair wind, which was now taking him into Tangier harbour.

It was true Hamut's passes for various courts and embassies across Europe offered a chance to explore many places of which he had heard only rumours and gossip. Perhaps the Duke really did trust him and was sending him, as they said, to learn of modern warfare and the political situations as listed in his assignment. On the other hand, travel was dangerous at the best of times and January was for certain not the best of times, they had given him no weapons and he could not turn the warrants for credit into cash until he reached his destination. All-in-all it did not feel like the golden opportunity His Highness professed it.

He stood on the poop deck admiring the mole growing out from York Castle and saw men working on a new wharf between the mole and the Queen's Steps. He raised his eyes to the town remembering his amours with the young ladies of Tangier and wondering whether Dover was still operating. If he got into the first boat ashore and was quick about it he could look up one of the officers he knew, borrow a few pistoles, buy a weapon or two and still have time to visit the Portuguese whore for a little light relief and a quick catch-up on the gossip and the latest news of the garrison and Ghailan.

***

Some hours later Hamut ran down to the shore wearing a cavalryman's cutlass and a pair of pistols, clutching a small bag of coins. He was no longer a slave, even though he was sometimes regarded as one, he had money and the means to defend himself. Assassination was now unlikely; he told himself he should stop worrying and start looking forward to his travel, just as the Duchess of York had advised.

WAXING SULTAN

March 1671

The officer had paid her well and she had tried everything she knew, but he could not settle to the task in hand.

Dover had never seen her best-paying customer distracted in this way. The peace treaty with Al-Rashid had been an insult to the garrison, giving away much-needed weapons and powder in exchange for food. Middleton was a drunken fool. Twelve months of Middleton's governorship had seen the incursions by the Sultan's men increase; they frequently appeared in great numbers at the boundary and loitered for no obvious reason. At the same time excursions by the garrison had decreased and the area citizens could safely ride was lessened.

Middleton said the garrison was at full strength – by whose measure her customer wanted to know. They had sufficient men to keep the enemy away from the city but insufficient to ensure the forts were fully manned; and nowhere near enough men, particularly cavalry, to control the fields and pastures needed to keep cattle and horses fed.

The Governor did not take care of the men who were here. The rations were already insufficient before he had given a great store to Ghailan. Those in hospital were on survival rations of watery gruel, while the Governor entertained officers at lavish banquets. Even the officers' finances had deteriorated. Some previous governors had tried to make good the lack of soldiers pay from England by using their own cash, and a few officers had tried to lighten the men's burden by offering advances of pay, but the Tangier treasurer in his comfortable office in Whitehall had decreed no advances were to be given.

Not wanting to upset the officer further she had eventually pulled on her silk pantaloons and sent him away calm if not satisfied.

His complaints were voiced by others; she had often heard tell Middleton was frequently drunk and many thought him ineffective. On the other hand, the constant arguments between officers and merchants had abated under his governorship, though probably because of the Mayor's absence rather than Middleton's presence. Perhaps the most useful thing he had achieved was in declaring the markets 'free', as they had always been by law but not in practice, which had immediately reduced prices to half.

Word was the Governor had complained to his masters in England many times of the poor food and lack of money, but in truth her soldiers were poor as church mice and could not afford to buy the local fruit and fish even now it was a good price. The army officers and wealthier merchants could live well; it seemed strange to see the soldiers and poorer citizens suffering malnutrition amid an abundance of fresh food.

June 1671

Palmes blinked; it was difficult to believe his eyes.

Late spring in Tangier and you could think it was a sunny summer day in Hampshire. The lush green meadow sloping down to the gently babbling river was scattered with men scything the grass. Draft horses from the quarry were waiting patiently while men pitched grass into their carts. The few remaining troopers' horses would be well fed. The land between Anne Fort and Kendal was fertile. The same soil around Whitehall supported an extensive garden and a small orchard supplying a variety of herbs and Mediterranean fruits for the officers' tables.

A shout from a lookout had alerted Palmes and an outstretched arm pointed to a large force of black-skinned skirmishers clambering from Anne Lane and preparing to attack the foragers. Before the English drummers had finished their call to arms, four or five hundred white-robed Sudanese had formed into three ragged rows beside their red and green standards several hundred paces from the Palmes' position. Distinguished by the colour of their sashes, the enemy musketmen stood tall in rank and file challenging his battalion at its own way of war. Never before had Palmes seen Moors fight with such discipline. It appeared Sultan Al-Rashid was intent on ejecting the non-believers from his lands using English tactics.

As soon as Palmes' three-hundred-strong battalion had fallen into line, lit their matches and doused their pipes he marched them towards the enemy confident no ambush by lancers could have been laid under the watchful sentries in the forts. Equally, the garrison had few Horse to call on and he had not ordered his men to bring grenades. It would be trial by musket-fire.

The two converging battalions came within range and stopped. The enemy front rank presented their muskets. Thinking he might yet persuade them to break and run, Palmes ordered his men to advance another ten yards.

The Sudanese stood firm. The Tangier battalion presented their muskets. The front ranks fired simultaneously. A cloud of smoke hung over them.

The Moorish first rank retired to reload; the Tangier second rank moved forward.

The English were more practised and fired their second salvo while their opponents were still moving into position, but the enemy stood their ground and fired soon after. Volley by volley, Palmes advanced. Realising his men were firing more often and more accurately, he halted. His men were still greatly outnumbered, and their hangers were nowhere near as effective as the Moorish scimitars in hand-to-hand combat. Content to hold position and exchange fire, he sent a rider off for more ammunition – it could be a long day.

Every time a Moor fell he was dragged away for another to take his place. They stood 'toe to toe' until the Sultan's men ran out of ammunition and started to withdraw, taking scores of dead and many more wounded. The Tangier battalion had suffered one wounded but, still wary of close combat, Palmes greeted the Moors' retreat with a rousing cheer rather than hot pursuit.

Later in the day, marching his men back to Katarina Gate, Palmes mused on a successful six months. The mole was making good progress and an increasing number of ships were using the harbour. A detachment of men had sailed to Old Tangier and burned the Moors' crops, though it would have been more to Palmes' liking if they'd had enough men to occupy the village. At least this was a start. Today's engagement was a significant success and may well discourage the Moors from trying the same tactic again – heaven forbid they should field the large number of men they had and make a well-organised concerted attack.

June 1671

London, England

Pepys was not pleased.

Midsummer Day and he had been called to Windsor for an extraordinary gathering of the Tangier Commission because Middleton had far exceeded his brief and spent a great deal of money without prior agreement.

It was difficult enough for Pepys to find the wherewithal to pay the authorised garrison costs, let alone extras whenever a soldier who knew nothing of the King's finances took it upon himself to throw cash at

TANGIER: THE EARLIEST BATTLE HONOUR

unnecessary defensive structures. He was totally opposed to encouraging Middleton to carry on in this way by reimbursing his so-called secretary, this John Luke upstart, who only got his job because his brother had been stupid enough to get himself killed along with Teviot, and had the nerve to attend the commissioners' meeting. How he could show his face in front of His Royal Highness the Duke of York, Prince Rupert and Lord Ashley and Admiral Sir Thomas Allin here in the heart of Royal Windsor Castle, Pepys did not know.

Pepys did not offer an opinion, of course, now the Duke of York had affirmed his Catholicism but before his arrival he drew the commissioners' attention to the high proportion of Catholic officers and men in Tangier. Once His Highness had arrived from his previous engagement with the Treasury Commission and formally introduced Middleton's request for reimbursement, the Prince and Shaftesbury had waded in with their argument that the strengthening of the citadel defences had severed the stronghold from the town; which was patently true. He proposed a motion to tell Middleton to stop the works immediately.

Others argued the citadel was the only part of the town that had modern defences against cannon, citizens would be taken into the citadel in an emergency and the inhabitants were in favour of the works. Admiral Allin said the new defences would help secure the mole as well as the town and Wren supported his argument. All the commissioners who had been to Tangier let their feelings override their better judgement and Pepys' cause was lost.

No sooner had Pepys spoken to the Treasury Lords than Howard and Luke accosted him and demanded an advance for Lady Middleton before she left for Tangier. He had explained to them the Lords had made no decision yet, nor had any order been given for paying the garrison. The insolent Luke had then gone to the Treasury Lords himself, who had told him they had passed an order for six months' pay at their meeting on the previous day.

Nonetheless, Pepys had delayed handing anything over, explaining he had to make numerous calculations concerning deductions and expenses before he could write the draft. Regarding the defence expenditure, there were many steps to take before any payment could be made. Luke and Lady Middleton would have to be patient.

Chapter 8

Spendthrift King

April 1672

London, England

Pepys threw the note onto his desk: 7 April 1672 would be a date to remember.

The purpose of a strong navy was to avoid war by intimidating others. The navy was a bargaining chip. And here was the King declaring war *again* on the Dutch. The Dutch who had defeated us, no, humiliated us only five years before. Five years of hard work for Pepys. Years when half the finance granted to the navy had been diverted to cover the King's extravagances and Pepys had been hard put to find sufficient resources to rebuild the English navy and provide for his own needs.

This was almost inconceivable. How could Protestant England be joining an alliance with Catholic France against the Protestant Dutch Republic? Even if de Witt had effectively supplanted the Stuart Prince of Orange, the United Provinces was still a natural ally of the English. The foolhardy Robert Holmes had started the war single-handedly by attacking a Dutch fleet on the excuse they did not strike their flags. Observers said they had. Whether he did it on his own initiative or on secret orders from the Duke of York was unknown.

This Treaty of Dover, promising to support the French against the Dutch, was suicidal. The King had no cash – he had frittered it all on his mistresses (one of whom was French and had spent her two years in Whitehall lavishing the King's money on converting her apartment into a French Palace, another was in Paris bestowing more of his gold on her new lovers). In addition there were rumours of large sums of cash from the Secret Service budget given to Nell Gwynne, an actress of ill repute, but the King resisted publication of those expenses on grounds of National Security.

The war was most inconvenient to Pepys himself. It was true the greater the spending on the navy the more room for manoeuvre in his accounts, on the other hand he was at the stage when other pursuits demanded his attention and this war made much extra work for him personally.

The King had found a way to borrow even more money in advance of his taxes being collected. Traditionally the Crown sold the rights of collecting taxes to 'farmers' at a discount. The King received the money in advance and the farmers suffered the cost of collecting the taxes and the delay in getting their hands on the money, but received a profit to compensate them. In addition to this His Majesty had been selling taxes to the Goldsmith bankers. He had given them tally sticks – pieces of wood with notches cut in them representing certain taxes – and they had given him gold. As the taxes were collected the interest and a small part of the capital was paid off. Unfortunately the King had sold more taxes than could be collected and accumulated debt much larger than he could service. There was no way out except greatly reducing his expenses.

On the contrary, he had declared war and greatly increased his expenditure. He turned to Parliament for more supply. They said he only called Parliament when he needed money and they turned him down. Rather than reduce his expenditure, the King declared a temporary suspension of repayment of his loans. The merchant bankers could not believe what was happening. The King had taken the keystone out of the arch underpinning the finances of the whole banking system. He had removed the trust in his word.

The stop was said to be temporary, but everyone knew the Spendthrift King would not, and indeed could not, curb his wild spending. No one would invest in the Goldsmith bankers' debt. No discount was sufficient to tempt buyers. The Goldsmith bankers were headed for bankruptcy as surely as the King was headed for another mistress.

April 1672

Tangier, Morocco

Dover pulled the little medicine chest from under her bed, flipped the lid and took out the green glass bottle.

She removed the cork and smiled to herself as she poured the clear liquid into the cut-glass goblet. She sniffed the flowery aroma and her smile turned

SPENDTHRIFT KING

to a laugh. It was certainly time for a celebration and she always celebrated with her favourite drink, genever.

She counted back on her fingers. Five days ago, on the eighth of April while she had been watching the married men defeat the bachelors in the annual bowls match outside the city walls at Whitehall, the Great Al-Rashid had been at his Ramadan prayers.

As midnight brought in the ninth of April the sighting of the new moon had signalled the end of Ramadan 1672, or 1082 in Islam, and the beginning of Greater Eid celebrations. While she had been entertaining her favourite customer and looking up at the silver crescent in the black sky, Sultan Al-Rashid had been entertaining a few of his closest friends at a drunken Id al-Kabir party.

She held up her glass and toasted the new moon.

At dawn on the ninth while she had been awaiting a local informant and had chanced to see someone suspiciously like Shere sneaking from a house and escaping over the garden wall, Sultan Al-Rashid had been spurring his favourite white horse around one of his immaculately maintained royal gardens in Marrakesh.

She raised the glass again and toasted Al-Rashid.

Galloping through an orange grove, the Sultan had careered into a low branch, smashing his skull. Now, four days later, the messenger had arrived in Tangier with the news of Al-Rashid's death.

She raised the glass once more and toasted the late Al-Rashid. What exquisite irony. The pious leader of Islamic Morocco had been killed whilst riding under the influence of alcohol.

But the most exciting news was that her father was alive – working in Marrakesh as one of the late Sultan's secretaries. As a scribe his price would be high, but she would write to the Redemption Fathers in Barcelona to open negotiations.

She refilled the goblet, toasted her father and drank the contents down in one.

Dover doused the candle in the window and released her body from the confines of her work clothes. It was time for a night off. She made little from whoring these days – only her intelligence activities kept her solvent. Her debtors' book had many pages; the soldiers had not been paid for more than two years. Their credit was exhausted with all the taverns and merchants, they were now selling anything they owned – she had a small store of uniform shirts and stockings and had even begun a pawn business.

If a soldier in her book got himself killed she received nothing; if he had pawned a watch or a gem, a roll of tobacco or even his spare clothes she had something with which to pay his debts.

She wrote a hasty note to John Luke, the Governor's secretary, informing him that one of the deceased Sultan's brothers named Ismail had seized Al-Rashid's treasury at Fez and declared himself sultan.

The streets to Jews' Lane were littered with idle soldiers drinking, smoking and gambling, playing Aunt Sally, wrestling or arguing. Tangier was becoming a garrison town without employment for its soldiers – a dangerous place. Hopefully the new sultan and Ghailan were likely to be occupied in competing for control of Fez. With any luck her father would find a way to escape. Or if Middleton were replaced by a competent governor this could be the moment the merchants of Tangier took a step towards security and prosperity and she would earn enough to buy his freedom. On her way home to continue her celebration she would visit her orange tree and say a prayer.

October 1672

The sun brought out the full beauty of the polished red cedar. She might be designed to bring death and destruction to the high seas, but she was a work of art. A Livorno galley fashioned for speed, with a sleek hull, a massive lateen sail to catch the slightest breeze and a small foremast to give maximum manoeuvrability.

Holding his son's hand, Palmes walked up the mole to join the group of officers admiring the latest addition to the Tangier privateer fleet. The ship had arrived years later than originally planned. Difficulties in obtaining the forty or fifty slaves needed to man the oars had only been overcome by sailing to Valletta, where the Knights of St John held a slave market well stocked with captured corsairs.

Captain John Holmes was inspecting the galley. Holmes had been given the task of protecting English shipping from corsairs. His frigate, the *Nonsuch*, had been built for speed and manoeuvrability and the galley would be joining his squadron of privateers to prey on Dutch merchantmen and protect English shipping from corsairs.

He had already claimed several Dutch prizes. Those cargoes had provided some small income for Tangier, which was as well given the Dutch success in intercepting what little supply had been sent from England.

SPENDTHRIFT KING

Intelligence sources reported the Moors were busy fighting among themselves. Al-Rashid's successor, Sultan Ismail of Fez, had suffered rebellions in Marrakesh and Tafilalt in the south, Taza, the Rif and the Gharb in the north. All the cities of the Gharb had declared for Ghailan who would be busy preparing for Ismail's eventual return. It seemed unlikely anyone would mount an assault on Tangier, and Middleton's peace treaty with Ghailan had proved a shrewd move, even though Palmes had thought it weakness at the time.

As always the relief would be temporary and Middleton must take advantage of the lull in fighting to build relationships with the local tribes. Palmes had heard Angera, Arzila and Tetuan were keen to establish ties with the English. Middleton blamed lack of money for his failure to trade with them, but he was a feeble governor who had no influence at court and lacked the diplomatic skills to forge alliances with local chiefs. More, it was the governor's proclivity for entertaining and drinking and his lack of any strategy for Tangier that saw the city wallowing in the doldrums when it should be pushing forward and leading the Gharb to become a thriving colony.

The city was a backwater where the governor and officers could live comfortably but achieve nothing worthwhile and the men and the citizens lived miserably and had no means of escape.

December 1672

Dover had bitten her fingernails to the quick.

The nine months since Al-Rashid's death had seen the Rif and the Gharb rebel against Ismail. Tetuan had asserted its independence by decapitating Al-Rashid's appointed governor and purging the Sultan's officials. It was now the biggest contributor to Ghailan's army but, uncertain of Ghailan's success, the new Qaid of Tetuan was secretly trying to negotiate a mutual support treaty with Tangier instead. By chance he had chosen a Jew named Jacob, one of Dover's contacts, to discuss terms with Secretary John Luke.

Unfortunately Ghailan's agent Mohammed Lucas was also visiting Luke. Lucas had been one of Al-Rashid's most brutal officials and was now equally vicious in Ghailan's service. Dover suspected Jacob was unaware of Lucas' new found loyalty and feared he would unwittingly reveal Tetuan's design to him. She had to warn Jacob.

She had been informed the turncoat was meeting Luke in the Mole Tap, a drinking house frequented by mole-men and sailors. This was the ideal opportunity to identify Lucas and his fellow agents, but the Tap was a dangerous place for a woman and it was also possible she would be recognised, fatally compromising her intelligence work. She should call on her Jewish agent and send him to spy on Lucas, but time was short and she might miss her opportunity. The question was whether it was worth the risk.

She changed into her dark brown dress, grabbed her black cloak and went out into the wintry night. She narrowed her eyes against the fine spray the blustery wind threw into her face as she hurried down to Sandwich Gate. Emerging at the top of Queen's Steps, the fierce westerly took her breath away, and she could see the Atlantic waves crashing into the mole and throwing water high in the air to drop like rain on the paving. She began to have second thoughts. This was a job for a man after all.

She turned back into the gateway.

But what if the Jew were not at home? What if he were too late? What if tomorrow Jacob was found floating face down in the bay?

She had a job to do. She wrapped her cloak tight, turned once again through the gateway and fought her way down Queen's Steps along the new quay to the mole. Other people were battling the wind to get to the ale house and she managed to grab the arm of a fresh-faced sailor and drag him into the Tap with the promise of a suitable reward if he bought her a drink.

A few seconds later she was in a dark corner shaking off her cloak and adjusting her scarf while he was ordering her a Blue John.

Lucas, deep in conversation with the Governor's priggish secretary, had leered at her as she entered, and then got back to his discussion. She had downed her first pint when two men joined Lucas and Luke. The older stooped one was balding with a scruffy gun-metal grey beard, the other a blear-eyed swarthy man with curly black locks.

She was kept busy amusing her own companion, trying to avoid the attentions of engineer Shere who was eyeing her up, and watching the younger rheumy-eyed one controlling Lucas with subtle looks and a kick of his foot under the table. Halfway through the next beer, when she realised how strong it was and began to regret her choice of drink, she belatedly noticed Lucas pointing her out to the older man who, in turn, was watching her from the corner of his eye. She pulled her scarf up, took her sailor by the arm and dragged him out of the door, slipped him a couple of groats and told him to delay the others if they followed.

She heard a scuffle and grunts and hurried on, blown along by the wind. She did not look back until she reached the top of Queen's Steps. Several

Above left: Henry Mordant, 2nd Earl of Peterborough, Tangier Governor 1661–63, removed. (From a contemporary portrait; CCPD)

Above right: John Belasyse, 1st Baron Belasyse, Tangier Governor 1665–66, resigned. (After Sir Anthony van Dyck; CCPD (CC BY 3.0))

Below left: John Middleton, 1st Earl of Middleton, Tangier Governor 1669–75, died in fall. (Attributed to Jacob Huysmans; CCPD)

Below right: William O'Brien, 2nd Earl of Inchiquin, Tangier Governor 1675–80, removed. (Artist unknown; CCPD original held by the National Army Museum)

Above left: Thomas Butler, 6th Earl of Ossory, died before taking up post as Governor. (Engraving by James Parker after copy of painting attributed to Peter Lely Wikimedia Commons original)

Above right: Charles Fitzcharles, 1st Earl of Plymouth, died of fever in Tangier before receiving his appointment as Governor. (after Peter Lely: Wikimedia Commons)

Left: Sir Palmes Fairborne (thought to be), died in battle before receiving his appointment as Governor. (Detail from 'Prospect of Tangier from the Land it being the South-West Side' W. Hollar; Rijksmuseum: CCPD)

Above left: Sir Percy Kirke, Tangier Governor 1681–83, with an image of Peterborough Tower, Tangier, removed. (Artist unknown; CCPD (original held in the Officer's Mess of the 2nd Battalion, Princess of Wales' Royal Regiment))

Above right: George Legge, 1st Baron Dartmouth, Tangier Governor 1683–84, appointed to destroy and abandon Tangier. (Peter Vanderbank; CCPD (original held by the National Portrait Gallery, London D34683))

Right: Luisa Francisca de Guzman y Medina Sidonia, Queen Mother of Portugal, mother of Catharine of Braganza. (Attributed to Alonso Cano; Museo de Bellas Artes – Cordoba, Andalucia, Spain: WPCD)

Above: Charles II and Catherine of Braganza double portrait. (Unknown artist: WPCD)

Below left: Al-Khadir Ghailan on horseback, overlord of the Gharb, northern Morocco, 1657–72. (from 'A Description of Tangier' (1664): CCPD)

Below right: Muley Arsheid Zerif (Al-Rashid), Sultan of Morocco, 1666–72. (Wenceslaus Hollar 1670; University of Toronto, Thomas Fisher Rare Book Library, Hollar Collection: Public Domain)

Above left: Muley Ismail, Sultan of Morocco, 1672–1727. (Unknown artist; Royal Collections Trust RCIN 619122: CCPD)

Above right: Edward Montagu, 1st Earl of Sandwich. (by Peter Lely; Yale Centre for British Art: WCPD)

Below left: Samuel Pepys, Clerk of the Acts to the Navy Office and Treasurer of the Tangier Commission. (John Hayls (1666); National Portrait Gallery: WCPD)

Below right: Henry Bennett, 1st Earl of Arlington, Sec of State for the Southern Dept, 1662–74. (After Sir Peter Lely: Getty Images)

Above: Tangier city and citadel. ('Prospect of the Inner part of Tangier from the South East' W. Hollar; Metropolitan Museum of Art, DP823363: Public Domain)

Below: Tangier looking towards Katarina Gate. ('Prospect of Tangier from the Land it being the South-West Side' W. Hollar; Rijksmuseum: CCPD)

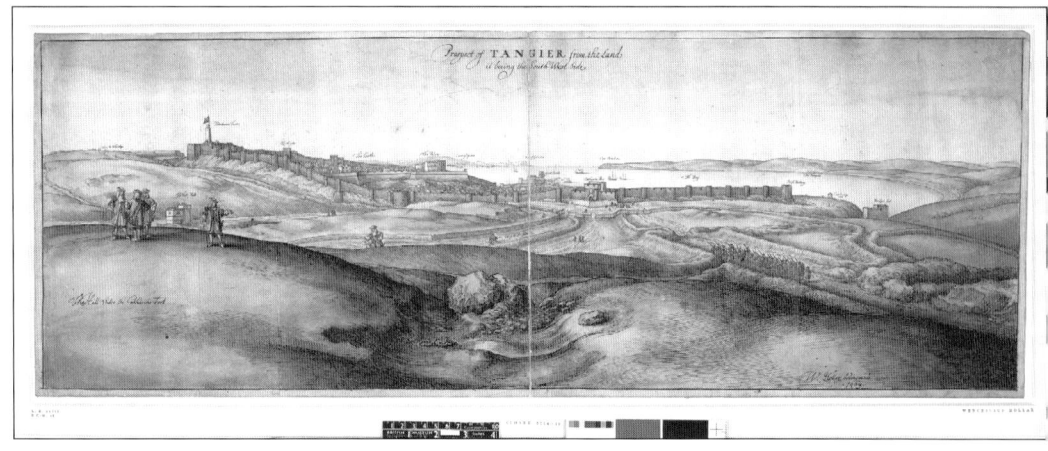

Above: Carting stone from Whitby Quarry to the mole. ('Prospect of York Castle at Tangier from the Strand' W. Hollar; Metropolitan Museum of Art, New York DP823362: WCPD)

Below: Henrietta Fort and Devil's Drop. ('Prospect of the grounds around Henrietta Fort' W. Hollar; Univ of Toronto, Thomas Fisher Rare Book Library, Wenceslaus Hollar Digital Collection: Public Domain)

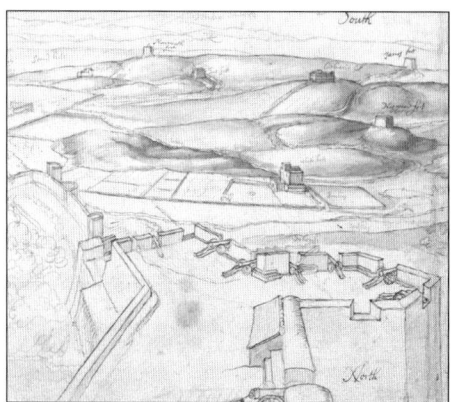 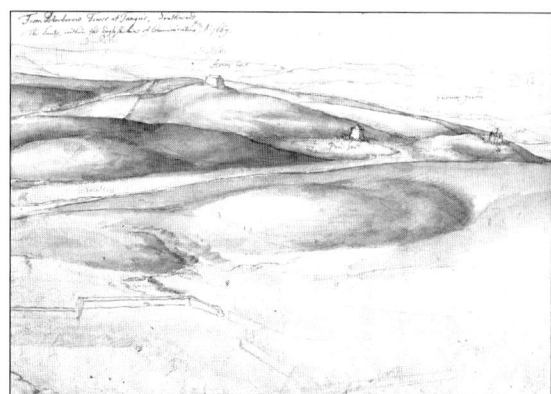

Above left: Later forts to the south-west of Tangier, Belayse to James. (Detail from 'A View from Peterborough Tower at Tangier' W. Hollar; Yale Centre for British Art: Public Domain)

Above right: Later forts to the west of Tangier, from Anne to Kendal. (Detail from 'A View from Peterborough Tower at Tangier' W. Hollar; Yale Centre for British Art: Public Domain)

Below: Later forts to the north-west of Tangier, Charles and Henrietta. (Detail from 'A View from Peterborough Tower at Tangier' W. Hollar; Yale Centre for British Art: Public Domain)

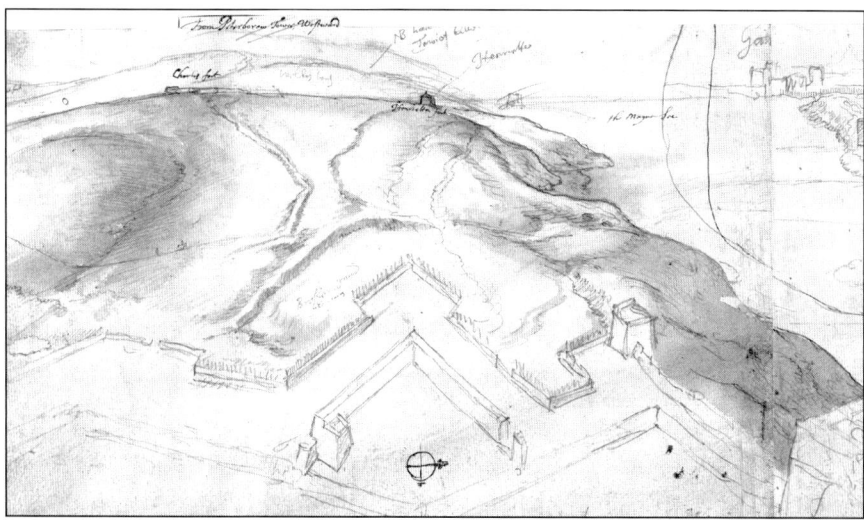

figures were still brawling on the mole. She had achieved her objective and could give Jacob a description of Lucas and his accomplices. She had escaped for the moment, but she feared Lucas had recognised her. Keeping to the shadows she took a circuitous route to Jacob's back door. He immediately offered her a large glass of wine and sanctuary for as long as she was in need.

Once she was calm and settled he imparted the wonderful news that her father had been moved to Ismail's offices in Mequinez. Once the new sultan had established his authority it might be possible to negotiate her father's freedom.

March 1673

London, England

It was heartbreaking for Pepys.

The war against the Dutch was proving an expensive mistake and had brought England nothing but pain.

Parliament had forced His Majesty to rescind his Declaration of Indulgence which would have allowed Catholics to follow their religion without persecution, and to introduce the Test Act, barring Catholics from public office which in turn made it abundantly clear that thoroughly Protestant England was allied with expansionist Catholic France against the Protestant Dutch.

In June of last year when the French, the instigators of the war, had run from the scene leaving their English allies to fight alone, Lord Sandwich had been drowned after his disabled flagship had been set ablaze by a fireship in the Battle of Solebay. Pepys would miss him terribly as a friend and mentor as well as a sponsor.

Last July William of Orange had become Stadtholder, so now Charles was at war with his nephew. That was a ridiculous state of affairs, even more so as William was proving a capable leader, forcing the French to retreat from his territories.

Several convoys to Tangier had been intercepted and shipments of silver to the garrison had disappeared into the Dutch war-chest. The expense of the war had put the King at the mercy of Parliament's fiscal power for no good reason. In addition his reversal of the Declaration of Indulgence had

TANGIER: THE EARLIEST BATTLE HONOUR

undermined the authority of the Crown. Parliamentary opponents of His Majesty were forming devious alliances with Stadtholder William in the United Provinces in an attempt to stop the fighting as soon as possible.

The emboldened Parliament had also tabled a motion proposing Tangier be brought under Parliament rather than the Crown, and to be governed by the Laws of England rather than the martial law of the Governor.

September 1673

Tangier, Morocco

It was a first-hand report, a document to be relied upon.

She had lived six months in fear of her life, holed up in a friend's house, watching every shadow. She wished no one harm, but this man's demise was good news for her; his agents would be dead or have tasks more urgent than seeking revenge on her.

What a relief, she could live freely once more – as freely as the English war against the United Provinces would allow, at least. The Dutch navy captured or sank much of the supply sent to Tangier – the soldiers remained poor, and life was barely tolerable. Still, she had to be thankful for small mercies.

She copied the letter carefully in her own hand, folded the sheet over and sealed it with a trembling fingerprint.

September 1673

Today Hamut had scored his first minor success in intercepting a letter sealed, intriguingly, with a fingerprint.

His tour of Europe had been highly successful. His experience of politics, diplomacy and war, as well as the carnal depravities of Christian states, had rekindled his zeal for jihad against the decadent Nazarani.

He had feigned a headache, left the governor entertaining everyone at lunch and retreated to his office. He reached into his waistcoat and pulled out the document. The seal had been applied in haste and he easily lifted it with a paper knife.

He read:

Whilst Ismail besieged Taza, Ghailan had sent his men out into the fertile countryside to help bring in the plentiful harvest and was relaxing with his concubines when a messenger burst in with terrible news. Ismail had undertaken a forced march through the blistering heat of the blazing summer sun and was only a few hours away with twelve thousand men.

Ghailan hurriedly drew up what men he had in front of the city, and saw Ismail's army moving into their traditional crescent formation. In the centre stood a black infantry unit with spears to the fore protecting musketmen and crossbowmen. On either side were Moors wielding bows and slings, clubs or long darts. Mounted Moorish warriors waited on the horns of the crescent with long muskets loaded and ready.

Ghailan caught sight of Ismail in the distance with his reserves of horse and a bodyguard of his famed Black Guard; knowing there was little chance of getting to the Sultan without breaking through the main body of his troops he fired a series of arrows high into the sky, more in hope than expectation. He sent his cavalry forward and advanced his infantry simultaneously. For a moment he could not see what was happening through the cloud of dust from the horses' hooves, but as the air began to clear Ghailan could see many of his lancers were missing, they had not attacked the enemy, but had ridden past them and kept going, paid off by Ismail or eager to escape what they saw as a lost cause.

Ghailan cursed those who had deserted him and shouted encouragement to those that remained. He charged angrily, his iron lance thrusting death to all who came near. The blade stuck fast in the chest of an enemy horse, he let go before it could drag him from his steed, swung his petronel into his hand and blasted an incoming rider off his foaming mount. He dropped the firelock and grasped his trusty scimitar; his most loyal men flanked him as he cut a swathe through the enemy horse. His first horse was felled and he jumped onto a second and grabbed another lance brought by an aide, continuing his wild attack. The battle was not going well, and he could see some of his skirmishers wavering under the push from the Sultan's Black Guard. His only hope was to get to Ismail.

Seeing gaps in the enemy infantry lines, now in chaotic melee, he rode his horse directly into them, forcing his way forward with

TANGIER: THE EARLIEST BATTLE HONOUR

his flashing lance. A second horse was cut from under him, then a third and a fourth. He was leading a charmed life, fortune was favouring the brave. His fifth horse was carrying him out of the melee towards Ismail and his reserve. The Sultan was sat on his favoured white stallion, Ghailan could clearly see his tawny face and forked black beard, his black eyes staring at Ghailan; one more push forward and his little group would reach the Sultan, it would only take one thrust of his trusty lance.

An enemy pistol was raised and pointed. His aide shouted a warning. Ghailan turned and ducked. Too late. The pistol ball struck into his chest. Falling sideways, he made a desperate grab for the saddle pommel, missed, and fell heavily. Undismayed, he was drawing his scimitar as he rose. Blood soaking through his shirt, he roared, hacking and slashing relentlessly until, weakened by loss of blood, his blows slowed; one of the Sultan's Black Guard stepped forward, blocked Ghailan's arcing attack and ran his heavy spear through the warlord's chest. The spearman pulled his short sword, sliced off Ghailan's head, rammed it onto his spear and held it aloft with a triumphant shout.

At the sight of their leader's eyes staring from his lifeless head Ghailan's men broke and ran.

What wonderful news. He carefully refolded the letter. He opened it again and savoured every word.

If Hamut had learned one lesson on his travels to England and Europe it was the need for Muslims everywhere to unite against the infidel, if not voluntarily then it must be by force. Morocco had been splintered by the revolt of Tafilalt, Draa, Sus and Marrakesh in the south and the Gharb and Rif in the north. While Ismail had been occupied elsewhere Ghailan had reclaimed his capital of Al-Kasr. As long as Ghailan was fighting the Sultan, the English and Spanish enclaves had been secure – with Ghailan's death the Sultan could pour all his energy into crushing the English.

Hamut folded up the letter and slid it into the drawer, unsure whether to pass on this news or hope Ismail would launch a surprise attack against Tangier before the Governor heard of the Sultan's victory.

Life at Whitehall Palace had been comfortable, but he knew Allah had sent him back to Tangier for a reason. The Duke said he was sending Hamut to assist the governor because he valued Tangier above all other places. This was difficult to believe when he looked at the succession of incompetent governors given the post as political favours.

Middleton would not welcome his advice; he had only installed Hamut as under-secretary to John Luke because the Duke of York had sent him.

Hamut would contact Sultan Ismail and offer his services. His knowledge of the English and Tangier would prove invaluable and the Sultan would, no doubt, reward him handsomely.

February 1674

The wait was interminable, but Palmes was confident he would be acquitted.

The facts were simple and incontrovertible. Ghailan had been dead for six months, but they were still at war with Ismail and with the Dutch and nothing Carr said could change the situation. As Captain of the Watch it was Palmes' duty to secure the safety of the city by ensuring sufficient men on watch in each appointed location. It was no part of Captain Carr's duty to question Palmes' authority or his decisions.

When Carr refused to show him proper respect in private it was a matter between the two of them; in front of soldiers it was insolence.

Eventually the Court Martial had completed their deliberations and called him back.

Half of the room was filled with Palmes' family and supporters, the other half with Carr's allies. Palmes' eldest son, Stafford, stood and gave him a salute, his wife smiled as she rocked their latest to keep him quiet, though his crying would not be heard above the noise in the courtroom.

Secretary John Luke stood up. The noise in the room slowly abated.

He ordered Carr to step forward first. In a clear strong voice the secretary stated the charge against Captain Carr of insolence to a superior officer had been dismissed.

One side of the room stood and erupted into a clapping, cheering, raucous crowd. The other half of the room sat in stunned silence; then burst into even louder catcalls, booing and hissing.

The court ushers eventually got everyone seated and quiet by threatening to arrest them for contempt of court.

Luke then told Palmes to step forward. He announced Major Palmes Fairborne was guilty of provoking an inferior officer and was suspended from duty forthwith.

TANGIER: THE EARLIEST BATTLE HONOUR

Palmes knew this was not about his run-in with Carr. His continuous stream of letters home had at last borne fruit and he had been awarded a commission to serve as Prize Officer – making decisions on prize ships and cargoes and earning a percentage of the proceeds. Governor Middleton considered that office to be one of the perks of his position. He had openly told Fairborne to relinquish the post and Palmes had refused.

This verdict had been mandated by Middleton to persuade Palmes to reconsider.

***

A few days later Palmes had been called before the Governor and once more ordered to resign his post at the Prize Office. If he refused he would face another court martial, this time for insubordination, a charge carrying the death penalty.

Palmes was a man of principle. He knew the verdict would be a foregone conclusion, but he had been awarded the commission fairly and honourably; he richly deserved the profits that would flow, and he needed the money to support his growing family. After much discussion with Marjory he decided to refuse the order.

Found guilty of insubordination, he was sentenced to be shot.

Not only was his career in ruins, his life was in danger. What the Moors had failed to do Middleton was about to achieve.

His only hope was for Middleton to grant a pardon either voluntarily or on orders from the Tangier commissioners in Whitehall Palace. He appealed the verdict to gain time and he and his wife spent every waking moment writing to anyone who might be able to help.

After three weeks under house arrest Middleton granted him a pardon, but he was still demoted and living under a cloud.

July 1674

Palmes was dismayed, but not surprised.

As soon as he had heard of the Governor's accident he had run to the palace, but there was nothing to be done. The surgeon said Middleton had tripped, fallen down the stairs, landed awkwardly on his shoulder and suffered internal injuries from which he would not recover.

Everyone told a different story, but it seemed the Governor had been drunk, as he often was. The Governor's Palace was set up for entertaining, discourse, dancing and sexual intrigues. The larder was full and the cellar handsomely stocked. Middleton was frequently indisposed, blaming various illnesses, but those who spent any time in the palace knew the Governor often drank heavily.

As soon as Palmes had been nominated Acting Governor he had set up office in the Palace and called for John Luke, the secretary, and Hamut York, the Moorish assistant. When he had quizzed them regarding diplomatic messages and activities they had looked at him blank-faced. When he had requested copies of recent letters to His Majesty and the commissioners they stood and stared. The verbose Luke had nothing to say. The reticent York offered nothing. When he had asked for the Governor's notes on developing trade, on negotiations with city states, he received nothing.

Sultan Ismail had killed Ghailan a year ago, the war against the Dutch had ended six months ago and he could find no evidence of a strategic design, no plan for developing the city.

Palmes called for the intelligence reports. He read of Ismail's cruel revenge throughout the Gharb and how Fez Old City, Taza and Tetuan had been frightened into submission. Ismail had moved on to Marrakesh, and on his way back was besieging Ben Abu Bakr's Dila. It seemed Tangier had missed the opportunity to strengthen Ghailan and now it was too late to weaken Ismail.

March 1675

Nine months after Middleton's death the new Governor, Inchiquin, arrived, bringing great optimism to Tangier.

He brought few reinforcements and a mere six months' pay of the thirty months owed, but a little was far better than nothing, and might presage more to come.

More importantly, Inchiquin brought papers for Palmes' reinstatement as major and, as proof of his rehabilitation and His Majesty's appreciation of his valorous conduct for the Crown, Inchiquin was to knight him.

The cloud had lifted; the sun was shining on him. Palmes' endless letters were paying off.

Chapter 9

Betrayal

September 1675

Tangier, Morocco

Hamut looked back with satisfaction, five hundred of the very best soldiers of the garrison marching under his orders.

It was true they were under Major Palmes Fairborne's command, but it was on his advice. Inchiquin had only been six months in post and had already shown his incompetence in numerous ways. He, Hamut, would demonstrate it to all and make himself welcome to the all-conquering Sultan at the same time.

Hamut had been caught preparing a message to the Sultan's appointed warlord of the Moors, Qaid Omar bin Haddu of Al-Kasr. What better alibi than saying it was a plan to entice the Moors into leaving their villages open to an English raid? Inchiquin was too lazy to open even his one good eye to see what was going on. He had accepted Hamut's word and committed his men without verifying his assertion the Qaid had ordered his whole army to Fez.

Fairborne had nearly wrecked his design by suggesting Inchiquin send a discovery force in advance, but the greedy governor had adopted Hamut's plan to ride out at night and insisted on speedy action to surprise the villagers, expecting to capture Moorish cattle and women.

Hamut had been unable to dissuade Fairborne from leaving a reserve company of a hundred men in Anne's Lane – a defensible position where help could be obtained from the nearby forts, the major said. Fairborne had then marched to the Great Hill and insisted on establishing two companies of musketeers and a company of pikemen into a great square with pikes pointing to front, flank and rear. Only then had he sent the Forlorn Hope with Hamut to carry out the raid. The night was not going exactly to plan, but he was nonetheless confident of success.

BETRAYAL

Hamut led the fifty Horse up the Great Valley in the bright moonlight and a hundred musketeers followed. The cavalrymen looked impressive with their shining cuirasses and polished helmets, but they were almost all inexperienced Gentlemen Volunteers brought to Tangier by Inchiquin. Hamut smiled, confident this would be the much-feared Fairborne's last day on Earth.

An hour on he saw Omar's signal and kicked his spurs; his English horse broke into a gallop. Taken by surprise, the cavalry were not sure what to do. They did not wonder for long. A startling volley of gunfire from hundreds of muskets all around felled many of the Englishmen before they knew they were under attack. The cavalry had no time to organise; no time to pull their pistols, the advantage of the charge of heavy horse and massed gunfire was lost. They were static as hundreds of horsemen careered amongst them; sabres flashed cold moonlight, but however fast a trooper wielded his sword he could not turn away the simultaneous thrusting lances and carving scimitars of three or four attackers at once; before long almost every gentleman volunteer had been brought down and hacked to pieces.

Many of the Foot died without firing their muskets, injured by the initial volley then run through by the Moorish lancers sweeping in among them. The officers shouted for the men to form ranks, but it was too late. Fewer than half made it into a defensive square; hundreds of muskets poured continuous fire from close range and more men dropped by the second. Every time a defender fell a lancer charged into the gap stabbing a spear or slicing a scimitar.

A thick pall of hot, black powder smoke rose into the cold night air. Within minutes there were too few defenders to fire a volley and the musket fire became ragged. Half a dozen cavalrymen rallied to help the Foot, firing their carbines and pistols, but as the last English musketeer was run through with a lance and the injured captain was dragged off, the troopers galloped away from the pursuing Moorish lancers.

Hamut accompanied two thousand joyous Moors careering down the valley to annihilate Palmes Fairborne and his three hundred men. He knew Fairborne would be there, mounted on his favourite grey horse, waiting for the Forlorn Hope to return. Even though the major knew Inchiquin was a fool he would carry out his orders to his last breath. A dying breath that was due shortly.

Energised by victory, reloaded, spurred on by the war cries of their fellow men, the Moorish lancers threw themselves at the square of redcoats, charging full-pelt to terrify the defenders. A split-second before they would have impaled themselves on the bristling wall of pikes they fired their muskets and turned away.

Palmes had doubtless warned his newer recruits of this tactic, but it was still difficult to withstand. At the very moment the horsemen slowed to turn there was a curt order; and a hundred muskets fired their deadly hail of shot and fifty riders fell from their steeds. Some jumped up and ran away, but not one redcoat broke ranks to finish them off. The only hope against insuperable odds was to maintain their tight defensive wall. If they held their discipline they were unbreakable. Hamut had seen it many times. Horse and shot could not break a square, it needed cannon or pikemen; but the local tribesmen had neither, they could only try to force a mistake.

A shout from Fairborne and an order from a captain; the square began a very slow movement down the hill towards the English lines. The major had obviously concluded his Forlorn Hope were without hope, beyond help. He was retreating. A mile was a long way to carry out a retreat in formation at night. Hamut had never seen it attempted, but if anyone could do it Fairborne was the man. Hamut recognised Captain Leslie's voice, he was controlling those facing Tangier and ensuring the movement was slow enough for the men moving backwards or sideways to keep in strict ranks in straight lines.

Hamut pointed out the men for the skirmishers to kill, but Fairborne and Leslie led charmed lives, they could not be reached; the musketeers reloaded, moved back and maintained a steady fire that held the attackers far enough away to keep the redcoats safe. The square did not falter.

After a seemingly endless crawling retreat the three hundred men reached the ditch and rampart of Anne's Lane. The lack of a quick counter-attack made it obvious Boynton's Reserves were no longer in the Lane. A few minutes later the sound of distant gunfire encouraged Fairborne to advance once more, presumably to help whoever was still fighting, whether Boynton's men or the Forlorn Hope. Incredibly he was leaving half his force in the Lane and advancing with only a hundred and fifty men. On hearing the welcome news of many Moors gathering in the Great Valley, Hamut knew his mortal enemy was doomed, and allowed Fairborne to advance with little resistance.

The major had just begun ascending the Great Hill for a second time when a swarm of white ghosts came screaming down out of the night, whooping and calling on Allah for victory. Fairborne at last realised he was once more entrapped and called a halt.

Holding the square formation, he waited for the Horse to come within range. Hamut's group charged the rear simultaneously. The redcoats held their nerve against the great horde threatening to engulf them and fired a well-timed volley. Horsemen dropped, but more took their place and still they attacked.

Fairborne's few once again retreated slowly and deliberately, making sure they left no gap, left no injured man behind, left no space for a lancer to encroach upon their square. The enemy horsemen attacked furiously and relentlessly. The British square withdrew painstakingly with unbelievable discipline.

At long last they neared Anne's Lane once more, having left fewer than a dozen dead behind.

The other half of Fairborne's battalion ran out to beat the lancers back and Hamut, knowing Allah for some reason wanted Fairborne to survive at least for the time being, withdrew leaving many hundreds of their own dead on the ground and Fairborne still standing.

Sultan Ismail had killed Ghailan and banished Ben Abu Bakr; he was undisputed ruler of the whole of Fez, and Marrakesh. Hamut was now firmly committed to the Sultan's cause, there was no way back to Tangier for him until the walls fell.

November 1675

Tangier, Morocco

Never had Barlow been so pleased to see a place; Tangier may have managed to lose a hundred and fifty of their best men, but it was still there, offering a haven from corsairs.

Life was hard and Edward had been desperate or he would never have signed on for such a voyage.

The short journey from the Downs to Glasgow had gone well, but once laden with eight hundred barrels of herring the *Marigold* had proved as leaky as his hat. The master, Capes, had refused all Edward's pleading to anchor somewhere safe in England to find the leaks and deal with them before setting out across the Bay of Biscay. Consequently the small crew of eighteen had been obliged to man the pumps for the whole journey, which by good fortune was less than three weeks.

TANGIER: THE EARLIEST BATTLE HONOUR

Now at last after two or three sleepless nights of watching out for Salli Rovers with all eight guns loaded, as well as keeping the pumps worked, they had arrived at Tangier. The most blessed of sights, apart from the safe harbour, were two King's frigates waiting to escort merchants through the Straits.

The crew had found what seemed to be the worst of the leaks, they had taken on water for the next leg of their journey and Capes had arranged to join a convoy due to leave in three days' time, given favourable winds.

Edward lay in Dover's arms, in her wild plot, under the orange trees, commiserating about the state of the world.

The Dutch War had been a disaster for both of them and neither of them could see any reason for it to have happened.

Edward had been captured at the beginning of the war, losing all his possessions and two years of his life. Now he had no savings for his old age and fewer years to accumulate any wealth.

Dover had lost most of her income. According to the Governor, Middleton, the King had bankrupted himself fighting the war and any money he had sent to Tangier had been intercepted and stolen by the Dutch. The soldiers had no pay, and supplies were scarce. Prices were high and she had spent almost all her savings. Middleton had no idea how to command an army and even less ability to run a trading port or control the Mayor and Corporation. The city was disorganised, merchants had lost money and were beginning to pack up and leave. The pitiable Governor had drunk even more than usual, tripped over a servant, fallen down the steps and died from his broken bones.

Fairborne, the temporary governor, was just getting things back under control when a new governor, Lord Inchiquin, had arrived and plunged the city back into chaos. After Middleton had wasted years when he could have been strengthening trade with the Moors and making allies, Inchiquin had trusted a traitorous turncoat and let him lead five hundred good soldiers into an ambush, from which a handful escaped. Dover had known many of them and would miss them sorely. Finally she had learned one of her best customers, a French merchant, was planning to leave on a ship named the *Marigold*.

Barlow said he had travelled worldwide and never seen a good war. The only way to happiness was to seek peace and understanding of other countries through travel and trade. He could see no reason why Tangerines could not agree to pay the Islamic toll and establish a market city for mutual benefit.

He grinned, the war had brought Barlow some benefit – he was visiting the white cliffs of Dover – and provided a Dutch prize frigate, now rechristened *Swan,* to escort the *Marigold* into the Mediterranean. Further, Dover's bad news was his good luck; Barlow's ship now had a French passenger to help pay the crew.

May 1676

Tangier, Morocco

'Fire!'

Faces set in defiant death masks, the two men tied to the posts sagged in their bonds, red life-blood oozing from their white shirts.

A barely audible sigh rose from the thousand assembled men.

Palmes showed no emotion. The firing squad awaited the order to reload.

Three more men stood ready, hands tied behind their backs.

Five nooses hung from a cross-beam. Five men stood near the gallows.

A wooden horse with triangular backbone stood ready to cut its way through two men's crotches.

Their pay might be more than two years in arrears, the garrison might be so short-staffed that soldiers had to do sentry duty or night duty as well as normal daytime work, but they were not permitted to complain. They had worked tirelessly for months on much-needed improvements to the defences without pay. The men had put up with miserable conditions that had worsened steadily since Colonel Norwood's departure more than six years before, and now had to exist virtually without provisions. Still, apart from increased drunkenness there had been a remarkable continuation of routine and carrying out of duty.

But now, with Governor Inchiquin absent on two years' leave after only one year in post, Acting Governor Fairborne's worst nightmare had materialised.

That morning, on assembling the men at five o'clock for fatigue duty, there had been cries of 'Home, home!'

When Palmes had asked the reason for their shouts one or two spoke up complaining of the want of pay and provisions and the burden of extra duties. Palmes knew the men were at the end of their tether. He had great sympathy for their situation. He had spent his own money trying to keep

TANGIER: THE EARLIEST BATTLE HONOUR

the improvements funded. He had spent his own money buying slaves for the mole-work. His family was destitute. Day to day he was living on credit with the merchants.

Once Inchiquin was safely on his way to England, Palmes had moved into the Governor's Palace determined to uncover the truth of Tangier's finances, to discover why the men's pay was so far in arrears. He had been shocked by what he found, though, on reflection, he should not have been surprised.

He already knew the soldiers' pay was almost entirely consumed by the victuallers in England, who charged excessive prices and delivered poor-quality food. He had not realised how much money was skimmed by others in England. The Treasurer, for instance, a man by the name of Samuel Pepys, who Admiral Allin told him was full-time secretary to the navy, took a salary of six thousand pounds for his occasional work for Tangier. That was more than twenty times what Palmes should have been paid as a captain leading a hundred men into battle, or the same cost as a hundred Horse with all their expenses. It was, in fact, about a tenth of the total annual cost of the whole garrison and defence of Tangier. The same man took a penny in the shilling of any payment sent to Tangier. A little bonus worth Palmes' salary as captain – to a man who had never set foot in Tangier and certainly never risked his life against a Muslim warrior out to cut his throat!

Nonetheless, Palmes knew his duty. He was a soldier. He was a King's man. He told the paraded men he would hazard ten thousand lives in the King's service if he had them. But, he said, he had stopped all extra work because of lack of money for supplies. In future they would be allocated to fatigue or military duties, but not both.

During the day his Egyptian slave had come to him. He was a young man of good family, a reliable servant for several years, unfortunate to have been an officer on a Turkish ship captured by a Tangier privateer. He had information, he said, but he did not want Palmes to think he was involved and he did not want to cause trouble. Reluctantly he told Palmes of a plot to mutiny. He gave the names of a dozen men who were planning to refuse to carry out orders until they had been paid.

Palmes immediately ordered the men arrested and summonsed a Court Martial. The officers' mess was cleared and the senior officers assembled. Courts Martial were held regularly. Most dealt with trivial offences, but the proceedings were always written into the court record book.

BETRAYAL

This day, however, was certainly not trivial. The men arraigned did not deny the charges and were unrepentant of their actions. The officers present had no difficulty arriving at their verdict. Soldiers, especially those in the face of the enemy, had no right to withdraw their services. Refusing to do their duty was mutiny, and conspiring to refuse duty was conspiring to mutiny, which was in itself mutiny.

The subaltern ringleaders were sentenced to be shot, the privates to be hanged, and those who were aware of the plot but failed to report it were sentenced to 'ride the wooden horse', which although not necessarily a death sentence, might well result in the victim being crippled for life, or even killed. The sentences were to be carried out at the next morning's parade.

With the two most vocal ringleaders dead, slumped at the wooden posts, he called for the remaining ten convicted mutineers to be brought in front of him.

Palmes was not a vindictive man. Nor was he a commander blessed with an excess of able-bodied troops. He was a practical man, pragmatic.

He offered to spare their lives if they would repent and promise obedience. Overawed by the speed and severity of the punishment, they all agreed to continue their duties as long as pay and provisions arrived. If they were kept without both they declared they could not remain passive.

Palmes had to decide whether ten men on active duty was better than ten dead men.

Although not entirely satisfied, he granted them temporary reprieve.

February 1677

Major Sir Palmes Fairborne, Lieutenant Governor and Acting Governor for the last twelve months, was not one to feel sorry for his fellow man.

He explained to Stafford, his curious twelve-year-old son, that people were born to a station in life as ordained by God. If one fulfilled one's role in the required manner, for the most part one could expect the life one deserved, just as Stafford was anticipating his well-deserved appointment as ensign in the Governor's Regiment. Slaves were either born to slavery or had done something to warrant enslavement. Many thousands of Christians and many more thousands of black Africans enslaved by Turks and Arabs suffered an almost intolerable existence, treated worse than animals. No doubt if a slave repented his sins he stood some chance of freedom; the Redemption Fathers did buy a few lucky Christian slaves from Muslim owners.

Yes, Palmes had bought and sold slaves but they were captured Muslims. In this part of the world it was catch or be caught. Despite that, he could not help feel some twinge of regret when he saw what Vicar Turner had referred to as 'noble savages' chained with Musselmen and black Africans. Muslims deserved slavery for their abhorrent religion and sub-Saharan Africans were lucky to be given the opportunity to work for Europeans rather than live as wild savages. The North American Indians, however, were Christians and it did seem harsh they should be enslaved by Christians. Apparently their crime was to be Native American at a time when the chief of one tribe, the Wampanoag, had rebelled against His Divine Majesty's rule. As a consequence *all* Native Americans were distrusted and many were transported as slaves, possibly some unjustifiably. But they did have a certain way of holding themselves, a certain pride and bearing that made you think they should be free, riding the open prairies rather than shuffling along in East Indiaman cotton shirts, knitted West Country stockings and Nottingham boots. Palmes sighed.

The slaves he was marching to meet engineer Shere were originally bought by the captain of the Duke of York's English galley to man its oars. It had proved impossible to maintain a sufficient supply of slaves and the expensive ship was abandoned in Tangier – where eventually it had been retired as unseaworthy. Palmes had bought the survivors from the captain to work on the forts. Now that work was finished the Commissioners' Secretary Samuel Pepys had ordered him to hand the seventy-nine surviving slaves to Shere to join with the three hundred slaves already working alongside another three hundred freemen on the mole.

Palmes had helped the engineer organise extra horses and carts and now a sensible box construction had been adopted you could almost see the edifice grow each day. All along the mole men were working, leading cartloads of stone, carrying tarris mortar from the factory or loading rocks into huge wooden chests on barges. Even though it was low water the fresh westerly was sending salt spray to make life even more miserable for the workers. The slaves were worked hard, but he supposed a life of hard labour breaking rocks was infinitely preferable to that of living every hour chained to the oars of a fighting galley.

BETRAYAL

Two very large wooden chests, Charles and James, had been constructed in England and sent out by ship. The design was to fill the boxes with stone and pour in tarris, a mixture of Roman mortar and lime, which would set underwater and bond the rocks into a solid mass. Placed on a foundation of compacted stones, these gigantic boxes – eighteen feet deep – would stand with their top surface three feet above the high water mark, presenting an area forty feet by thirty feet ready for the building of a roadway and gun emplacements.

The men were currently working on smaller boxes mounted on barges that would be sunk once the block was bonded with tarris. Even the Atlantic would have difficulty shifting this massive edifice.

Shere, who had replaced Cholmley as the chief contractor, nodded to Fairborne and made a show of trusting him to have delivered the correct number of workers, but the major had seen him carefully counting every one before they reached the jetty. Palmes held out the ready-prepared receipt and Shere led him to the mole office to complete the paperwork. Stafford followed, checking his graffiti on the mole that marked its length on every one of his birthdays.

He had been eagerly looking forward to the promised tour of the tarris works where mortar and lime were mixed and beaten, but he quickly emerged hot, red-eyed and coughing. He pitied the slaves who had to heat the mix and beat it for eight hours until it was the consistency of wax, ready to be poured into the chests to cool and set.

Once more in the fresh air, Shere showed them York chest, the one great monolith already in place, standing proud and extending the mole seaward. Two smaller chests beyond it had lost their wooden encasements but the tarris work, hardened by the salty sea, was holding the rocks together, proving the value of his construction method. Three other small chests could also be seen firm and entire. A total of six large chests were planned, after Peterborough came Anglesey, Coventry, Craven and, finally, Charles. Charles would be placed on the seaward end sometime in the summer and would mark the end of the mole in the sense of completion as well as its furthest point. Shere's contract stipulated he would only be paid once Charles was seated.

Shere had bravely taken the whole financial risk and it was no small achievement to design and oversee the building of a structure to stand against the mighty Atlantic storms. The engineer was obviously proud of his achievement, and knew Palmes reported back to the commissioners regularly.

TANGIER: THE EARLIEST BATTLE HONOUR

June 1677

The quarry was silent. Dover could not remember the air ever being so still.

Day after day the continual clunk of sledgehammer on iron, the hammering of mallet on chisel, the shout of commands, the continual creak of cart and rumble of cart wheel, all punctuated by the occasional explosion of gunpowder packed into crevices and the tumbling of stone on stone as the small landslide released boulders down the rock-face, were ever-present sounds drifting up from the quarry. But not today.

Whitby was always busy with the sound of women chattering over their washing, children at outdoor lessons, men commanding pack horses. Not today. The flag at Whitby tower hung lifeless. Not a breath of wind from the Atlantic. Perfect peace.

The only sound from the seashore was the gentle lap of wavelets rattling shingle.

Dover's revealing off-the-shoulder top was attracting the attention of all those gathered on Peterborough Tower. While she was pretending to marvel at the panoramic view of the forts marking the boundary of civilised

The Mole, 1666. (Detail from 'Prospect of Tangier from the East' Wikimedia Thomas Fisher Rare Book Library from Univ of Toronto Wenceslaus Hollar Digital Collection)

BETRAYAL

Tangier, those officers not invited to the Governor's Palace were enjoying a view of her powdered cleavage. With soldiers' pay now three years in arrears she had to find more customers with cash. Bought to entice men of private means, successful merchants or even a ship's captain or two, Dover had chosen this momentous occasion to try out her new pink satin bodice on the lesser commissioned officers.

The flags on Henrietta, Charles, Kendal, Pond and Pole hung like rags. No Levant today. An eerie silence had descended on the countryside as well as the shore. There were no patrols around the perimeters, no work parties toiling in the hot sun, no locals bringing their wares to sell in the market square, no one tending the herb gardens at Whitehall, no burial party at the cemetery.

The whole sky was a blue void, even the hunting hawks had gone elsewhere today.

Looking over the town to the bay she could see ships riding at anchor, and sailors in the rigging all looking across the harbour towards the mole. Every soldier not on duty at a fort was watching what the sailors were looking at.

Down on the mole the teachers had special permission to bring their classes to watch the event. An undeclared holiday had been taken by the whole town. Two thousand people were crowded on the sea walls, on the seafront, on the quay, and the lucky ones were on the mole.

Everyone was watching. Eighteen months of Palmes Fairborne as Acting Governor had seen great progress and everyone knew today was a turning point in the history of Tangier.

They had prayed in church for this, and here it had arrived; the first calm day for months; with not even a ripple on the flat harbour water, it reflected the few fluffy white clouds in perfect detail.

Engineer Shere was in charge. Sailors from a visiting frigate manned the oars of cutters at the four corners of the barge, each taking the strain to keep it in place while Shere measured the location precisely with marked poles and knotted ropes. He had measured the base time and again to ensure it was horizontal; tested the depth so many times to ensure it was exactly as he wanted it. He had driven piles into the foundation on three sides of the barge to position the chest and guide it as it sank, to keep it in place, to ensure it was upright and perfectly positioned. Once sunk there would be no moving this concretion of rock and mortar.

TANGIER: THE EARLIEST BATTLE HONOUR

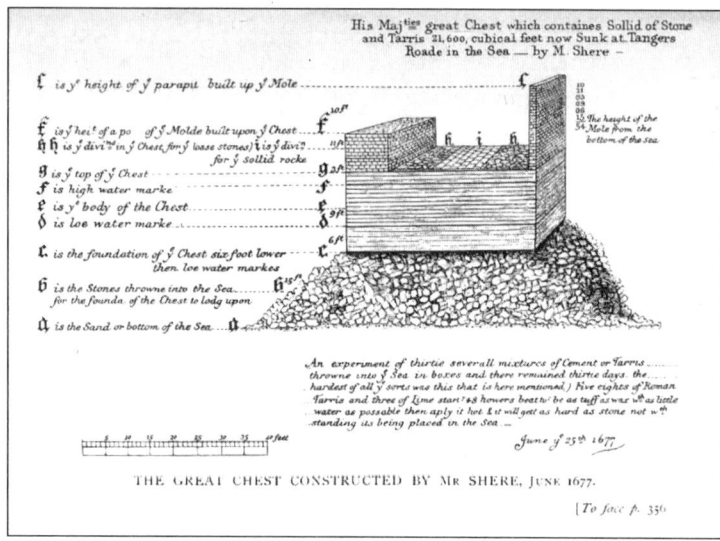

Diagram of chest construction for the mole. ('The Great Chest Constructed By Mister Shere, June 1677' CCPD)

This was the final piece of the amazing building that would out-wonder the seven wonders of the ancient world. Not the Romans, not even the Egyptians, had built a wonder as wondrous as this mole. The endpoint of this amazing structure was Charles Chest.

Finally, as convinced as he could be that all was as it should be, Shere gave the signal for the barge to be sunk. Two thousand people held their breath. Slowly the seawater swirled in; the barge began sinking. It was obvious to everyone that if the massive block shifted, the oarsmen in the cutters would not be able to stop it. But it did not shift. The huge conglomerate mass of rock and mortar descended slowly. Lower and lower it went. Nine feet of masonry dropped below the waterline. As the water reached the marked line the block stopped, at precisely the correct place.

The block was level, and stable, with nine feet of block above sea level. The charismatic Shere jumped from the mole to the ladder ready positioned for him on the side of the chest and climbed up onto the top. He stood, turned all around admiring the view in all directions, and then held his arms aloft, almost bursting with pride.

Two thousand people cheered him and his achievement. Five hundred yards of mole completed! Now he could begin work on the next phase to extend the edifice in a south easterly direction to enclose the bay within a protecting arm.

BETRAYAL

The massed drums and pipes struck up a tuneless cacophony and the celebrations began. On her way home Dover picked oranges from her trees. She had saved half the money she needed to buy her wild plot, but much of it was now invested in jewellery, watches and trinkets pawned by her customers. She needed one of the two officers who had been admiring her today to become regular visitors, or one of her merchants to strike it rich.

July 1677

Under the fierce summer sun five hundred Moorish lancers, muskets on their backs, lances held high, splashed their way across the trickle of a stream left by the recent drought without dismounting. Five hundred skirmishers followed them across the Jews' River. Warned of their coming, Palmes had assembled a battalion in Charles Fort to mount a counter-attack. He watched the Moors heading for the hillside between Henrietta Redoubt and Devil's Drop, confident the garrisons of the two forts could repel the invasion.

It was one thing to agree a peace treaty, it was quite another to keep to it. Good intelligence had warned Palmes to expect an attack and having seen Moorish Horse watching the positioning of Charles Chest a few weeks previously he had guessed the assault would target the quarry.

Palmes had been in Africa long enough to know Morocco was no more a country than was Britain during the King's War. Ghailan had always been struggling to keep the confederation of tribes together. Sultan Ismail had bribed Ghailan's mountain strongholds to step aside and that had seen the end of the warlord Ghailan. Now Ismail was perpetually fighting to keep his territories together. He had the advantage of an army of slaves based not on tribes but on personal loyalty, even so it was difficult for an Arab to subjugate Moors and he had appointed a local dignitary, Qaid Omar of Al-Kasr, to oversee the Gharb.

Angered by news of the progress of the mole, but fully occupied suppressing a rebellion by his brother in his trans-Atlas territory of Tafilalt, Ismail had demanded Qaid Omar retaliate against Tangier. Palmes knew of the Sultan's absence and was determined to impress the capabilities of the English soldier on the mind of the Omar; he vowed to give him a beating he would never forget.

Although Palmes was not happy with Charles Fort being so far out, it was a substantial building with palisade, trench, bulwarks and ramparts; it would take heavy cannon to breach the walls and it was impossible to scale

TANGIER: THE EARLIEST BATTLE HONOUR

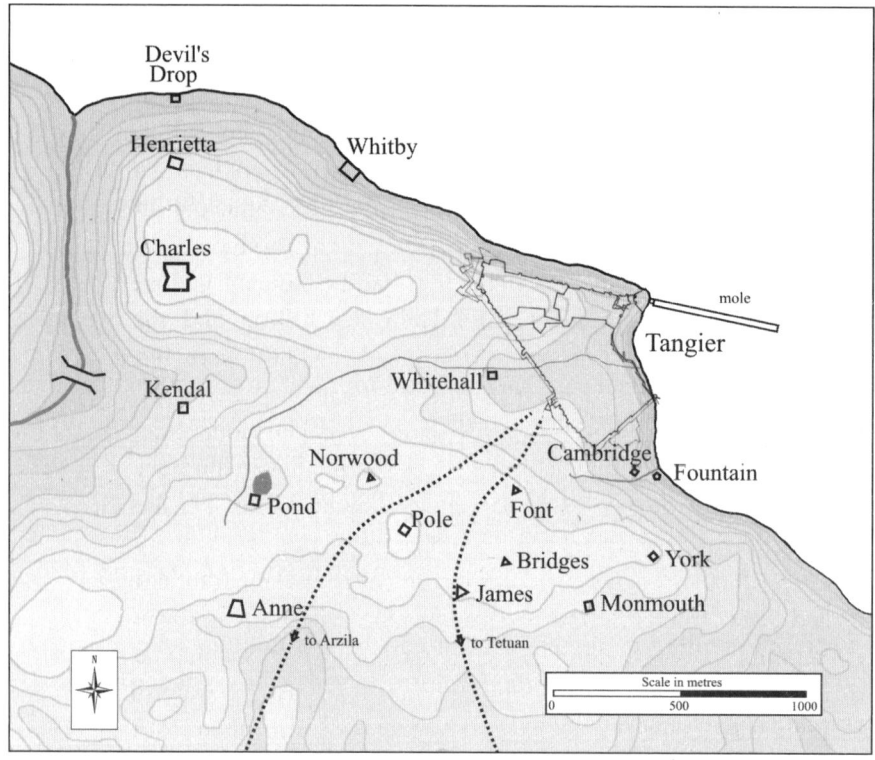

Forts, 1676. (Author)

without ladders. Henrietta Redoubt was much smaller but with no entrance at ground level any assault would need cannon or ladders. Whitby itself was a fortified settlement with Devils' Drop as an outpost and together they could fend off a significant enemy force until reinforcements arrived.

The first few Moorish skirmishers across the river ran for cover below the trench and palisades of Charles Fort and began working their way forwards from rock to rock. The crack of an English sharp-shooter's musket whenever a white scarf or red turban appeared was occasionally followed by a cheer from the ramparts.

The lancers' leader with violet sash matching the flag bearer's pennant twitched his gold-embroidered reins to ride along the riverbank and directed his horsemen to stay out of range of the small arms of the fort. A long line of white-wrapped figures ran behind with powder horns and small-shot pouches bouncing on their hips, clutching muskets.

BETRAYAL

A shout from one of the Moorish leaders and the first couple of dozen Foot ran to attack Henrietta while the lancers and more than four hundred Foot continued along the river and quickly rounded the hill to disappear from view.

Signals from Henrietta kept Palmes informed of the action beyond his sight on the shore. The men there knew the skirmishers had been deployed to distract them while the main force swept by to attack Whitby, but the garrison of the redoubt would not be diverted nor subdued by musket-fire.

Waving their muskets on high, the leading lancers galloped between the palisades running down from Henrietta hilltop and the barricade around Devil's Drop, but as the gap narrowed they were funnelled into a tight passageway and forced to slow to a canter. A series of explosions sent shrapnel ripping through horses and men. The riders hung on as the frightened animals reared and bucked, twisted and turned to get away from the terrifying carnage. More grenades rained down. Musket-fire from Devil's Drop added to the killing and the mayhem.

Riders further back gained some control over their frantic animals and headed back, following the barricade around the outpost towards the sea. More grenades with fizzing fuses landed among the escaping lancers. They directed their steeds towards the flat rocks out by the waterline, but the seaweed was slippery and the going slow, exposing them to the musket-fire of the garrison. Once past Devil's Drop the horsemen rode in circles between the outpost and Whitby, regrouping ready for the assault on the settlement, but they would be unable to launch an effective attack without their infantry. When they looked back they saw they were alone.

The Moorish Foot were trying to filter past the outpost by clambering up the hillside, unfortunately for them the bushes and grass inside the palisade had been burnt off and there was no cover. They were exposed to enfilade fire and only the bravest or most foolhardy could make progress. But these were not jihadists inspired by Ghailan's religious rhetoric; they were part-time soldiers who although loyal and steadfast did not intend to die for the cause. Under fire from Henrietta above and Devil's Drop below they made little progress. An hour into the attack few had made the passage past Devil's Drop to attack the fortified village. The small band was certainly not enough for a mass attack on Whitby. The trumpeter sounded the retreat, the flag bearer led the Horse back along the waterline and the shadowy white figures of the skirmishers withdrew, running the gauntlet of shot and grenade once more.

When Palmes saw the Moorish battalions in full retreat he knew it was the time to lead his men out of the gate to cut them down as they ran.

He looked across the river at the rising ground, wooded with thick undergrowth of brushwood, and beyond that was Teviot's Hill where the extraordinarily brave, usually cautious (but on one occasion not cautious enough) Teviot had met his death in an ambuscade especially prepared to slaughter him and five hundred well-armed, hand-chosen veterans, the likes of whom had not been seen in Tangier since. If Ghailan had managed to ambush and annihilate such a force, what chance did Palmes' relatively inexperienced men stand if there were a trap prepared now?

The question was, was it worth the risk, to catch and kill a hundred or so enemy against losing half the garrison? Perhaps discretion was the better part of valour. He would send a small discovery party of Horse up the Great Valley alongside Teviot's Hill. They could observe the enemy retreat from a distance, unseen, able to gallop away at the first sign of trouble.

***

An hour later he had his answer. The retreat had been into a prepared ambush of another thousand enemy lancers hidden around the dry riverbed that the English called Blaney's Bottom. For certain Palmes' Foot would have been surrounded and wiped out.

Palmes crossed himself and whispered a prayer.

September 1677

Dover had been getting desperate.

Surely her customers might expect a few pence in their pockets.

She had chosen her most alluring bodice and ribboned shoes and spent an amusing couple of hours watching the auctioning of wine and brandy from a captured ship. Even after the Governor and the Mayor had taken their share, and all the officers of the military and the corporation had been satisfied, there would be enough cash to provide the soldiers a few months of the twenty-four they were still owed. Praise the Lord they had received a year's back pay last month, and some had managed to clear half of their debts, but the pawn box she kept with her Jewish friend was still almost full. Credit was scarce and Inchiquin had been reluctant to pay for intelligence – even for news of Hamut's presence at Sultan Ismail's court. She needed her soldier boys to start paying in more than promises or she would be back to living on credit notes.

BETRAYAL

The auction was not yet finished when a salute of cannon-fire from the citadel heralded the return of two Tangier privateers. A great cheer went up when the gathered citizens saw they were accompanied by a handsome merchantman flying the crescent moon of Algiers alongside the ensigns of England. A second prize within a few days of the last and she was sailing low in the water, obviously well laden.

The success of these privateers meant more wealth coming into Tangier. The King of England might not be able to provide for his army in Africa, but it seemed it was capable of looking out for itself and more captured Turks meant more slaves to work on the mole. More free labour meant more cash for the mole-men.

A hint of a smile turned into a broad grin. One way or another, from soldiers or mole-men – hopefully both – Dover was confident she would be paid at least some of her arrears, and possibly find a bargain length of calico or silk in the market to enliven her wardrobe. She would enquire of the commissioners whether she might make a payment to secure a lease on the wild plot.

September 1677

London, England

It was typical of soldiers, always complaining and never to be trusted.

They lacked gratitude for the luxury of living on dry land, safe from the elements, with regular duties. They lacked appreciation for all the Admiralty did for their benefit. They were always trying to grab more. They complained about the victuals they were sent. They complained about lack of pay. And all the time they were robbing the Crown.

Pepys had heard of the capture of not one, but two Algerine merchantmen. They were reportedly both sizable ships of twenty guns, carrying full cargoes, one laden with wine and brandy, the other with deal, iron and pitch. These cargoes should have been auctioned off and the proceeds sent to England. It was perfectly clear in the Governance of Tangier.

With sailors you knew where you were. They captured a prize, they brought her to port, the prize money was distributed. The sailors got their fair share and expected no more. Given the capture of two or three decently priced ships and cargoes a sailor might earn enough to see him through his old age, should he live long enough to have an old age. A captain might retire on the proceeds of one decent prize, but that was right and proper, it was the captain's skill and ingenuity that made the capture of a prize possible. And a goodly prize would bring a worthwhile bonus to the hard-working staff at the Admiralty, and offer some recompense to His Highness and His Majesty for their labour and investment on behalf of the navy.

Pepys had been informed the wine and brandy had been requisitioned by Lieutenant Governor Fairborne, sold privately and the proceeds distributed amongst the military! The building materials had been used in construction works in Tangier and the forts around! He would raise the matter at the next meeting of the Commission. The finances of Tangier were in a poor enough state without a petty lieutenant governor taking the pay of the garrison into his own hands. The Duke of York would be interested to know how matters were conducted in Tangier; he would no doubt instruct Inchiquin to discipline Fairborne on his return.

A recent letter from Fairborne said Sultan Ismail was in full control of Marrakesh and Fez including the Gharb, and had troops skilled in mining, trenching and the use of great guns. It seemed England had missed the opportunity to conquer Barbary, or even negotiate an equitable peace. If Fairborne's report were accurate they would be fortunate to agree any terms at all. He did not believe His Majesty had been informed of the situation. He would not want to be seen to suffer a humiliating defeat; however much His Majesty professed to love Tangier, it was certain he loved himself and his reputation better.

Tangier was in a parlous position.

December 1677

Tangier, Morocco

Tensions were high. Some back pay had been distributed, enough for men to get drunk, but not enough for them to feel their grievances had been heard.

The corporal's stubbled chin was set. Musket in hand, stood at the door of the Governor's house at the head of a dozen armed men, his demand was clear and concise. Captain Scrope was wrong. The prisoner Scrope had arrested was falsely accused. The Governor must have him released immediately.

BETRAYAL

Palmes was unarmed. When the servant had told him there was a group of armed men wanting to talk to him Palmes, always a man to defuse a situation, had deliberately gone to the door without his pistol. He looked the corporal in the eye and shook his head. This was not the way. He took a step forward to placate the man.

Some of the men stepped back, but the belligerent instinctively raised his flintlock. Quick as a flash Palmes grabbed the barrel of the musket. He pulled it from the soldier's grasp and turned it on the man himself. The corporal had hold of the end of the barrel and was struggling for control of the gun. The men either side were raising their weapons.

Palmes forced the barrel under the corporal's ribs and pulled the trigger. The click of the flint, the puff of smoke, the crack of ignition all seemed in slow motion. The corporal's face screwed up like a rag, his mouth fell open. Hands still firmly grasping the musket barrel, blood pouring from his chest, the man slid to the floor. Major Daniels was elbowing his way through the stunned group of men to smack his cane down on the hands of the man one side of the Governor, then the one on the other side. While the rest of the men stood in shock, the major pushed the two against the wall and the Governor knelt to put his hand on the corporal's neck pulse, and declared himself sorry, but the surgeon could no nothing for the man was dead.

Other soldiers had heard the commotion and come running. The group offered no resistance and were quickly escorted to the gaol.

Palmes called a council of war and the two men were condemned to be shot the next day, subject to further investigation. However, subsequent enquiry determined that the corporal held a grudge against Captain Scrope from a previous encounter and had been the agent provocateur. Taking that into consideration, Palmes pardoned the two and cautioned them for future behaviour.

The man who Captain Scrope had caused to be arrested for disobedience was found guilty and sentenced to be whipped in front of the regiment at parade.

Chapter 10

Ottoman Tactics

January 1678

Tangier, Morocco

The cold wind brought the feel of snow from the mountains; the damp cold that chilled you through to your bones – the wind of change was blowing over Tangier.

No Moon. No stars. The night was as black as coal. It was impossible to see your hand in front of your face.

The wind also brought sounds. The sound of gunfire. First musketry from Henrietta, and shouting – Berber and Arabic voices encouraging each other – then heavy cannon booming from Charles spraying sparks into the night. Anne's cannon broke into action, muskets joined in from Kendal and Pond.

The Officer of the Watch had called the Governor, who had turned out the regiment. They stood inside Katarina Gate, apostles full, grenade pouches bulging, matches lit, ready to go, but the gates remained closed.

The Governor was on the Upper Castle ramparts watching. He could see little in the blackness, but he suspected ambushes were laid.

Things had changed over the years. No longer a garrison of three thousand that could move in great force and repel any enemy. No longer an enemy who fought with outdated weapons and threw themselves at the massed muskets of disciplined ranks.

Palmes had only a small garrison of less than a thousand, made up of a few experienced veterans, some inexperienced but able-bodied men but the great majority fit only for work as builders' labourers. He would not say as much in front of his officers, but the last two shipments of recruits were barely of use in any service. There had even been two women disguised as men! He could not afford to take any sort of risk. He had not even felt able to impose a death sentence on mutineers. Veterans were, in practice, irreplaceable.

A bright flash ahead and to his left was followed by an almighty explosion and something bursting into flame. The cannon-fire on Charles Fort was straight ahead, the fire must be Kendal. Largely made of wood, the Moors had mined it or hit a powder keg. Either way it was unlikely any of the garrison had survived that devastation. There was nothing Palmes could do to help any of the forts. Anne and James were more substantial and close enough for mutual support. Charles could stand alone unless the enemy brought up siege equipment. He was just wondering about Pond when someone pointed out a light in Henrietta. The only access to the tall square stone-built fort was by raising a ladder to the first-floor door. It looked as if that door was open. There would be no way to put a scaling ladder up with defenders firing down. All those inside must have been killed. Maybe the attackers had used captured grenades.

If Henrietta had fallen it seemed likely they had captured Devil's Drop and were even now in the process of taking Whitby. The possibilities did not bear thinking about. He paced to and fro.

But still he could not take the risk. He had so few men. Even if he took the Horse they could not see enough to be sure there was no ambush, and he was convinced the enemy would be lying in wait. No. The forts would just have to look out for themselves until daybreak. He sent word the regiment was to stand down and reassemble an hour before sunrise. But he remained, like a sentry at his post, lost in thought. He pictured each individual who had manned Kendal. He brought to mind the names of all those in Henrietta. He stayed there trying to remember everyone on all the forts until the gunfire stopped three hours later. Then he walked slowly back to his house for an hour's nap in his favourite chair, before turning out for the reconnaissance ride.

***

At first light Palmes led the Horse out of Sandwich Gate onto the seashore, followed by Captain Leslie with two hundred of the most trustworthy Foot. The remainder of the regiment was left in reserve in Katarina Gate. They took ladders and marched around the quay and along the quarrymen's shore road to Whitby. The little settlement had survived the attack, but the inhabitants were desperate for more soldiers to be stationed there. Palmes continued on up the cliff path with the Horse, exploring every hidden nook and cranny on the way, before waving Leslie to follow.

The men who put the ladder against the wall of Henrietta were in no hurry to climb it, fearful of what they might find. From the top rooms they reported two dead, lying amidst glass fragments and an unfamiliar lingering smell.

Heavy-hearted, the party continued to Charles Fort, who reported they had got through the night without casualties, but said the Moors had used long forked sticks to drop glass containers of toxic chemicals through the openings in the walls of the fort. The bottles broke, exploding glass and releasing gases that made it difficult to breathe and irritated the eyes. It seemed the attack on Henrietta had employed Turkish suffocation bombs to incapacitate the garrison before storming the redoubt. Once the defenders had been rendered unconscious it would have been easy to scale the building with ladders and take the survivors prisoner.

They could see Kendal was a smouldering ruin and were sure there could have been no survivors, though they did not dare venture out to confirm it. Pond had signalled they had repelled the attacks, but feared the Moors were still in the vicinity.

Palmes promised to send relief before long, and told them to keep a lookout for Moors returning round Kendal Hill to attack his patrol. He looked all around before waving his cohort on down the covered way towards the pond. The day was dull and the clouds reflected in the pool made the water dark and uninviting, but being close to the spring he knew it was always clean. Palmes told the men to be on their guard while they allowed their horses a few minutes' drink and waited for the infantry to catch up.

Receiving confirmation from Pond Redoubt that their hill was free from enemy soldiers, Palmes led the Horse and Foot together beside the river; then spread out in battle formation with Horse on both wings in anticipation of an attack by lancers or skirmishers. They advanced up the hill in formation to what remained of Kendal.

As they breasted the hill a sorry sight met their eyes, with charcoaled beams still smoking and palisade stakes scattered far and wide. Only the stone foundation remained standing. Palmes rode his cavalry on to look down over the edge of the hill into the valley, and as he had suspected, a mass of five hundred Moorish Horse were withdrawing, having given up hope of catching Palmes' men unawares.

On picking through the ruin they found the bodies of all ten defenders. Some had apparently died of wounds before the explosion, but all were burned beyond recognition. They wrapped the corpses in sheets to take them back to the burial ground by Katarina Gate. There would be even more widows wearing black in Tangier tonight.

The Moors were learning the art of siege warfare. Palmes' doubts about the defensibility of the forts were being realised. A garrison of a thousand men was insufficient to defend the long perimeter against determined attacks by the Sultan's professional soldiers now they had modern weapons. The Tangier commissioners had to send more men or risk losing their city.

February 1678

The spots were a worry. She had never had a rash like this. She tried to examine her customers before allowing them liberties, without being too obvious about it, gently feeling about the place and keeping her eyes open. She talked to others of her profession and they kept each other informed of ones to avoid, passed them on to the French madam, and advised their own customers to avoid her. You had to look after yourself and your friends. It was all in a day's work.

She had thought maybe she should stop working for a while, wait and see what developed, but some of the soldiers' back pay had arrived so it was the very time she needed to see her customers. She had to collect from those who had been visiting on the slate, and encourage those who had been holding back for want of cash.

Her need for cash had become urgent. Merchants had been voicing concerns about the garrison's ability to defend Tangier against a Moorish attack and some had even taken their goods and left. The price of property was declining and the commissioners had accepted her proposal for leasing the wild plot; at the same time the Redemption Fathers had agreed to include her father on their next mission to Fez and Mequinez.

The Jewish doctor had said there was no cure for the plague. If that were true it was down to God, so she had started going to church twice a week instead of once, and asking forgiveness for having that English priest Turner as a customer, but he did seem so much in need of a friend. So here she was on her way to the English church dressed demurely in her only cover-all top and long ankle-covering petticoat with her thick cloak of best English wool in case she needed a Protestant god to forgive her for a Protestant priest, clutching a letter for the Governor's secretary.

TANGIER: THE EARLIEST BATTLE HONOUR

In it she reported disturbing developments. First, the duplicity of Qaid Omar bin Haddu of El-Kasr, who had not only led the night attacks against Henrietta and Kendal while negotiating peace with Governor Fairborne, but then presented the brass cannon from Kendal to Ismail, who had been so pleased with the victory that he had put it on public display and promoted Qaid Omar to Viceroy. Second, the fighting against the Rif, which was supported by Ottoman advisers, may have weakened Ismail's army, but captured Turks had taught him new techniques of siege warfare including the construction of ladders that could support many attackers at once and a type of glass grenade that could render men unconscious. The Turks called them 'stinkpots' because they smelled ill.

It was as well Lieutenant Governor Fairborne had rebuilt Kendal and Henrietta – now a much more solid fort some called 'Palmes Fort', strengthened others, and had yet more wooden redoubts built to repel skirmishers.

Outside the church dedicated to Charles the Martyr, not to be found in her book of saints, she stepped smartly out of the way of the Mace, who was leading the Governor and Mayor and their train of scarlet-gowned aldermen and purple-cloaked councillors. Almost falling into the fawning group of women surrounding Mister Shere, now promoted to Engineer in Charge of the Mole, she was caught by a well-dressed gentleman who had been giving her the eye while his wife was looking the other way. Nodding a 'thank you', she wiggled her way to a pew one row in front of him on the left side of the church, which was, she had been told, reserved for non-military people by order of the Tangier commissioners in England despite squabbles from the officers.

Halfway through a tedious sermon on Sunday being made for man, not man for Sunday, a nice-looking officer came in and spoke to Governor Fairborne, who immediately upped and walked off. On the way out he tapped a couple of others on the shoulder and took them out as well. Dover had to satisfy her curiosity; she crossed herself casually and followed them.

Officers in their Sunday finery were running in all directions. Striding down Misericordia, Fairborne was pointing at the naval sloop raising its sails and weighing anchor. By the time he was through Sandwich Gate and at the top of the Queen's steps the *Chatham* was leaning with the wind and starting to make way towards the end of the mole. Fairborne broke into a run. Shouting that Turks were making off with the King's ship, he sprinted to the shore and round the quay, gesticulating for the gunners to fire on her.

OTTOMAN TACTICS

The blast of cannon and the scream of flying shot announced the opening up of York Castle battery, and by the time the Governor arrived on the mole the big guns there were swinging into action. The decent westerly was in the Turks' favour, helping them out of harbour, and they were already on their way across the bay as Dover reached the top of the steps.

It was a beautiful spring day, white sheep clouds chased each other across the bright blue sky; the air was so clear it felt as though you could see forever. She could clearly see the Turks working the sails frantically to squeeze maximum speed from the English ship. The first cannon on the mole sent a splutter of sparks and a white stream of smoke chasing after the cannonball hurtling in the direction of the escaping vessel, and the ear-splitting crash of the explosion echoed back immediately from the castle behind.

Dover was jostled and bumped as more people came running to the sound of cannon-fire; the churches must be empty by now. Children cheered with each shot fired; men and women pointed and chatted; soldiers lined the city walls and a merchant was shouting odds on whether the Turks would escape and raking in the bets. Anyone not on the walls or the citadel must be crammed onto the steps or running around the harbour for a closer view.

More cannon burst into life. Fairborne was directing the gunners, though they seemed to know what they were at without his advice. A shot hit the *Chatham*'s rigging; slowing her somewhat; more splashes all around the hull showed the master gunner had her range, though she must already be at their limit.

The gunners were all reloading and that seemed to give her the breathing space she needed; the fleeing sloop was nearly across the bay and headed for Cape Malabata. She was going to slip through their fingers and make the escape of a lifetime – taking an English naval ship from an English port. The Governor would be in a foul temper, he was famous for hating to lose, and this loss would be trumpeted throughout the English-hating world.

One crashing boom sounded louder than the previous cannon-fire, perhaps they had used more powder on this one. Dover craned forward as if that would help her see further. There was a delay that seemed like hours, then a fountain of water right next to the bow. The whole ship shuddered; it seemed to stop dead in the water as if it had been shot in the heart. It began to wallow. A tremendous cheer went up from the gun battery crews and swept all round the delighted crowds.

TANGIER: THE EARLIEST BATTLE HONOUR

The mortally wounded sloop turned her bow away from the freedom of the Mediterranean, swinging back to point to the shore. She was sailing palpably slower than before as she sank lower in the water.

The cannon ceased firing. They need waste no more powder and cannonballs, the *Chatham* was done for. The spectators could see figures jumping from the deck. Much as they wanted to prevent the Turks escaping, no one wished to witness the death of fellow men, but now, in front of the whole of Tangier, the ship foundered on a reef some way from the shore, the tide was running strong and it was clear that only capable swimmers stood any chance of surviving the wreck.

A few days later two English survivors sheepishly made their way back to Tangier and had to explain to the Governor how they had been surprised and overcome by their Turkish prisoners. Luckily for them almost all the Turks had perished either by cannon-fire or in the sea after the wreck.

Fairborne had once again proved that as long as he was in charge the Tangerines had nothing to fear. Unfortunately Inchiquin was expected back from his two-year sojourn in England and it was rumoured that Fairborne was due an equally long leave.

November 1678

London, England

Pepys' lunch with Palmes Fairborne, on two years' leave in England, had not been as successful as he would have wished.

He had confirmed Palmes' twelve-year-old son had been made ensign in Captain St John's Company, but Pepys had been distracted all evening. It was ridiculous, but it did cause him to lose sleep. There were always people who resented the success of others and were jealous of those who acquired wealth. His closeness to the Duke of York and his recently delivered well-crafted speech in Parliament had upset the great and powerful Howard, Auditor of the Exchequer who accused Pepys of speaking more like an admiral than a mere secretary, and accused him of Catholicism.

Titus Oates' accusations, naming him as a participant in a Catholic plot to assassinate His Majesty, were plainly ridiculous. He was a Protestant and had always been a faithful servant of the King. The whole thing was obviously fabricated, but Lord Shaftesbury had seized upon it to stir memories of Catholic persecutions and designs against Protestants and he had launched an attack on Catholics in general and the Duke of York in particular. The recent burning of the Pope's effigy in the streets of London and the celebrations of Good Queen Bess had stirred the apprentice mob.

Pepys had not been too concerned until his secretary had been arrested as an accessory to the murder of the magistrate investigating the plot. Pepys had given poor Sam advice on how to provide an alibi and was paying for counsel to help him prove his innocence, but the man was not the brightest of candles and might well be persuaded to say something incriminating.

May 1679

Calamity!

He, Samuel Pepys, had been incarcerated in the Tower of London, refused bail. St Michel, his French brother-in-law, had offered to cross the Channel to dig up evidence of his accuser's bad character and unreliability as a witness. Pepys had always treated St Michel well; he was a close friend who could be relied upon to pursue his many contacts and make diligent enquiries. Hopefully His Majesty would signal his faith in Pepys by agreeing St Michel could postpone his planned mission to Tangier and undertake Pepys' more urgent assignment. The Duke of York would have intervened on his behalf, but the King had packed his Catholic brother off to Scotland to avoid inflaming anti-Catholic sentiments.

He prayed for his brother-in-law's success; he was confident he could prove his innocence if anyone was listening, but many innocents had been executed for this King to keep his crown.

October 1679

Pepys sighed. He had been ejected from his posts at the Admiralty and the Tangier Commission, and had to move out of the Admiralty house in Seething Lane, but at least his brother-in-law's enquiries had produced sufficient evidence of his accuser's misdemeanours for Pepys to be granted bail and released from the Tower.

Since the death of his wife he had come to realise work and money were not everything. He had accumulated sufficient wealth to rent a comfortable

TANGIER: THE EARLIEST BATTLE HONOUR

place, enjoy life with his lady friend and use his idle hours to write the memoirs of his time at the Navy Office.

Although no longer employed on the Tangier Commission he was still interested in its progress.

The battle between the Crown and Parliament was at the root of every issue. It was clear the King despised and feared the Commons. Of course, Parliament had murdered his father and was now trying to control him, demanding he renounce his brother's right of succession. He would never surrender his divine authority to the whim of the Commons but he needed Parliament whenever he needed money.

Pepys could see the answer was to manage his finances in such a way as to live within the income from his existing grants of taxes. Those grants were worth more now booming trade was bringing in more customs and excise; and his expenditure must be less due to declining forays with fresh mistresses and the lack of wars.

Tangier had nearly been thrown a lifeline when, in an attempt to ensure it could not be sold to France, a Bill had been introduced to Parliament annexing the city to the Imperial Crown of England and making Parliament responsible for Tangier's finances. Such a move would have relieved the King of the expense. Unfortunately before the Tangier bill had been passed Charles had prorogued Parliament to prevent any discussion of the Duke of York's exclusion from the succession. Pepys hypothesised that the King was trying to rule without Parliament by securing a fresh promise of gold from Louis.

Unfortunately it was unlikely to be sufficient to enable him to continue funding Tangier.

Chapter 11

Tangier Besieged

May 1680

Tangier, Morocco

By the time he had returned from leave the damage was done.

It was a grim irony how Palmes had argued over many years that Tangier needed a commander-in-chief who remained in post for more than five minutes. Inchiquin had been Governor for five years and the place was in more danger than ever. They were stuck with a man who was afraid to confront the enemy. As long as Inchiquin was Governor they would lose more of their fearsome reputation, more of their land and more of their most precious commodity, veterans.

Palmes had seen lives of hundreds of battle-hardened soldiers thrown away by incompetent commanders. Peterborough had handed the initiative to Ghailan. Teviot could be considered unlucky, but had sold his soldiers' lives dear. He was followed by a series of governors who failed to show the determination to win a decisive victory and follow it up with authoritative diplomacy to gain a mutually beneficial long-term peace with the Moors and to secure the future of Tangier. In truth the failure did not only lie with the governors themselves. Lack of direction from a King too much occupied with his own problems, and from commissioners seeking personal gain, were equally to blame.

Now Inchiquin. Inchiquin who had virtually abandoned Tangier's defensive ring of forts and their garrisons of four hundred men.

Omar knew the forts were essential to the security of Tangier. Without strong outer-works the small city would be indefensible against an enemy with even a passing knowledge of siege warfare. But he had apparently decided he was losing too many men assaulting forts in direct attacks, and changed his strategy. Reinforced by thousands of men from Sultan Ismail,

Omar had begun systematically digging a network of trenches to isolate individual forts before besieging them and forcing their abandonment.

Inchiquin's failure to react to this new strategy had led to the loss of Kendal and Pond and the abandonment of Anne and James. Then, incredibly, Sultan Ismail's sappers had been permitted to dig four rows of wide and deep trenches from Pond across the Marshan Plateau and from Jews' River bisecting the space between Charles Fort and Henrietta Fort. The two forts on the far end of Marshan were cut off from the city by a virtually insurmountable barrier. No cannon-fire had been directed against the enemy, no disrupting sallies from the city. Inchiquin maintained that two hundred and fifty men with supplies for three months could hold the forts.

Palmes knew it was dangerous to leave an enemy undisturbed. The Tangier Regiment had few enough men, to lose more than three hundred in manning Charles and Henrietta took all flexibility from the garrison, and meant the marooned men had no respite, no access to medical treatment and no time to relax or recover. They would be worn down or the fort would be destroyed. It had been a strategic blunder to allow the Sultan's men to dig their trenches unmolested.

He had tried to encourage Inchiquin to be more aggressive. He had ridden out every day to look for a weakness in the enemy disposition but with so few men he could not risk a sally against a more numerous enemy now they were firmly dug in.

A few days earlier Omar had tried to repeat his earlier success against Henrietta by bringing up siege towers to breach the walls and drop in stink bombs, but the thicker walls Palmes had ordered in the rebuild had given Lieutenant Wilson and his thirty defenders time to drop grenades on the attackers. When the assault faltered Wilson's men had burnt down the wooden towers.

Palmes put the glass to his eye. Today he had been called out to Pond to see what he made of feverish activity below Charles Fort. It was clear to him. Things were going from bad to worse for the poor occupants of Charles and Henrietta. The Moors were mining. He would use the megaphone to advise Captain Trelawney and his garrison to listen carefully and to counter-mine.

May 1680

Hamut knew Allah had told Sultan Ismail he had been chosen to eject the Christians from the Muslim lands of Africa. Hamut could help him.

TANGIER BESIEGED

Ismail had subjugated the rebel lands and brought his huge army from the Atlas Mountains and the Sahara desert; Moors of the Sanhaja, light-skinned Sarhawi, dark-skinned Tuaregs and black-skinned slaves from further south.

Omar, Qaid of Al-Kasr, knew the Gharb and Tangier. Hamut had learned warfare from the Italians and Germans. He had shown the Qaid how to defeat men who hid in forts and refused to come out and fight like honourable soldiers. They had burned down the wooden redoubt of Kendal and used alchemy to render soldiers unconscious before scaling the stone walls of Henrietta.

Ismail had fought the Ottomans of Algiers and captured Turks knowledgeable in siege warfare. Hamut knew the methods used by the Turks against Christian castles all across the Mediterranean from Istanbul to Malta, Candia to Chyhyryn. Together Hamut, Omar and Ismail's siege engineers would build machinery and dig tunnels to undermine the forts and bring the walls of Tangier tumbling down.

Intelligence from within Tangier said Devil Fairborne was absent and Inchiquin was irresolute. Now was the time for the Sultan's men to fulfil their jihad.

Hamut had been sent to guide the Sultan's spade men. New to Qaid's army, they called themselves 'sappers'. These huge, strong men shifted more soil in an hour than Hamut could dig in a day and the sappers worked all day with little rest. They dug deep, wide trenches and threw the soil up as a wall to stop the English horsemen and to protect the workers from musket-fire from the forts above. They had worked for days before the English seemed to have noticed anything was happening.

The men in the forts built high platforms above their ramparts and fired down on the sappers, but the Sultan's men erected wooden roofs and work continued. Hamut praised Allah for persuading Inchiquin to keep his redcoats safely inside the city walls, for failing to fire cannon from the city walls.

By the time Fairborne returned and came riding out to see what was happening they had four wide parallel trenches completely isolating the forts. Within the trenches there were wooden strongholds and pathways defended by the Sultan's soldiers and Omar's skirmishers. It would be impossible for the English to relieve those in the forts.

Meanwhile, unseen in the Jews' River valley, miners had been burrowing into the hillside below Charles Fort.

TANGIER: THE EARLIEST BATTLE HONOUR

The tunnel had been filled with gunpowder kegs and all was ready to bring the walls down. Hundreds of the Sultan's infantrymen were waiting in the valley below ready for the assault.

Hamut was watching Pond Redoubt, the only enemy fort visible from the valley, when he saw a chilling sight. Dressed in Tangier Officer grey and wearing his distinctive bright green sash and red feathered hat, it was Commander Palmes Fairborne, the Englishman every Moroccan knew by name, by sight and by reputation.

Hamut's nemesis would see the mining and without doubt find a way to prevent its success.

At the same time the Sultan's men were escorting two redcoats from Charles back to the fort under a white flag; having shown them the mine, it was hoped they would persuade the captain of the fort to surrender.

Sometime later a trumpet and drums accompanied the hoisting of a company flag and shots were fired from the ramparts by belligerent defenders.

Men came running from the mine. There was a huge explosion, followed by a blast of wind as the air was filled with a black dust. A great cheer went up and peering through the swirling cloud, anticipating the sight of a shattered castle, the besiegers were greeted by three hurrahs from the ramparts. The walls were standing as defiant as the defenders.

All the sappers were lined up to watch the humiliation of the chief miner, who after confessing his failure to dig far enough under the fort was hanged from a tree.

Hamut suspected some trickery by Fairborne.

May 1680

The splinters of rock flew in all directions. The retort from the captured cannon echoed round. Another part of the wall fell away.

Hamut was well pleased with life. His work was proving fruitful. Once captured, Henrietta would be a useful platform for firing on Charles Fort. Tangier itself would fall soon, and Hamut would be lauded as a great jihadist.

Mercenaries from Spain were manning the falconet captured when Fort Anne had been abandoned. The retreating English had not disabled the cannon properly and now it was being turned against their fellow defenders. It was not a powerful weapon, but it was chipping away at the corner of the

TANGIER BESIEGED

walls; as stones were knocked out, masonry higher up tumbled down the facade. The redoubt could not last much longer and there was no hurry. At the same time, miners were tunnelling from several directions and the explosions above and below would have their effect before long. This destruction was possible because of Hamut's study of siege warfare and he looked forward to a handsome reward from Sultan Ismail, certainly a wife, maybe a thoroughbred horse from the Sultan's famous stables.

The defenders knew their governor had abandoned them. It was too late for even the resourceful Fairborne to mount a rescue operation. The besiegers were well dug in and there was no chance the city garrison could break through the series of trenches surrounding the fort. The defenders' only means of communication with their compatriots was by speaking trumpet. They used Irish rather than English to try to confuse the Moors, but Omar had Irish deserters working for him and, unknown to the English, had no difficulty understanding the messages going back and forth.

Inchiquin had tried offering the fort in exchange for his soldiers' lives, but the stone building was replaceable, the men were what Omar wanted. He was depleting the city garrison and there was always a chance that some of the captured men would save themselves from the desperate fate of a galley slave by being circumcised, accepting Allah and reinforcing Omar's growing army of highly useful European mercenaries. He demanded unconditional surrender. Fairborne's response was to organise a breakout from Charles and Henrietta for seven the following morning, supported by a sally from the city.

Another one pound cannonball smacked into the corner, sending half a dozen rocks crashing down.

A white flag appeared at the top of the fort. They could not hold out any longer.

A few hours later a forlorn-looking bunch of about thirty redcoats marched out of the fort, carrying their wounded, holding their heads high. Abandoned by the cowardly Inchiquin, they had fought long and hard until their ammunition had run out. Now they would be presented with a difficult choice – but no harder than the choices Hamut had made.

Everything went black.

Finding himself lying on the ground, ears ringing, Hamut tried to understand what had happened. He had been thrown in the air and knocked down by a massive blow. Debris was landing all around. He wrapped his arms over his head for protection. It had been a huge explosion.

When he looked up he saw Henrietta had disappeared. The departing soldiers had left a slow fuse to destroy the fort and kill any Moroccans who were near. He should have known the redcoats would destroy the fort they abandoned.

May 1680

Palmes was fuming, fists clenched, condemned by an over-cautious commander-in-chief to stand and watch from Peterborough Tower!

Through the crystal clear morning air that follows a night of rain he had witnessed the destruction of Henrietta. He had used a glass to see the survivors marched up the hill on the far side of Jews' River. Now he saw a churning stream of white-clad figures running down the hill towards the battleground and a white tornado of horsemen galloping up towards Charles. The Moors obviously knew of the planned breakout, they could no longer count on the element of surprise.

Inchiquin wanted to abandon the escape attempt. Palmes knew it was the last chance for the beleaguered garrison. Four trenches filled with thousands of well-armed enemy foot-soldiers and the Marshan Plateau awash with Moorish lancers were almost insurmountable obstacles to the safe return of a hundred and seventy men escaping from Charles. Should they leave them to their fate or gamble on a rescue mission?

Admiral Herbert, always keen to help the city, had provided six hundred mariners to man the palisades in case of an attack on the city, which released the whole Tangier Regiment for outside action. Even so, with near four hundred men stationed in forts a total of a further four hundred brave fighting men was all they could muster for this action. Hume's company of Dumbartons, just arrived from Ireland, had been pressed into service, adding seventy invaluable veterans to the rescue effort.

What hope did they have against the thousands gathering on the plain in front of him? But who knew how many more men the Qaid could assemble if Inchiquin delayed. Palmes felt a desperate sadness that things should come to such a pass, but the plan must go ahead. Palmes said he would take responsibility.

He took out his pocket watch. Seven o'clock. He willed Boynton to begin the sally, every minute's delay allowed more of the enemy to reach the field of battle. He knew his major well and did not doubt his ability and steadfastness.

TANGIER BESIEGED

The familiar starburst yellow, red and green company flag issued from Charles' gate, followed by Captain St John and a stream of grenadiers running at the enemy trench.

At that instant Hume's fearless Forlorn Hope, led by Lieutenants Bayley and Pierson, issued from Katarina Gate; keen for their first encounter with the enemy, matches glowing, new white cuffs gleaming in the morning light, they hoisted their white saltire and marched forward. The nearest Moors ran to attack them. As soon as they came within lethal range the Scots stopped, presented muskets and fired a deadly volley. Those attackers not felled ran back to the safety of their trench. The Scots quick-marched after them, the row of pale grey stockings catching the sun as they strode forward in unison.

The one hundred and seventy-four men from the fort ran across the muddy plateau firing muskets and throwing grenades, making enough noise and creating enough mayhem for a thousand. The flag disappeared into the trench followed by all the men. As the last man dropped out of sight the fort behind them seemed to rise off the ground, as a series of explosions reverberated around the hills. The last man out had set short fuses to blow up the bastions and deny Charles to the enemy.

Five detachments of the Tangier Regiment emerged from Katarina Gate, unfurled their colours and three companies of a hundred and twenty men, with forty on each wing, strode after the Dumbartons' Forlorn Hope, flanks protected by the thirty remaining Horse.

Palmes was cheered by the sight of the first red coat appearing from the far trench; more followed and he counted above a hundred and fifty who made it into the second trench, and after a few minutes almost as many topped the second, swinging swords and muskets and running to the third.

The Forlorn Hope was in good formation at the lip of the fourth trench pouring continuous fire into the enemy lying in wait for the men from Charles. The last trench must be twenty feet wide and more than fourteen feet deep. Palmes could see sun glinting off the expanse of mud in the bottom. His escaping garrison would have a desperate task crossing that quagmire under the scimitars and muskets of hundreds of Moors and climbing out of the trench.

Boynton drew up the main body of the Tangier to fire volleys into the Moors who were attacking the flanks of the Dumbartons. As the first refugees plunged from the marshy plain into the mud of the last trench

TANGIER: THE EARLIEST BATTLE HONOUR

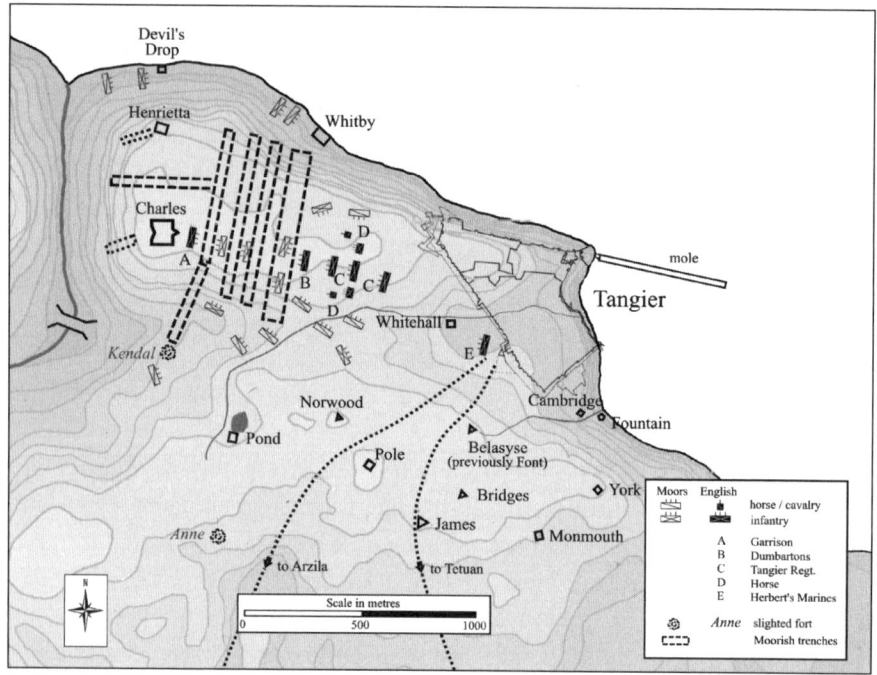

Escape from Charles, 1680. (Author)

the Forlorn Hope came under a ferocious attack from Sudanese Foot and waves of Moorish lancers led by numerous richly garbed generals. Palmes thought the Dumbartons would be lost but an ensign from the Tangier led a company forwards and courageously drove into the Moors' flank, inflicting devastating losses and forcing their retreat.

Palmes saw St John jump into the last trench, furiously hacking at Moors with his hanger. For every Moor cut down it seemed two took his place. More of the garrison followed, but there were so many of the enemy lining the trench it seemed impossible for anyone in red to emerge. Bright flashes of musket fire, flashing slashing blades, shouts and screaming. He saw Captain Trelawney lead the last group into the trench with his young son. Such a mistake to have taken a young lad into the fort. It was impossible for people on the ramparts to help for fear of killing their own; all they could do was watch and pray. For the most part it was not enough. St John emerged covered in mud and turned to help others. Through the smoke and haze Palmes saw another ten, twenty, thirty men of the fort appear from the last trench, helped up by their comrades and protected by the Forlorn Hope. He prayed, he cursed, he swore, but after about forty it was clear no more were coming. Neither Trelawney nor his boy had emerged.

A multitude of Moorish Horse swept down on the Dumbartons, but Hume held his pikemen steady while the muskets reloaded and fired time and again. Once they knew no more could be rescued from the pit of mud the Scots began their withdrawal. Seeing his opportunity, a brave Moorish lancer with the rich horse trappings and colourful robes of a leader looking for glory, charged at Hume. The captain fell to the ground clutching his leg and the lancer rode over him. A Scotsman thrust his pike between the horse's forelegs, bringing mount and rider crashing to the ground; another Scot ran forward and smashed his rifle butt down, caving in the rider's head, then hoisted his captain across his shoulders and carried him to relative safety in the midst of his company.

The orderly withdrawal continued, with St John one of the last, reluctant to admit no more of his men could make it. A groan escaped Palmes' lips as he saw the heroic captain himself go down. But two men lifted the injured hero and dragged him into the group of burly Dumbartons. The Forlorn Hope pulled back further. The main body of the Tangier Regiment held their ground as the Forlorn Hope withdrew with their dead and injured. The Moors had lost a great many men and, on seeing such a determined force of redcoats covering the retreating survivors to the welcoming cheers of the seamen, they gave up their pursuit and began recovering their own innumerable injured and dead.

Palmes breathed a sigh of relief, but more than a hundred of his garrison had not made it back; whether dead or captured he could not tell. A hundred good men lost due to Inchiquin's timidity. The Lieutenant Governor clenched his fists. He would do everything he could to be rid of Inchiquin as soon as possible.

Palmes hurried along the city wall to Katarina Gate to greet the returning warriors, shouting encouragement and congratulating them on costing the enemy so dear, looking for his son. When he had seen Stafford and all the other survivors safely back inside the city gates he strode down Katarina Street and turned right into Rua de la Duana.

The guards saluted him and opened the doors of the hospital. Inside the clerk handed him a list of all the new admittances and told him Captain Hume was in with the surgeon who was operating on St John.

TANGIER: THE EARLIEST BATTLE HONOUR

Palmes passed through the consulting room, full of pipe smoke, beer fumes and injured men being diagnosed by orderlies, into a room with three large tables where surgeons and their mates were operating on the seriously injured. Hume sat with his bandaged leg up on a stool drinking a mug of rum and smoking a pipe of tobacco. He waved Palmes over. He was in good heart, recovering from having a musket ball dug out of his leg.

He pointed his pipe at the table where St John lay strapped down, and told Palmes the surgeon was trying to remove a lead ball from under St John's shoulder blade, but he shook his head, thinking his fellow officer's chances of survival slim. Hume told Palmes his men had fought well – he had lost more than a dozen men and half the beds were filled with his wounded, but they had held their ground against concerted fire from the enemy and several attacks from lancers.

Palmes handed the lieutenant the list of those in hospital, then visited every bed and spoke to each of the men before going down to York Castle to order a roll call.

***

An hour later Palmes dismissed the unhappy parade. He had lost one hundred and thirty-two men and Trelawney's boy from the fort, and seventeen from the Dumbartons. A seaman saluted and handed him a note. The green silk ribbon indicated it was from Qaid Omar. He untied the parchment. Omar agreed to the English retrieving the bodies of the fallen under a white flag and informed Palmes they had captured thirteen men and Trelawney's boy.

Some hours later the quarrymen brought in several cartloads of bodies. All had been decapitated. A short while later another cart arrived carrying all the heads. The Sultan Ismail's men were taking the heads to him as grisly proof of the victory. If they dared return without this evidence the Sultan would personally behead the messengers without a second thought. Omar sent a note to Palmes saying he had personally written to Ismail telling him Fairborne himself had requested the heads be returned.

Palmes ordered the preparations for a military burial in two days' time. Trelawney was to be interred in the cathedral grounds, all subalterns and privates in the cemetery outside Katarina Gate.

The loss of the forts was bad; the loss of men was worse; but allowing thirteen cannon and a mortar-piece from Charles Fort to fall into enemy hands was disastrous. Increasing numbers of skilled gunners were selling themselves to the Sultan and even spiked guns could be brought back into use. No doubt those from Charles would soon threaten James and Pole as the one from Kendal had been used against Henrietta.

Without even one full troop of Horse to challenge the enemy in the field the future of Tangier was bleak indeed.

***

Palmes had been summoned to dinner at the Governor's Palace. Whenever he entered the cathedral of the dining room his eyes were drawn to the windows. Not stained glass, but a mesmerising view out across the choppy waters of the Straits, framed on the left by the restless Atlantic, always shifting and changing colour, ahead to Spain and Tarifa, and to the right the North African coast. It was a picture created by the greatest artist of all. Inland, if you could put the Moors out of your mind, the nearby hills, backed by the distant mountains and topped by the ever-changing sky, were an unforgettable sight.

In peacetime this room must be one of the most coveted places in the world.

The parchment hit the table with a hollow smack. There were two parts to the letter from Omar to Inchiquin. The first listed fifty-seven prisoners the Moors had captured from Henrietta, Charles and Giles Fort. The second part Inchiquin quoted word for word:

> If his Lordship has a mind to be eased of his troublesome war he should quit all the forts and be content to keep the place as the Portugalls had it, otherwise he (the Qaid) would not stir from hence till he had reduced them all. If His Excellency does not accept these terms the next business will be the town for since they are both skilful in mining and great guns you cannot hold out long if they proceed after the rate they have done.

Inchiquin agreed with Qaid Omar.

It was Palmes' task to give the Governor a spine.

Sometime later, after a dinner of river fish and wild boar followed by dates and spiced chocolate, the Governor's secretary was called in. Palmes sipped the excellent Madeiran Malbec and listened to Inchiquin dictating a reply based on their discussion. After thanking the Moor for his civility, he continued: 'As to quitting the forts, it does not consist with the Honour of his Majestie nor my owne and though I know them not to be impregnable, yet would sell them as dear as I can.'

Palmes knew it was whistling in the dark, but Tangier's only hope was the heavy toll they had taken of the Moorish fighters. The enemy man-to-man fighting was undisciplined and they lost many more men than they should have. Qaid Omar's own army was composed of irregulars, much like the English militia. They were artisans and farmers; they had businesses to run, crops to tend; their families could not sustain unlimited losses. Ismail's siege men were also limited in number. His army was huge, but he did not seem inclined to commit too many of his favoured black infantry to this arena. A few more battles like the last might persuade the Qaid and the Sultan that Tangier was not worth the cost.

***

A week later Inchiquin called a Council of War. This time it was no intimate dinner where Palmes could gently persuade the Governor to his viewpoint.

Captain Leslie, Lieutenant Fitzgerald and Merchant Luddington had been sent to Qaid Omar to discuss peace terms. They had been shown the expert tunnelling into solid rock and sapping under the walls that had been the downfall of Henrietta. Ismail's engineers confidently predicted the undermining of the upper castle within twenty days. They had shown the envoys a score of heavy guns mounted in batteries ready to fire against Pole and Norwood.

For fear of the enemy taking Pole and gaining the vantage point from which to bombard the city at will, terms had been proposed for the English to abandon and reduce all the forts excepting Fountain and those guarding the water supply there. This effectively repeated the terms the Qaid had proposed previously that Palmes had rejected. Nonetheless, some respite was gained. A four-month truce lasting until September would allow Qaid's men to return to their homes for harvest, and permit the mole-men to resume their quarrying and work on the harbour. The Moors would move their guns away and the English would not be permitted to make any improvements to defences in terms of forts or city walls.

Palmes could see these terms gave respite to Qaid and gave virtually nothing to the Tangier garrison. On the other hand, even with the four extra Dumbartons companies they had received, without Horse they could not challenge the Moors' positions. An artillery battle would lay waste the city walls and expose the inhabitants to a mass attack from the Sultan's army.

Palmes accepted defeat in the council and wrote a detailed letter home telling the commissioners if they failed to send four thousand Foot and five hundred Horse Tangier would be lost. He sent the letter express by land and by sea.

The future of Tangier was in the balance.

Chapter 12

Tangier Relieved

20 September 1680

Tangier, Morocco

The usual lanterns were giving their meagre light in the darkest lanes and alleys, and the hillside township was almost as quiet as usual, but there were noises – door latches softly clicking, boots on cobbles, creaking saddle leathers, murmurings from the lanes.

It was as if the city of Tangier itself was holding its breath anticipating something special now the truce had expired.

A double bell echoed around the bay.

Another two bells, a pause, two bells, a pause, two bells … Silence.

Eight Bells. It was four o'clock; the beginning of the morning watch.

The lights on the fleet moved in concert in Tangier Bay as the men-of-war rode the swell, the remnants of an Atlantic storm that had long since blown itself out, the long, leisurely waves were creeping around the harbour mole giving life to the silver moonlight reflected from the black water. Moored in line on the chained anchors, Admiral Herbert's squadron of nine frigates was an impressive sight, each ship with two decks of guns, instilling confidence in the European inhabitants of the city.

The scent of orange blossom drifted up to Dover, who had come to the tower of York Castle for an assignation with a militiaman. Down in the bay the mole stretched out as a symbol of English determination to make the city a successful centre of mercantile and naval activity. The city looked the same as always; the solid mass of the citadel, reinforced but the same reassuringly familiar shape, the medieval walls embracing the terracotta roofs, the cobbled streets and gardens sprawling up the hillside to the solid castle that was Katarina Gate. Within the embrace of those walls all the inhabitants of Tangier huddled together, walls that provided comfort for its

TANGIER RELIEVED

willing population, a prison for would-be deserters desperate to escape the carnage of battle, and an obstacle for those with information to sell to the Qaid. Beyond the city wall the heights of the Moroccan hinterland, where unknown thousands of Moorish soldiers awaited the chance to expel the Christian interlopers from this tiny foothold on Muslim land.

But Tangier had changed. Fearing for their lives and livelihoods under uncertain and aimless governance, most of the merchants and traders had left, to be belatedly replaced by the army that would have given them the confidence to stay. They now had the army they had longed for over the last twenty years, said to number nearly five thousand. All those newcomers had money in their pockets – certainly she had never been so busy. It was a pity the original garrison was still living on credit. Training and drill had been stepped up, no more inebriated soldiers on the streets, every station was manned, any person attempting to leave the city under cover of darkness was to be shot on sight.

In the few weeks since her slaughter-man had joined the militia he had taken the night watch for the coolness of the night air and the peace that replaced the chaos of the daytime township, and she came to join him whenever she could. She slipped her arm around his waist. Tonight was different. Her eyes swept back across the jostle of houses perched on the hillside.

In the pale light of the waning moon she looked down on the Parade Ground of York Castle. She stood in awe. Three regiments, more than two thousand men, had assembled in almost complete silence. Now they stood waiting quietly.

The sound of horses' hooves clattering on cobbles. The sentries guarding the storehouse moved aside to make way for an imperious figure riding an immaculately turned out dark grey stallion.

Sir Palmes Fairborne on Storm. Everyone in Tangier and outside it could recognise Sir Palmes Fairborne, the man rumoured to be the next governor following Inchiquin's ignominious removal. Resplendent in his new moss green silk coat and silver-edged baldric, the Acting Governor cut an impressive figure. Not tall in stature and lacking the fashionable affectations of a wig or face whiskers, but still immensely imposing, he was much respected and admired. All eyes were on their commander-in-chief as he joined his commanders. The militiaman pointed out Admiral Herbert, Major Sir James Halkett and Lieutenant Colonel Boynton; but her

TANGIER: THE EARLIEST BATTLE HONOUR

companion was no more aware of the Governor's designs than the rest of the city, although it was clear something special was coming their way.

She watched Sir Palmes Fairborne ride along in front of the ranks of scarlet coats. He stopped in front of the green colours of his own First Tangier Regiment and spoke quietly to Boynton, commanding the Governor's Company this morning. He then moved alongside Halkett in front of the Dumbartons' blue and white colours. He spoke in a measured voice, clearly, without shouting. The gentle offshore wind carried his words up to Dover:

> Countrymen and fellow soldiers, let not your approved valour and fame in foreign nations be derogated at this time, neither degenerate from your ancient and former glory abroad; and as you are looked upon here to be brave and experienced soldiers – constant and successive victories have attended your conquering swords hitherto – do not come short of the great hopes we have in you, and the propitious procedures we expect from you at this time. For the glory of your nation, if you cannot surpass, you may imitate the bravest, and be emulous of their praise and renown.

Admiral Herbert, looking incredibly uncomfortable on a docile mare held steady by an orderly, fidgeted with his eyepatch and fixed the Marines with his one good eye. His facial scars were testament to his own bravery. He reminded them they had demanded to be allowed ashore to prove themselves the equal of the land-lubber regiments. He exhorted them to seize this opportunity as if it were their last, for it may well be so. He told them to follow Captain Barclay's commands and said he expected reports of their valour on his desk before the end of day.

Fairborne's little group rode out of York Castle to visit the other regiments. Dover caught a glimpse of Sackville's hat above the redcoats crammed into the market square as he began his address to the King's Battalion of Guardsmen, but from such a distance she could catch only a few words; 'My Good Fellows', 'worthy of being called the King's Guards', 'glorious and everlasting fame', 'stand well together'.

Dover shivered with anticipation, and drew the militiaman into the shadows. The quicker she gave him satisfaction the sooner she would get to see what the Governor was planning.

***

TANGIER RELIEVED

This was Palmes' moment; the end of the ceasefire. This would be the ultimate test of his abilities.

Thirty years of active service had prepared him for this moment. From a volunteer at Putney Heath to colonel of the Governor's Regiment in Tangier; from a supplicant with whom the Sultan's general would not deign to negotiate to the commander-in-chief poised to conquer untold lands, from commoner Fairborne to Sir Palmes Fairborne. He had been proved correct. Without sponsorship ability was nothing. He had both. Thanks to his constant stream of letters to people in power, Inchiquin had been retired and Tangier had received a sizable reinforcement of experienced soldiers. Today he would achieve complete victory over the combined Moorish armies of Omar and Ismail. Today he would prove his ability as commander-in-chief of five regiments, the most numerous English army fielded since the King's War.

Palmes looked up at the clear black Moroccan sky. A myriad of twinkling stars; the star at the end of the tail of Ursa Major was especially bright tonight. 'Alkaid' the Arab astronomers called it, the last of three mourners following a coffin they said – whose coffin? Not his, maybe Qaid Omar's. Storm snorted out a white cloud of droplets and pawed impatiently at the ground. Palmes patted the horse's neck and spoke a few calming words as he surveyed the ramparts, watching the silhouettes of the city militia, grateful their presence released regulars to join his outside party.

He had ordered the regiments to assemble at their designated places at three in the morning in complete darkness to ensure there was no possibility they could be observed from outside the city. The men massed in front of him were silent, as commanded, but the flexing and shifting of thousands of bodies produced its own kind of music, like the restless ocean down on the seashore.

Palmes surveyed the First Tangier Regiment; the green of their colours and facings appeared black in the faintest red lightening of the sky, he could not make out the men's faces, but these were his men, men he knew and trusted; men he had trained and fought with. He could address every one by name. He had joined them as recruits at muster twenty years ago – a seventeen year old captain, already with experience of fighting the Turks. Since then they had been through much together. They had been treated harshly; men lost in battle not replaced, supplies late in arriving, pay almost always in arrears, sometimes by years. But twelve of his sixteen companies were veterans of battles in Tangier. Now, even stood

TANGIER: THE EARLIEST BATTLE HONOUR

easy in the darkness he could feel their eagerness to engage the enemy. They wanted revenge for the mauling they had suffered in the spring while Palmes was absent; revenge for their sacrificed comrades. The four new companies had seen service in France or Virginia. He knew their muskets would be clean, their apostles full. His newly formed grenadier shock troops were fingering their hatchets or touching the soft leather of their grenade pouches for luck; the pikemen envisioned their planted poles keeping the enemy lancers at a distance to be cut down by musket fire. He had fought many battles and lost few men, he knew they would stand firm confident in his leadership.

His regiment needed few words of encouragement and after a brief reminder of what was expected he had addressed the Dumbartons, reminding them of their glorious history, Hume's company's courageous action in saving men from Charles Fort and their own fearsome reputation fighting for the French. He had then listened to Herbert exhort his Marines before leading the three regiments up the dark winding cobbled streets lit by night lanterns, past the gathered women and children waving good luck to their men, to the King's Guards Battalion in the market square.

The first chirpings of a dawn chorus. In the strange twilight the silver coats gave the pikemen an eerie presence, like a gathering of ghosts – but having watched their training Fairborne had ordered his regiment to follow the same regime. Standing proud, the Guards were, to a man, tall, broad, strong and capable of deeds beyond most men. And these exceptional soldiers had been joined by a company of York's favoured Marines in their yellow coats flying newly awarded colours of lemon and white waves backing a red cross of St George. This regiment knew it was expected to go one step further, stay longer, never flinch; Palmes was eager to see this King's Battalion in action. Despite Palmes' instruction for silence, Sackville's voice rang out in the confined space. Sat astride his black stallion, wearing full wig, in a cloth of gold coat with waist scarf of the King's blue edged with gold, he harangued his men – reminding them they should act like Guards and bring credit to themselves and the regiment. They in turn were watching their colonel. The men eyed him warily; he was the most senior officer in Tangier but he was a parade colonel, and had seen little action. Now, recalled from five years' retirement for this mission, they were wondering whether he was fit for command. Some doubted he had the knowledge, let alone the desire, the fearlessness and the presence of mind. They would find out soon enough, but it may be at the cost of their own lives.

TANGIER RELIEVED

Still, better a senior officer than the callow eighteen-year-old Charles Fitzcharles, Earl of Plymouth, love child of the King, who was leading a corps of the volunteer regiment as part of the Forlorn Hope. Palmes acknowledged Sackville's battalion and rode on up Katarina Street to the heavily barred gate of Katarina Gate, where Tollemache was addressing his vanguard of Coldstreamers and Gentlemen Volunteers along with more than two hundred cavalry.

Palmes pirouetted his steed and cast his eyes over the Volunteers. Inexperienced sons of gentry, their horses and equipment were expensive and beautifully turned out. They wore the best-quality crimson coats with the King's blue facings and breeches, and silver edgings to their fashionable waist scarves and hats, but their effectiveness was unknown. The Earl, all in blue and gold, seemed to be enjoying Tangier; they said he had his father's manner, easy going and friendly to people of all standing, witty and always affable. It remained to be seen how he performed in battle, but he would receive no special treatment from anyone.

At the councils Sackville and Tollemache had criticised every design Palmes had put forward, every disposition he had proposed. Sackville acted as if he had ten years' experience in Tangier, rather than barely ten weeks without a weapon fired in anger. He had been intimidated by the Moorish lancers demonstrating their riding skills outside the city walls and wanted to await the arrival of cavalry reinforcements. Halkett of the Dumbartons had agreed with Palmes, asserting the urgency of re-establishing forts. Fortunately it had not come to the test. Palmes had been lucky the promised Horse had arrived a few days before the end of the ceasefire.

The bright red line of the eastern horizon across the bay was now surmounted by a yellow band of sky that shaded into the deep blue of the heavens. It was nearly time. The familiar pre-battle tightening of the stomach was returning. Palmes grinned to himself. Today he would get his first taste of revenge on Tollemache for his unfounded criticisms. He had placed him in the vanguard with his company of Coldstreamers to drive the enemy off and establish an outer ring of fire to ensure the sappers could rebuild Pole Fort without hindrance. Palmes had given him the Gentlemen Volunteers to oversee as well. That should keep him occupied. Revenge too on Qaid Omar, the enemy commander who had exacted a bloody toll on the garrison. Now Inchiquin's negotiated truce had finally followed its instigator into retirement Fairborne was determined to show Omar the Tangier garrison was well up to the task of repelling any attack he could launch.

TANGIER: THE EARLIEST BATTLE HONOUR

But this was more than a revenge mission. Today had to be a success, his reputation was on the line. Fairborne had used every day of the ceasefire to prepare for the resumption of hostilities, just as he had previously used every day of his leave of absence in England to garner support for the colony. In London he'd had to counter fierce resistance from Pepys, that miserly pen-pushing Tangier financial administrator who could see no more profit from the colony, and suspicious Shaftesbury, who saw Tangier as a training ground for a Catholic army to suppress opposition to the government. Pointing out the value of the city as a harbour for the Mediterranean Fleet in their war against corsairs and as protection for the Duke of York's Royal African Company ships, he had persuaded the King and his brother to bolster the garrison.

Both Pepys and Shaftesbury had since got their just deserts, Pepys sent to the Tower of London and Shaftesbury removed from the Privy Council, so neither was on the Tangier Commission now.

Three days ago Palmes had stood on the ramparts and watched Qaid Omar's lancers remove the red flags that marked the boundary during the cessation of fighting. He had heard the cannon fired to formally declare the resumption of hostilities. For two days his men on the city walls had watched the daily displays of the enemy's equestrian prowess as lancers rode in intricate patterns across the hillocks. That and the occasional cannonball fired into the city. No attack. Those cannonballs were a warning; he had to re-establish the forts Qaid Omar had reduced. Without that defensive line Tangier would always be vulnerable. Today he had to push Omar's forces back from Pole and make it clear he was able to reclaim lost land.

Fairborne knew the war against the Moors would never be won; there would always be another battle. He had tried to negotiate an extension of the ceasefire, but Omar had heard of Teviot's deceit many years before and knew a governor might be overruled by the King or even a new governor. Even so, if the city's defences could be strengthened the Sultan might be persuaded the price of outright victory was too high and an indefinite ceasefire might lead to eventual acceptance of the English presence, or the Sultan might be overthrown by one of his numerous rebellious relatives, or the Moors might decide they could profit more from trade with a thriving Tangier, than from war with an ailing city. He, Colonel Sir Palmes Fairborne, might hand his regiment to another and become merely Governor Fairborne, to spend his remaining years passing time in polite conversation and negotiations,

TANGIER RELIEVED

ordering the domestic affairs of a prosperous colony and enjoying family life.

He was concerned about what would be facing him when the gates opened at daybreak. In the early days of Tangier he could have relied on the Moors being at Fajr prayers as the dawn broke, but now the Qaid had the Sultan's mercenaries, black-skinned Sudanese and pink-cheeked Europeans, so you were never safe, not at prayer times, not even during Ramadan. He had not sent scouts out for fear of warning the enemy of what was about to happen today. Surprise was the key.

The crimson above the hills east of Tangier Bay was turning yellow, and the firmament was brightening to a dark blue, blotting out the stars. Men and horses could now see clearly enough to move swiftly over uncertain ground. He pulled his pocket watch from his waistcoat. Five o'clock. It was time. Time to discover whether these regiments were up to the task Palmes had set them.

He signalled to the cornet to get the Horse mounted, turned Storm towards the gate, held his carbine aloft, following his time-honoured tradition and nodded to the gatemen. The bar was lifted. The heavy oak gates swivelled silently open on greased hinges and Palmes led his men from the safe haven within the city walls through the ravelin outer bastion and into disputed territory.

The cool night-time offshore breeze sent a shiver across his face and down his spine that added to the adrenalin-induced excitement of anticipation. His eyes darted over the stark ruins of Pole Fort ahead, searching for signs of lurking Moorish defenders. Nothing. He looked back at the cavalry brigade; so many flags, the green of his own Tangier Horse surrounded by numerous red guidons of the King's men, all with breastplates and helmets glinting in the early light, well prepared and eager.

Never before had he so many cavalry at his disposal, never led this many Horse into battle. The new troops of a hundred and eighty Horse had arrived in good condition considering the long sea journey. These men had fought alongside the Duke of Monmouth, a fierce leader who had won many encounters against the French, Spanish and Dutch. They arrived much better equipped than other reinforcements, with horses, armour and weapons from the King's own Horse Guards. Palmes had them train with the half-troop of thirty Tangier Horse, who gave them much good advice on how to fight the Moors. They had the experience, the equipment, the knowledge, did they have the courage?

TANGIER: THE EARLIEST BATTLE HONOUR

He waited until Tollemache's vanguard had cleared the ravelin and was ready to advance, then squeezed his knees and urged Storm into a trot, then a canter and waved the Horse forward. Fairborne led the charge between the two trench lines, up the grassy hill to the ruins of Pole Fort. The few desultory defenders, awoken by the thundering hooves, were reaching for their weapons and running for cover as a hail of carbine shot blasted them. The firefight was brief and one-sided. Within minutes the riders were drawing their cutlasses to finish off the survivors of the small garrison.

Fairborne's saddle complained as he twisted round. His heart leapt to see the massed scarlet coats of the regiments of Foot flowing out of Katarina Gate, colours held high. He waved Tollemache forward and saw him and Plymouth kick their horses into a canter. Immediately a drumbeat echoed up off the city walls, giving the three hundred Coldstreamers and Gentlemen Volunteers a controlled urgency as the green coats of the pikemen and redcoats of the musketeers broke into a quick march, following their red and white colours up the shallow valley. When they divided into three and began swarming up the hill to occupy the fort and around it to block the roads and old trenches, Palmes knew they would be in position before the enemy forces could respond.

He sent a troop of Horse to secure the hillsides against lancers, ready for the Marines and Dumbartons, and waved Barclay and Halkett on. Even louder, the insistent beat of 'Dumbarton's Drums' sounded out, setting the rapid pace of another twelve hundred men, as the Marines unfurled their yellow ensign and the Dumbartons let fly their blue and white colours. Next he signalled to the First Tangier and the Battalion of Guards.

The head waters had burst the dam and a river of red, green and silver was flooding the land in all directions. Palmes' chest swelled, the magnificence of the spectacle was almost overwhelming. Three thousand troops all moving to his purpose, colours flying, drums pounding. He could see the citizens of Tangier on the city walls watching the grand display. Highly irregular – he must chastise the militia commander this evening – but what a sight they were watching!

Satisfied he had caught Omar by surprise and all was going to plan, he left a few Horse to ensure engineers Shere and Beckman could safely begin the work of assessing Pole and took the remainder down the far side of the hill towards James Fort to hold the inner valley, pending the arrival of the Forlorn Hope of Tollemache and Plymouth.

TANGIER RELIEVED

A shout went up from one of the Horse who was pointing northward towards the horizon. Peering into the distance, he now saw signs the Moors were beginning to react. A few of the enemy were assembling around Charles Fort. Palmes assigned a troop of Horse to reconnoitre in that direction and towards the Moors' encampment beyond Jews' River and continued his tour.

Scrutinising the hills rolling down from James and Anne Forts, he still saw no sign of movement, but confident as he was of his own regiment, he did not yet know or dare trust the new men. He judged he had time to review the southern flank before anything serious was likely to evolve from the enemy to the north. He turned his remaining cavalry to the left and trotted around the hill to the Forlorn Hope, who were establishing their positions. He pushed his horse on and rode his men behind the various units. Some were lucky enough to find themselves old trenches, some were taking cover behind rocks or in dry gullies, others were hastily shovelling soil for new foxholes while comrades fired at the few of Omar's men foolhardy enough to come within range.

Seeing Tollemache directing operations effectively, he voiced his appreciation of the Coldstreams' speedy arrival, assigned him a half troop of Horse and asked after Plymouth. He rode in the direction indicated and found the youthful Fitzcharles busy placing his musketeers to cover the road that led from Fort James to Pole. Fairborne spent some time encouraging the young man, repeated his advice on dealing with the heat and rationing the water and left him twenty cavalry, telling him to send for help if needs be rather than retreat from this key position.

He rode up along the side of Pole, observing his own First Tangier alert and ready in their ranks on open ground, pikes to the fore, awaiting developments. He saluted Giles, his lieutenant colonel, and continued round towards the south-west corner of the city. The distant sound of muskets told him Halkett and Barclay were having to fight for territory. He nudged his horse on, keen to discover whether these regiments were pushing forward or withdrawing. Halkett should be starting his attack on what remained of Fort Monmouth.

He breasted a small knoll as the sun's disc slid up from the horizon. Straight ahead, the tall uncompromisingly rectangular Irish Battery stood on the rise beyond the dry moat that surrounded the city; he was relieved to see Halkett's Dumbartons forming up in three lines on the hillside opposite.

***

TANGIER: THE EARLIEST BATTLE HONOUR

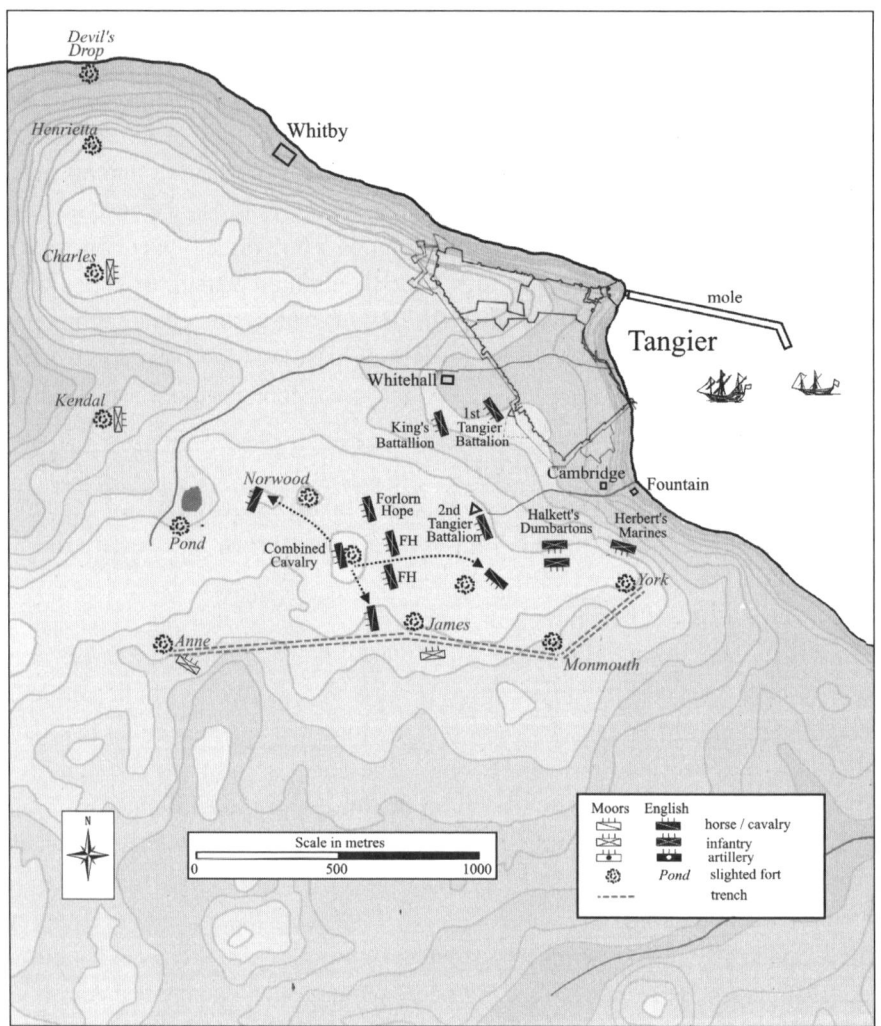

Pole restored. (Author)

Major Sir James Halkett had studied the lie of the land from the battlements of Irish Battery, discussing the opportunities and risks with Commander Fairborne. Despite his great experience fighting in Europe, James knew he was a beginner against the Moors. The advice was that the enemy lancers were accomplished riders and could arrive at any moment, seemingly materialising from nowhere, but the Foot would not come forward in any numbers because they were within range of the cannon on the city walls.

TANGIER RELIEVED

He had to occupy the high ground before lancers or skirmishers arrived. As soon as the last of his men had emerged from Katarina ravelin he signalled the drummers to strike up the famous 1 … 2 …, 1-2-3 of 'Dumbarton's Drums' the regimental quick march.

He followed the First Tangiers along the outside of the palisade, but continued straight on when Giles led his men up the shallow valley to the right. On his left he could see the Marines had made good progress and were spreading out ready for an assault against York Fort. To his right a troop of Horse were holding the high ground between First Tangier and his eventual target, Fort Monmouth, protecting his right flank. He shaded his eyes and gave a final wave to Hunter, the Master Gunner high up on the tower of Irish Battery, who replied by discharging a hand drake to reassure him he was ready to provide covering fire with half a dozen heavy cannon. Halkett knew time was of the essence and, satisfied everyone was in their allocated position, he headed towards the bluff of exposed rock on the way to Monmouth. At the foot of the sharp rise he ordered the lieutenants to form his company into ranks, pikes to the fore, ready to advance through the tall dry grass.

A sergeant in another company shouted. Everyone turned to see him pointing at Sir Palmes Fairborne astride his famed stallion rounding Pole, high above the lines of the First Tangier, watching the Dumbartons advance. Halkett removed his hat, enormous white ostrich feather shivering in the breeze, and raised a cheer, acknowledging the commander-in-chief who had sent the Horse to help them, and was clearly organising the whole encounter. Fairborne acknowledged their salutation, and the men quickly moved into position for the advance.

On the initial approach Halkett had seen several white-robed figures scampering about near the top of the rise, their crimson fez caps showing up well against the blue sky. His Dumbartons had a well-earned reputation for fierce fighting, but despite the men's desperation to prove themselves to their Governor and commander, Halkett was determined not to suffer unnecessary casualties. He took the advance slowly, giving the enemy time to realise they were greatly outnumbered and make a timely escape.

Once he judged the more timorous enemy had retreated, he sent a detail of grenadiers to deal with any remaining foolhardy defenders. The strapping men, distinguished by their unusual brimless caps of red and white bearing a silver Royal Cypher and Crown, chosen for their physique and fierceness and always keen for action, moved swiftly from one place

TANGIER: THE EARLIEST BATTLE HONOUR

of cover to the next until they were within lobbing distance of the few lingering Moorish musketmen, then tossed their deadly missiles. The hail of shrapnel and agonising screams were followed by the grenadiers' charge, swinging their axes and bludgeoning the life from any who had survived the grenade attack.

Without pause Halkett ordered his lines forward, muskets armed ready.

To his left, the company of Marines, yellow coats almost glowing in the bright morning light, were already halfway up the rise heading towards the ruins of York Fort. The crackle of each volley of their advance was followed by a cloud of smoke. They were coming under heavier fire than the sporadic resistance the Dumbartons faced, but the seamen were still advancing more quickly, even without the reassurance of pikemen. Admiral Herbert had told him the Marines were keen to show themselves more than the equal of any land-based units, and Captain Barclay was proving the point this morning, clearly determined to take York before the Dumbartons reached Monmouth.

Halkett turned back to the job in hand; the front row was moving back to reload, leaving the next line free to fire their fusillade. There was another cry and the Marines let out a mighty cheer. The drumming of hoof-beats announced the charge of another troop of Horse, this time riding uphill between the Dumbartons lines and the Marines'. Red guidon flying, brawny horses striding out, manes fluttering with blue ribbons and tails strung out like pennants, the cavalry were waved on by Barclay's men. The Sudanese Foot took one look at the concerted charge of carbine-firing horse soldiers and, knowing they were defenceless in the absence of Moorish lancers, discharged their muskets in a ragged volley, scrambled from their trenches, drew their long knives and ran for their lives, stumbling through the scrubby grass and leaping across trenches. The Marines' colours streamed ahead, seemingly filling the sky, as the battalion surged after them, screaming like the devil and wielding their muskets as clubs.

Now with both flanks secure, the lieutenant colonel pushed his men quickly. 'Onward the Dumbartons!' Halkett shouted as enemy skirmishers were cut down in full flight.

A joyous shout from five hundred men announced the planting of the yellow flag of the Marines on York hilltop.

A few moments later, disappointed to be second to their objective, but pleased he had lost no men, Halkett stood on the highest remaining section of Monmouth Fort as the ensign beside him raised the white cross of the Dumbartons' St Andrews flag. Halkett surveyed the triangular line of the low surviving walls surrounded by a deep ditch. He swiftly deployed the battalion within the walls, in the ditch and among the network of trenches dug by the advancing Moorish sappers six months earlier.

The Troop of Horse cantered over and offered themselves for reconnaissance or taking messages. Halkett sent them to discover the enemy deployment and movements and then settled back to take in the full vista.

The Marines were spreading themselves among the mining works and rubble of the lozenge-shaped building that had been York Fort, preparing for the attack that was sure to come. The black hats of his Dumbartons were visible in the trenches around Monmouth. Down to his right, at the far end of the vale between Monmouth and Pole, he could see the smoke of musket fire rising above the Flags of St George, flying over the Forlorn Hope. The advance units were dug in and trying to pick off the Sudanese musketmen edging down from James and Anne forts. Nearer, the bright colours of the First Tangier Regiment fluttered on the hillside between him and Pole Fort. On the far side of Pole he could make out the right wing of The King's Battalion stretching almost to Whitehall. The Second Tangier Regiment stood by outside Katarina ravelin, guarding the city gate and providing a reserve, with the remainder of Dumbartons working shifts labouring on Pole.

Not much more than half an hour after they had opened the gates, Sir Palmes Fairborne had near three thousand troops perfectly placed to repel any Moorish assault, and now the miners and mole-men slaves would be on their way from the city with materials to refortify Pole under the direction of engineers Shere and Beckman.

Thankfully the morning continued dry and comfortably warm. Halkett heard the sound of continued skirmishing as the Moors tested the advance units, but he could see work continuing on Pole Fort. In the late morning, as the land warmed and the breeze turned to onshore, the Horse advised him that Moorish infantry were moving closer. He alerted his men and whenever they sighted a flash of white or red they loosed a volley. They repelled several assaults, and twice he had to send for fresh apostles of powder and supplies of shot, but his men were firmly entrenched and in no danger of being dislodged by a few hundred skirmishers. Likewise, the Marines held steady under fire. About two o'clock the sound of the call to prayer drifted up from Old Tangier across the bay and the attacks ceased. Halkett stood his men easy and rotated his sentries to give everyone time to relax, eat and drink.

TANGIER: THE EARLIEST BATTLE HONOUR

Under the protection of the Forlorn Hope and all the other forces deployed he watched work on Pole advance quickly. A strong palisade was erected around the old fort. Judging by the stone carted up into the palisade, a breastwork must have been built by the time the setting sun was suffusing the gathering clouds with a pink glow. There had been several stretcher-bearers carrying casualties from the Forlorn Hope, but Sackville's Guards had seen little action that day as they marched up to the newly fortified Pole to defend it overnight before the trumpets recalled the Dumbartons and other regiments to their barracks.

***

With his objective achieved a greatly relieved Sir Palmes Fairborne ensured Pole was well defended overnight and withdrew all his other forces into the city.

He knew Qaid Omar had spent the summer truce watching the build-up of British forces with great frustration and growing anger. If the Moorish general had any hope of defeating the city he would surely have devised a plan to attack as soon as possible before the new arrivals were acclimatised and trained. The lack of an attack at the expiry of the ceasefire and the limited response today made it seem the enemy commander had no new initiatives to cause concern to Palmes.

He was now supremely confident he had raised the siege of Tangier. With his First Tangier Regiment up to strength and the addition of the new regiments he would continue the reconstruction of forts in his plan to reclaim the line of British defences. If he received the full complement of reinforcements he had been promised he would defeat Qaid Omar's army and force the Sultan to sue for terms.

Chapter 13

Military Success

24 October 1680

Tangier, Morocco

So near to a permanent peace, yet so far.

After the successful attack a month before, Palmes had been hopeful of a treaty but Sultan Ismail was still awaiting a reply to the letter he had written to the English King and Qaid Omar would agree nothing in the meantime.

The Qaid was not labouring under the uncertain conditions Ghailan had suffered; the Gharb was united in its jihad against Tangier, Omar had the resources and the time for a protracted siege – Palmes would have to prove Tangier's ability to defend itself before the Qaid would agree a truce.

He and the Qaid were both well aware Pole Fort was the key. Palmes had to make the fort impregnable.

The letter from His Majesty had not materialised, nor had the promised reinforcements; Palmes was short of men, heavy cannon and above all cavalry.

Some cannon had been supplied. Palmes had come close to being a victim of one when it exploded, killing four of the crew and injuring engineer Shere. Several other artillery pieces had blown themselves apart, consequently none of the newly supplied heavy guns could be used for fear of the same result. He had moved cannon from the mole to the city walls, but he was in desperate need of long-range guns.

His cavalry was far short of the number he had sought; only a hundred or so of the promised six hundred had arrived. Luckily, perceiving the Spanish had finally come to accept humiliating peace with England, Palmes had secured an agreement for two hundred of their famed cavalry to be sent across the Straits to his aid.

Nonetheless, he had continued work on Pole. Beckman plotted and planned, still working towards his original aim from twenty years earlier, constantly strengthening the fort, extending the palisades from Katarina Gate to Pole and improving the entrenchments.

The Moors had been equally tireless in their efforts to impede Beckman's work, carrying out innumerable attacks, digging trenches and bringing up cannon to fire on the fort and the town itself. They had two batteries of cannon within range of Pole, and had begun undermining the fort. As a further distraction they had reoccupied their trenches on the Marshan Plateau and begun directing cannon fire from the heights.

The situation had now become desperate. Palmes needed to inflict a heavy defeat on Omar to persuade him to agree a peace treaty on acceptable terms. Now the Spanish Horse had arrived it was time to finalise plans and mount a decisive attack.

Whilst mulling over ways to launch a devastating attack, Palmes had thought to secure the Marshan Plateau by renewing the earthworks outside the citadel. At seven in the morning he took fifty Spanish Horse and a fatigue party of a hundred and fifty Foot to begin work.

He had deployed a defensive screen of pikes and muskets, set up the cheval de fries on each side to prevent a flanking attack and was deploying the workmen when he felt a pain in his chest. He had been hit. Blood was oozing from his jacket. He cried out.

He opened his eyes and looked into Marjory's worried face.

27 October 1680

Tangier, Morocco

This was it. The culmination of everything he had worked for over the last eighteen years. All on the turn of one card, one throw of the dice.

Palmes had often said he would willingly give his life in the service of his King. His own carelessness had allowed the offer to be taken up. An enemy marksman had recognised his distinctive horse or his attire and had managed a chance shot, hitting him in the chest. Surgeon Spotswood had declared it a mortal wound and told him he had only a few days to live.

His life's work of defending Tangier was being literally undermined. The Moors had to be pushed back, their cannon captured, the mines filled, the trenches defended. They had to be soundly defeated, to be shown the deadly

MILITARY SUCCESS

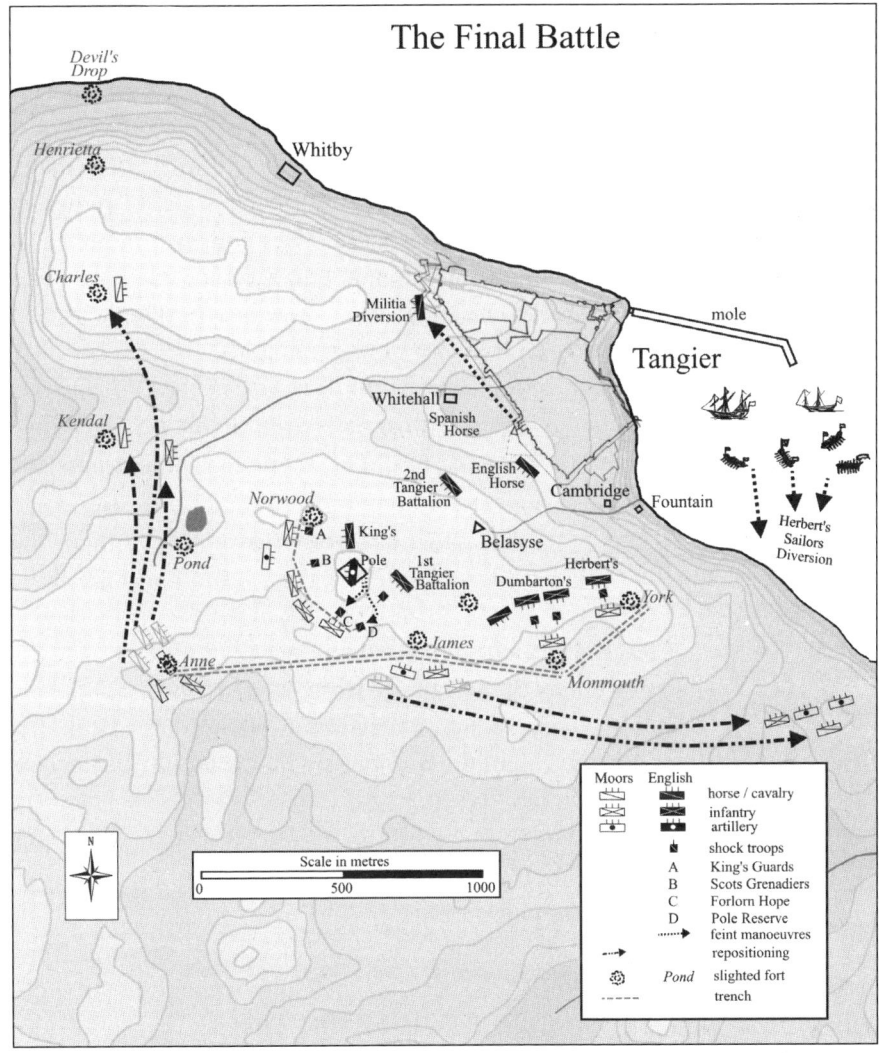

The final battle. (Author)

resolve of the garrison to defend the city and inflict a mortal wound to the army of Omar and Ismail.

The ferocious actions of the last month and bad luck with illness had already reduced the garrison to less than half. Attrition would make matters worse; now was the time for decisive action. Palmes was no longer a threat to Acting Commander-in-Chief Sackville's perceived seniority and the Guards' colonel had come to him for advice. Together the Council of War had planned the day in detail, knowing this was make or break.

TANGIER: THE EARLIEST BATTLE HONOUR

Sackville did not seem to believe the Moors could be beaten, but Halkett had supported Palmes and when it came to the final reckoning Sackville did not want to be the person who gave the King's Christian city to the Muslims.

The simplicity of Admiral Herbert's idea had impressed Palmes, and Sackville had accepted the suggestion with open arms. It was a brilliant stroke, costing nothing, but possibly gaining everything. Three in the morning and boats were now being launched from every ship in the harbour; sailors in clothes mimicking military uniforms filling every cutter, every longboat. The whole swarm of boats, flying what appeared to be regimental colours, apparently trying to move in secret, but making too much noise to be unobserved, were being rowed across the bay towards the Sandhills beyond Fountain Fort where the Moors had erected a battery of eight large cannon to deter a landing on the beach. If that was what they expected, that was what Herbert would give them – a whole regiment of soldiers trying to outflank the Moors and take their cannon.

On the other side of the city outside Katarina Gate another regiment was being assembled by McKenny of the Tangier Horse. Smartly dressed in their red coats several hundred men set out, with a whole squadron of Horse, to the beat of the drum and the call of the trumpet, marching alongside the city walls up the hill to the Marshan Plateau.

High above in Peterborough Tower, Palmes winced in pain as he put the spyglass to his eye. The effort made his chest heave, but he could not miss this action. The Moors had seen the boatloads of soldiers deploying across the bay. A large contingent of Moorish lancers was moving from James Fort down the Sandhills towards the bay. There were more stirrings and several hundred skirmishers followed the Horse. The feint was working.

Palmes turned his attention to McKenny and his militiamen approaching Whitehall. Moors beyond Kendal and Anne were tracking the soldiers northwards. This distraction by men not able to fight on the front line and the 'Horse' of mole-men carthorses and donkeys was persuading Moors to move away from the garrison's planned point of attack.

Palmes sent a message to Sackville. The simple plan of distraction was working better than they could have hoped.

**

MILITARY SUCCESS

So many fewer than the previous full-scale advance a month ago. The parade ground this morning was barely half filled. Stafford Fairborne shivered involuntarily. It was cold, not fear. He was ensign, fully experienced officer of the Governor's Regiment of Tangier. He carried the company colours. He led the attack. He did not know what fear was. He was a Fairborne. His father's son.

Sackville was a loudmouth, but he had a point. The Tangier Regiment had not performed well in recent encounters. The men needed a reminder of what was expected from them. If he were older, with a little more authority he would have said the same things. His horse moved sideways, eager to get on with it. He spoke softly to her. She nodded her head, as if in understanding, and stood still.

The utter darkness lightened a little as the crescent moon escaped from the cloud. The rain lessened.

At last Sackville led them up to Katarina Gate. Stafford wondered what his father was thinking. Was he still alive? Would he see Stafford leading his men from the front, fighting bravely?

The seven Troops of Horse were first out of the parade ground, followed by the Forlorn Hope, then the King's Battalion. Next was the Governor's Battalion and at last he was on the move. They marched up through the town in silence. The streets lined with well-wishers, almost all wives and children this time as most able-bodied men were outside the city walls with the militia, and the remainder were on sentinel duty.

The silence was broken by the distant boom of cannon. Admiral Herbert's men must be on the move, and their distraction was working. The noise would help cover the garrison's movements. Stafford had great admiration for Herbert – he was a man of action like Stafford's father. Having spent his life looking out over the Straits, Stafford had often thought of running away to sea. A career in the navy must be wonderful, moving from place to place rather than being besieged in one city. He could be a Rupert, taking prizes, a Holmes, capturing Dutch forts, an Allin, sinking corsairs, or a Herbert, defending besieged outposts.

The men were practised at assembling at Katarina Gate, and it seemed to take only five minutes to get the three hundred Horse and fifteen hundred Foot out into the palisade and formed into ranks, ready for the advance.

So the new commander-in-chief was stuck with Fairborne's plan.

Surprise and speed were essential, his father had told him. Each battalion was drawn up with its own detachment of shock troops at the front, fifty

TANGIER: THE EARLIEST BATTLE HONOUR

men with captain and lieutenant accompanied by a troop of Horse. They would rush the battalion's objective and make the first devastating blow; hopefully the unexpected shock would put the enemy to rout. The rest of the battalion would follow as it could to back up the initial thrust.

The assembly had been so quiet and the success of the feigned attacks so complete, the enemy were only just beginning to react when Sackville gave the signal to the men in Pole Fort.

Captains Lundy and Hume burst out of the door, leading their chosen Forlorn Hope.

The Scots on Stafford's left immediately sprang forward, led by Halkett, their fiery major. No one could keep up with him, but his attached Horse tried their best, and his Foot charged like furies.

Realising they were being made to look like laggards, Bowes shouted to his drummer to beat the quick march and the King's Battalion headed up the shallow valley between Pole and Whitehall.

Not to be outdone, the First Battalion of the Tangier followed Boynton to the left of Pole Fort. At the same time, Herbert's seamen and the second battalion of Dumbartons Scots struck up and charged after their rapidly advancing colours.

Grenades exploding in the first trench must have taken the Moors by surprise. They were suddenly face to face with seventy brave Scotsmen of the Forlorn Hope charging them with pike and musket. But Stafford could see they were putting up fierce resistance; there must be more of them than expected. He saw Lundy and Hume both shot down in quick succession and the Scots' charge stalled. The lieutenant, Robinson, took over and encouraged the men forward. White-robed figures began climbing out of the trench to attack the small group of screaming redcoats. The Moors could see they outnumbered the musketeers and were trying to surround them. Robinson fell and it looked as though the Forlorn Hope would be wiped out before the First Tangier shock troops could reach them, but then the Pole Fort reserve materialised, running at the Moors' wings, throwing them back and saving their Forlorn Hope. Moments later the First Tangier arrived and the Moors broke and ran.

Fawtrey led the King's Guards' advance corps with those of McCracken's Scots Grenadiers to attack a heavily guarded gun emplacement. Their initial success was halted by the sheer number of the enemy, who fought back with captured grenades and grapeshot. The main body of Guards was too slow and with no place to take cover the shock troops fell back behind Pole.

MILITARY SUCCESS

In the distance the Scots who had charged Monmouth Fort with Coy's Horse in support kept themselves in good order. Two detachments of shock troops, with half a company of grenadiers and Horse, instilled fear into the enemy defending the ruins of Monmouth Fort, and they quickly broke and ran.

But despite the speed with which Monmouth had been won, the Moors had brought up reinforcements from their encampment beyond the Sandhills to defend the trenches that stretched from James Fort to Monmouth. This line enclosed the English forces and at the same time protected the Moors' camp. The Moors who had fallen back from their positions around Pole regrouped in the trench lines between Anne, James and Monmouth.

***

Hamut had been relishing the thought of the imminent destruction of the new Pole Fort. The English reinforcements treacherously brought in during the truce, followed by Fairborne's aggressiveness, had given the Tangier garrison a temporary advantage, but Hamut's cleverly designed trenches and gun emplacements had put Omar's men on the front foot again. They were only one or two days away from bringing the carefully constructed edifice of Pole Fort crashing down on the heads of its arrogant builder, Beckman, and those suicidal screaming Scots who manned it. It was the will of Allah and Hamut was the servant of the one true god.

Tonight those very Scots he hated with a vengeance had come charging out of the fort expecting to find a few sleepy defenders to murder. They had been in for a shock. Hamut knew what to expect and had advised Omar to prepare for a sally. He had reinforced the trenches and posted men to defend the battery, issued grenades captured from the magnificent victory of Charles Fort, and ordered sentinels for every watch.

When the Forlorn Hope came charging out of Pole they had no hope. Their leaders had been cut down, they had been driven back; the valiant Sudanese had leapt from the trenches to surround the vanguard to finish them off. The brave Muslims had repelled the much-vaunted grenadiers with their own grenades, with massive firepower and religious zeal. But at the very moment they had gained the ascendancy they were hit by another mass of screeching, screaming Scots stampeding from the fort along the trench from the side – a totally unexpected flanking attack. They found themselves trying to push forward at the same time as defending from the side. His men

TANGIER: THE EARLIEST BATTLE HONOUR

had been halted by the fury of the new attack and were fighting back bravely when yet another squad of grenadiers and heavy cavalry crashed into them; they had no choice but to retreat, leaving the trenches to the English.

Then the grenadiers who had been beaten back from gun emplacement were reinforced by the full regiment of King's Guards and now resumed their assault. Attacked by the Guards from the front and the victorious Forlorn Hope from the side, the Sultan's men defending the guns broke and ran, abandoning their trench and their cannon. A huge cheer arose from the English, who sent shot and missiles after the fleeing men.

All of the trenches around Pole Fort were lost.

Hamut did not stop running until he reached the old James Fort.

Here he was safe. Another horde of Sudanese Foot was streaming down from the encampment to man the old lines of trenches between James and Monmouth. The cannon set up on this hill commanded the whole area to York Fort and on to the sea. Musket fire from James would devastate any army and halt any attack. No one would be suicidal enough to attempt these trenches.

Nonetheless, the foolhardy Dumbartons Scots drew up in ranks in front of the first trench. Their captain ordered the pikemen to stand alternately with musketeers in the front row, with more musketeers in the second. Some distance behind, a second company drew up in the same manner. The captain shouted, the drums rolled, but instead of the line moving forward as the defenders had expected, grenadiers ran from the wings, tossed their grenades and retreated swiftly. The skirmishers in the trenches were still trying to recover their senses and aim at the fleeing grenadiers when the drums rattled out their quick march and the redcoats advanced at the double, colours flying, pikes forward. The first row of muskets fired and stood aside, allowing the second row to advance with the pikemen. The second row fired and immediately, through the cloud of smoke, the vicious thrusting spikes charged the trench, impaling anyone too slow to escape.

The speed of the charge gave the defenders no time to reload. Desperately clubbing musket butts and slashing scimitars at the sixteen-foot pikes being thrust into the trenches, the Moors were horrified to see scores of grenadiers jumping down into the trench and coming at them with hatchets swinging. The skirmishers gave up any pretence of defence and ran to find refuge with the Sudanese in the next trench, leaving the Scots to be targeted by small-shot and cannon from Monmouth and James.

MILITARY SUCCESS

In front of James Fort the colours of the Tangier battalion flew above the ranks of redcoats with familiar green facings and green breeches advancing towards the fort, but before they got within two hundred paces a multitude of lancers swept down from Anne's and attacked their exposed right flank with a furious blast of musket-fire. With no Horse to protect them, few pikes and no time to form into a square, the officers were confused. The musketeers managed one shot before being overrun by lancers firing pistols, throwing lances like javelins and slashing scimitars from all directions. The Tangier men drew their pistols and swords, but Hamut smiled to see the Moors literally cutting their way through the redcoats. In total disarray, the English ran with the lancers in pursuit.

The brassy call of a trumpet, followed by a cacophony of shouts, warned the escaping men to get out of the way of the heavy cavalry charging through the chaos, sabres at the ready. The thundering Tangier Horse swept the lances aside and hacked at the vulnerable Moors, who, knowing they could not prevail, galloped off, pursued by the cavalry.

The second battalion of Tangier advanced in through the first to resume the attack on James. A couple of hundred yards from the fort they were stopped short by a fusillade of small-shot, and a hail of grenades. Disinclined to move forward against such devastating opposition, they stopped and fired a series of volleys. Hamut could see they would make no progress, but they were absorbing defenders' fire that was giving the Scots relief and allowing their attack to proceed without interference from James. The English had to be broken soon or the Scots would be through.

Another swarm of lancers swept down the hill and circled the Second Battalion Tangier's lines, attacking the flanks left exposed by the absent cavalry. The Tangier had stood and absorbed gunfire from thousands of muskets but when men started falling from this fresh assault they began to falter. Ignoring their officers, they turned their backs on the enemy and ran. The Moorish lancers immediately swooped in, riding stragglers down and killing them at will. The Tangiers had failed again and it seemed few would survive, but the captain of the second company of Scots turned his men about and fired a timely broadside at the lancers. Horses stumbled, riders fell, some turned to face the new enemy, some retreated, others milled about uncertain what to do, the pursuit ground to a halt. No longer harried, the Tangier captain regained control of his men, turned the fifty that remained to face the enemy and held his ground.

The impetuous Dumbartons had been repelled by the Sultan's Sudanese and trapped in the first trench to be enfiladed from James at one end and

TANGIER: THE EARLIEST BATTLE HONOUR

Monmouth the other. Caught in the deadly crossfire, they were taking casualties until the Tangier drew fire from James. Hamut screamed to the lancers and skirmishers to cease their pursuit of the Tangier. He prayed to Allah to turn them back to attack the rear of the Dumbartons.

The Scots' captain saw the danger. He ordered his men to reload, shouted to the grenadiers to light their murderous spheres, called for the drums again and the whole battalion arose as one from the deep lane and moved forward to the fast march of the drum. There was time for one shot from each of the defenders of the second trench before they were in danger of being skewered by pikes, battered by musket butts or butchered by an axe. Swords were no defence against being run through by a thirteen-foot pole. The pure fury of the attackers was terrifying. Even the Sudanese were no match for this wave of death. They ran.

Hamut was incredulous. He had seen the redcoats defeat his men when they were outnumbered, but had not believed they could sweep aside so many well-entrenched professionals of the Sultan's elite.

The Scots emerged from the second trench to be greeted by hundreds of lancers charging at them. The Scottish pikemen formed a defensive ring for the musketeers and grenadiers, and the lancers circled like vultures ready for the kill eager to claim a redcoat life to ensure the approval of Allah and an eternal life with innumerable virgins at their call. Skirmishers and Sudanese ran to attack with musket-fire.

Seeing the Dumbartons in danger of being swamped, the fifty remaining Tangiers threw caution to the wind, ran forwards and leapt into the trenches. Swinging shovels off their backs, they began constructing a causeway for the Horse. A few minutes later the trumpet called and a pennant-waving cornet was followed by two troops of heavy cavalry charging across the crumbling earthwork and hurtling into the Moors. The lancers lacked nothing in skill and bravery, but their small horses, light weapons and fragile shields could not resist the weight of the Tangier cavalry. They feigned retreat, galloped this way and that, ducked and weaved, but when the Spanish Horse came charging in Moorish lancers on their small Barb horses could do nothing more to protect their retreating Foot. The lancers fled, leaving the skirmishers and the Sudanese to the slashing sabres of the cavalry.

The English and Spanish cavalry combined to create mayhem, chasing Omar's retreating army over the Sandhills towards their encampment.

To Hamut's great surprise, the brassy blare of trumpets recalled the Horse and most of the cavalry left the Moors to their hasty retreat.

MILITARY SUCCESS

Hamut knew it was time for him to leave; Sultan Ismail would not be pleased. Heads would roll; his honorary wife and horse seemed far off now. It would be wise to escape inland to the mountains and lie low.

***

Despite his exhaustion, Stafford ran up the steps onto the city wall and charged around the ramparts as fast as he could. Elated by the great success of the day's action, he was desperate to tell his father all about it.

He found Palmes on the balcony at the top of the Governor's House. The commander-in-chief could see the whole battlefield and had watched the unfolding action, witnessed the decisive victory, the rout of the enemy, the recovery of many guns and the winning of so many enemy standards.

Shere had fought bravely in the Forlorn Hope that charged out from Pole, and reported back to Palmes 'that we should at length with a handful of men take the field, repossess and fortify an eminent post they had taken from us, give them battle, defeat them, taking their cannon, colours, prisoners, level and demolish their works and trenches and pursue them to their very camp. Nothing but Divine Providence and protection could have brought so great a work to pass.'

After he had listened to his son's account, Palmes said, 'I have been in this garrison a long time, many a times flattered with the propitious smiles of Fortune's favour, and sometimes endured the lowering umbrageous frowns of her adverse and fatal eclipses, doing my endeavour for the advancing of the King and Master's interest, to withstand the Moors' attempts and gain myself reputation; but I must now pay the debt of all men, and yet I think it rejoices my dying spirits to see this subtle enemy so bravely conquered; only I complain on my own sad destiny that during all the wars and encounters with them, I had not the happiness to obtain such a glorious victory over them. But I am most glad that a person I respected for his great parts ever since he came here has snatched the honour out of my hands.'

Soon after his speech he breathed his last, and Stafford was pleased he had not told his father how Halkett was saying Sackville had been too cautious. If he had ordered the Guards to press home their victory with the other regiments instead of standing around guarding the captured cannon, if he had let loose the cavalry instead of recalling them, they could have destroyed the retreating Moors. It would have been the end of Qaid

TANGIER: THE EARLIEST BATTLE HONOUR

Omar's army and much of the Sultan's. Halkett said if Fairborne had been in command the war would have been ended on that day as the Sultan himself must have sued for peace for lack of fighting men.

This time the brave commander Palmes Fairborne could not visit the wounded and dying, nor congratulate his men on their hard-earned victory.

Stafford walked slowly to the hospital and spoke to each of the men there expressing his father's gratitude for their courage and the worthy victory that killed well above a thousand of the enemy, captured many cannon and took half a dozen colours.

Chapter 14

Diplomatic Failure

December 1680

London, England

Pepys was not entirely unhappy to be relieved of his Tangier duties.

His Majesty was severely displeased with the humiliating terms of the treaty Inchiquin had agreed with Sultan Ismail. In response, the King had raised finance to send three thousand reinforcements and Fairborne had given the Moors a beating. But now Parliament had refused to support Tangier unless the King agreed to exclude the Duke of York from succeeding to the Crown of England.

This was the final insult. Charles would never agree to such terms. He had instead instructed Pepys and Shere to help L'Estrange launch a campaign in London's *Observator* newspaper to stir public opinion to support Tangier and decry Parliament.

To Pepys, L'Estrange's words appeared more designed to damage Parliament's reputation than save Tangier.

February 1681

Tangier, Morocco

Dover had to admit he did strike a most imposing figure, something the garrison had lacked since Fairborne's disastrous death four months previously.

He had a reputation for sweeping women off their feet, figuratively and literally. She was not sure she liked the look of him, but he did have a presence, a self-confident swagger. He had the arrogance of a cavalry officer rather than the pride of a Foot regiment. His uniform was immaculate with

TANGIER: THE EARLIEST BATTLE HONOUR

his grey silk coat and crimson sash and she could see some women might find him attractive, with his big brown eyes, full head of hair and broad shoulders.

This Percy Kirke was being sent to treat with the Sultan. How he was chosen she did not know, but she wished him 'God speed' in securing a lasting peace on favourable terms. He would need all the help he could get if he were to gain favour with the unpredictable Sultan, but they might find common ground in their adventures with women. Knowing Kirke's weakness, she had sent him a note promising him unheard of pleasure if he could negotiate her father's freedom.

Alongside him Qaid Omar was second best despite his magnificent robes and jewel-encrusted Tuareg headdress. The parade of Tangier Horse, led by the pipes and drums of the Dumbartons, marched up Misericordia, followed through the market place by the elite Moorish horsemen and Sudanese Guard in their immaculate white robes, for all to admire. The dignitaries and their retinues swept on up Katarina Street to leave by Katarina Gate.

The musketeers of the Tangier regiments stood to attention two deep each side of the street to impress Qaid Omar with their numbers, even though he must suspect, as Dover knew, that the men in Katarina Street had run up through the back streets from their previous posts in the parade ground.

Why they put up with it she could not understand. Here were more than a thousand men who had risked their lives; fought fierce battles, been shot at, bombarded, attacked by lancers, seen their friends die and lived in worse conditions than she, a common whore. Their king and country thought so little of their sacrifice and labour their pay was two years in arrears, and if she had not the softness to give them credit they would not even have the comfort of a woman's love to see them through. The Muslim men had houris to look forward to; Christian men had to get what pleasure they could in this life before an utterly celibate eternity among saints and martyrs. She was doing what she could to provide earthly delights.

The English King might be poor as a church mouse but he had sent her some more customers, enough to complete a second regiment. Now they had the Governor's Tangier Regiment same as always, but it had to be called First Tangier, because they now also had a Second Tangier, and she had donned her newest silk bodice and fancy Venetian hat in the hopes of attracting some of the new officers to her love nest … perhaps even the colonel, Mister Trelawney, as in Charles Trelawney, as opposed to Captain Francis Trelawney, who was buried after trying to save his son in the escape from Charles Fort.

DIPLOMATIC FAILURE

This Sackville got his wish to be in charge. He had spent all his time criticising that lovely Captain Fairborne, or commander-in-chief as he got to be. Sackville was commander and Governor and from what she had heard he was not so keen on it now he was responsible for the whole place. Easy to criticise them what's in charge, not so easy to be perfect when you have to do it yourself.

Anyway, talk was Sackville had been too timid in the October victory and if he had let the cavalry pursue the retreating Moors it would have been the end of Qaid Omar. It could be true, because Omar had accepted a six-month peace allowing the English to cut wood, pasture cattle, catch fish and trade with the locals for provisions, all in exchange for a few barrels of gunpowder and a hundred muskets.

But there was still hope; the treaty gave time for these extra boys to sail out to make up for her lost customers, and life was getting back to normal. News was Qaid Omar had told Ismail most of his army had been killed or deserted and he was in no position to fight Tangier without great assistance from the Sultan. Ismail had other troubles and Tangier would have to wait; his Imam had told him the English would be defeated in due course, and he was content to leave it to Allah's will.

Unfortunately, the English King had, for some unknown reason, chosen this smug fellow Leslie to be Ambassador to Sultan Ismail. She had known the young Leslie back in sixty-four when he bought his commission in the cavalry. She had watched his career, along with many others. He was brave enough, had accompanied an earlier embassy, and made it to captain in Middleton's Tangier Regiment; now he had been made major and knighted. Such things would not impress Qaid Omar or Sultan Ismail, but Leslie had started getting above himself, full of his own importance. He thought he knew better than everyone else and was causing great upset.

She heard he had told Sackville he could have agreed better terms than his, that no one should agree to such disadvantageous conditions. The Governor was mightily upset, said he had negotiated a more beneficial treaty than the much-vaunted truce Fairborne had agreed, and was well satisfied, especially given the condition of the garrison, which was precarious to say the least. But if Leslie could get more advantage he had better get on his horse and prove it. At this Leslie had apparently calmed down and said he would not go to the Sultan before the promised gifts from King Charles had arrived.

Dover's sources told her Qaid Omar had refused to tell the Sultan he must wait on Leslie, for fear it would cause great offence. That, apparently, was why the ebullient Colonel Kirke was being sent.

February 1681

Mequinez, Morocco

Kirke lay perfectly still; it was impossible to know whether he was paralysed by fear or genuinely unmoved.

A thousand shrieking warriors were hurtling towards him, their horses wild-eyed, straining at the bit, foam flying from their mouths, hooves beating the packed earth. The fiercest fighters, the most accomplished riders, the best shots the Moors could muster, were all simultaneously attacking Englishman Kirke. Fifty yards away, they thundered closer, forty, thirty yards, still he remained unmoved as the noise became deafening. Now releasing the reins, some were standing in their stirrups, some kneeling on their saddles, a few of the bravest standing on bare horseback. As one they raised their silver-chased muskets with both hands and fired them over the heads of the dignitaries.

And, at the last possible heartbeat of a second, swerved their steeds to a halt without reins.

A great cloud of dust continued forward, hiding the Sultan and his honoured guest from view.

As the air cleared, Percy Kirke stood up, bowed to the throng of horsemen, grinned his huge smile, cheered and clapped his enormous hands together in enthusiastic applause.

The Sultan's full lips widened and his dusky face beamed. More than anything, he sought praise. And the admiration of this proud beast of an aristocrat, son of King Charles' Groom of the Bedchamber, with the King's ear, was worth more than almost anyone else's. Kirke's reputation as a womaniser had gone before him, impressing the Sultan in advance, and his straight-talking lewd and humorous banter that had shocked the translator had quickly endeared him to the Moroccan ruler.

Kirke's willingness to travel a hundred and fifty miles to Mequinez to meet him, followed by this fearless confrontation and enthusiastic approval of the Sultan's entertainment, had cemented the friendship.

Hamut had thought better of trying to run away. Omar had laid blame for the defeat on the Qaid of Tetuan's shoulders and the ignominious retreat of

DIPLOMATIC FAILURE

the Sultan's own forces had been pivotal. Little blame had been apportioned to others. When Hamut heard Sultan Ismail had borne news of the defeat with equanimity he had decided he could return safely. Hamut's trenches could not realistically be seen as the reason for the loss.

Far from accusing Hamut, Ismail had been delighted to see he had escaped the slaughter and had rewarded him with another wife, who was by no means undesirable, and told him Allah had chosen some other time for victory over the English.

And so Hamut was here sat among the favoured ones, watching Ismail entertain this envoy of dubious reputation who was fast becoming the Sultan's bosom friend.

Under Ismail's constantly twirling red sunshade they strode around the lofty stone-built city walls, so much more solid than those of Tangier, as Ismail pointed out. 'English-built', Ismail explained, a grin creasing the dark skin at the corner of his sparkling black eyes, pointing to a group of emaciated white-skinned slaves toiling to place a large sandstone block precisely where the mason indicated. Everyone kept their eyes down, knowing the price for looking upon the Sultan might well be instant decapitation if they were lucky or long drawn out torture if the Sultan felt the need for amusement.

The tour had been punctuated by stops at each of the city gates, where seats and drinks had been arranged for the Sultan's refreshment. Lounging on enormous silk cushions in front of one gate, Ismail pointed out exquisite pillars salvaged from a Roman town for the quality of the marble, surpassing anything found in their own quarries.

In the Grand Mosque Ismail drew his attention to the minbar he had designed personally, and the ablutions courtyard he had provided, with fountains gushing water onto Zellij tiles of blue, black, terracotta and turquoise. Even in the height of summer water was provided for all, he stated proudly.

The Sultan showed his trust in Kirke, taking only two of his black bodyguards on the tour of his famed Royal Mews, petting every horse and telling stories of each animal. Hamut heard Ismail had roared a hearty laugh when Kirke told him King Charles had sold his horses to maintain his mistresses, or as he put it 'sold his stallions to pay for his mares'.

He finished his tour with a stroll around the palace grounds. These were full of fragrant white orange and lemon blossom, with subtly pink and purple buds and bright yellow stamens, variegated ornamental bushes,

TANGIER: THE EARLIEST BATTLE HONOUR

lush green grass, enclosures of lions, leopards and elephants, golden cages with song birds of all colours and paths of Islamic-patterned mosaics, with seemingly hundreds of fountains linked by rivulets and streams, and endless alcoves and bays each with its own statue.

Finally the great feast laid out with pigeon, partridge and pheasant, fish delivered fresh from the coast that afternoon, fruit of every sort, dishes of different dates, marzipans and nuts, all washed down with a variety of coffees Kirke had not known existed.

Then came the acrobats and dancers. When Kirke showed obvious appreciation of a pair of female dancers wearing only beads and diaphanous skirts, Ismail waved them over and gave them to him to keep him warm in the winter night. Not wishing to wait to sample his new companions, the Englishman retired with a woman on each arm and a lascivious grin on his face.

Never before had the Sultan been known to display his palace gardens and harem for another man's eyes. This Percy Kirke had found the way to Ismail's heart, and he had caused a stir among the Sultan's confidantes.

***

Some weeks later on his return from a tour of Fes with Qaid Omar, during which the warlord gifted an English boy slave to the visitor, Kirke was told by Ismail that the truce would be extended from six months to four years, and as long as Kirke was in Tangier the Sultan's forces would not attack.

This was no way to pursue a jihad, but Kirke had promised Ismail if he ever foreswore Protestantism he would become a Muslim. Perhaps the Sultan was planning a bloodless coup to win Tangier.

March 1681

Dover's intelligence on Kirke's visit last month had proved accurate. Now even before Leslie had returned to Tangier she knew the envoy's boast of bettering Sackville's terms had been hollow.

Qaid Omar and the Sultan Ismail saw Leslie as a person of little consequence and gave him little time. He had nothing to offer. The Sultan would stand by his word to Sackville and Kirke and therefore expected His

DIPLOMATIC FAILURE

Majesty to fulfil his side of the bargain and deliver the promised weapons and powder.

Dover had seen letters from Sackville requesting a weightier ambassador from the King but none had been sent. Perhaps despite his queen's wishes and those of the Duke of York, the King himself was more devoted to his mistresses, his whoring and his racehorses, as people said, or maybe it took time to choose someone of sufficient importance.

When Kirke had visited her he told her Governor Sackville had requested permission to return to England. The Guardsman had never seemed comfortable in Tangier. He was retired. Sackville said he had only come to please the King; his great experience had been ignored from the start; his advice had not been sought, nor the wisdom of his suggestions recognised. Even in final victory the honours had been accorded to Fairborne's plan rather than his own command. Indeed he had even been criticised for being too cautious when, in truth he had ordered an appropriate and safe pursuit and avoided what might well have been a disastrous trap. Tangier may be a fit posting for dedicated enthusiasts like Fairborne who were prepared to sacrifice everything for their misplaced honour, but in truth this place was too far from court to be visible to His Majesty. He might espouse support and give praise, but little materialised by way of hard cash.

The committee His Majesty had set up was (as everyone except the King knew) corrupt from its founding chair to its overblown treasurer. Any funds due to the patriotic garrison not siphoned off by the committee for their own enrichment had been pocketed by successive governors. The city itself had remained handicapped by the lack of a coherent design for its development. The Governor saw the King's appointment of a mere major for his envoy as evidence His Majesty had given up on Tangier.

As if to confirm Kirke's reporting, Sackville had soon returned to England, Leslie resumed his duties as Major of the Tangier Regiment, and Kirke of all people was nominated Governor. He said he had seen her father among Ismail's scribes but had failed to gain his release; she did not know whether he had even tried. Since Sackville's victory and peace treaty no one was interested in buying intelligence, but there were plenty of customers for her boudoir.

She had written to the Redemption Fathers yet again begging them to secure her father's freedom from the Sultan at any cost. She would work as long as it took to repay them.

TANGIER: THE EARLIEST BATTLE HONOUR
November 1681

Kirke had finally recognised what Stafford had known all along – Qaid Omar and Sultan Ismail only respected force. At last it seemed he had learned the Moors were not the 'great friends' he had been fooled into believing during his visit to Sultan Ismail. Sackville had dealt Qaid Omar a great blow but had failed to follow up on the day of battle and had equally failed to lay down tough conditions afterwards. The Moors could see he was weak-kneed.

At least Kirke was a successful soldier who had impressed the Sultan and Qaid. He would, no doubt take advantage of the four years peace of which he boasted to complete the impressive mole and the city could look forward to a peaceful and prosperous future as an indispensable naval base and a valuable trading city so lucrative to the English and the Moors that His Majesty and the Sultan would continue in peaceful cohabitation.

Qaid Omar had been keeping the terms of the peace treaty by allowing trade between the locals and the city, but he had broken the spirit of free trade by imposing a ridiculously high personal levy on cattle brought in for slaughter. The garrison were forced to pay many times the market price for their meat. At Stafford's suggestion, Kirke had sent agents to the market place in Al-Kasr. When Qaid Omar had objected, Kirke had the perfect reason to withhold the muskets and gunpowder promised in the treaty. As Stafford had predicted, the Sultan was greatly displeased with Qaid Omar.

When Stafford heard through the spy network in Tangier that one Prince Shereef was looking to escape the Sultan's court he had suggested giving him sanctuary and then using him to bargain with Ismail, but the Sultan's rage had resulted in Qaid Omar suffering serious illness. The regimental doctor sent to his aid found the Qaid 'much indisposed with a feverish distemper and weakness and coldness of the stomach' and was told his survival depended upon him satisfying the Sultan's demand for a huge sum of money to compensate for his inability to produce both the gunpowder of the treaty and Prince Shereef. Shortly afterwards Qaid Omar had died of suspected poisoning, to be replaced by his brother, Qaid Ali Benabdala.

A few weeks later, Stafford watched the new Qaid with two hundred horsemen escort the Moorish ambassador, Qaid Ben Haddu, and his retinue of twenty dignitaries and servants across the Sandhills to meet Kirke. The Governor rode out to Fountain Fort to welcome his guest. Kirke's escort of fifty grenadiers, thirty gunners and thirty negroes all in new uniforms and two hundred Horse matched the ambassadors' in magnificence.

DIPLOMATIC FAILURE

The Qaid's men saluted the English with small-shot powder play, Pole Fort discharged a cannonade, and another from the citadel greeted them as they entered Katarina Gate. The streets of the city were lined with foot soldiers and the mayor and aldermen in robes welcomed the Moors with a speech.

After a salute from cannon around the walls the procession continued down to York Castle, where the escort formed an honour guard and the ambassador led his retinue up the great steps to the citadel and into the Governor's Palace.

From the gallery the dignitaries looked out over the harbour filled with the English Fleet and ships from all parts of the world as three volleys rang out.

After a bounteous reception, the evening was rounded off with a magnificent firework display.

Governor Kirke knew how to present an impressive front and there was no doubt he made the most of his resources to show the ambassador the strength of purpose of the garrison.

***

Among the retinue Stafford recognised a Moorish turncoat named Hamut, who, it was said, Kirke tried to get excluded from the delegation, but the ambassador insisted and there was little the Governor could do without causing a major incident.

Two weeks later the Sultan's ambassador and his party set sail for England on the frigate *Hampshire* and the Algerine prize the *Golden Horse* of forty-eight guns.

January 1682

London, England

Resplendent in his new coat and reformed wig, Pepys looked down on Lord Chamberlain Arlington from a window of the mezzanine gallery of Banqueting House, pleased to be in the warmth and even more pleased to be back in favour with His Majesty and placed above Arlington for once.

After a seemingly endless wait the door on the opposite side of the court opened and Pepys recognised the Duke of Grafton, Colonel of the Footguard, emerging in full dress uniform, followed by the honour guard, and then at last, he caught his first glimpse of the Moorish ambassador, his Excellency Ben Haddu Ottor. A high green turban with red Mohammedan cap sat atop a face the colour of light oak that seemed to confirm the rumour of Ottor's English mother. His white woollen djellaba edged with green and gold was tied with a wide silk sash.

A few moments later Arlington led the ambassador into the reception hall, where the King and Queen were sat on the raised dais under the Royal Coat of Arms.

His Majesty posed in robes of state, the Queen was dressed in red, white and blue, her head and neck covered in glittering jewels. The Royal couple were flanked by the gentlemen pensioners with highly polished gilt poleaxes. Beyond them the Yeomen of the Guard in their flat black velvet hats, scarlet and black coats all richly embroidered gold, held gilded partisan polearms. The hall was lined with the nobility and gentry, paraded in their most expensive finery, all straining for a sight of the strangers. His Majesty gave the signal and Arlington accompanied the ambassador on his walk up the deep blue silk carpet.

Pepys could now see more detail of the ambassador's splendid attire. A string of large pearls was woven into his turban; his sash held a richly inlaid scimitar in a scabbard decorated with gold and silver wire; leather sandals encased his feet and the lower part of his otherwise naked calves.

On reaching the foot of the dais the ambassador bowed and Charles doffed his large brimmed black hat and then replaced it. The ambassador made a short speech in perfect English, then reached into his sleeve and produced a large scroll tied with green and gold ribbon, which he said was a letter to His Majesty from the King of Fez and Morocco. Charles accepted the document and handed it to Secretary Jenkins. The King asked after the Sultan's health and after a few more words exchanged between them the ambassador was escorted away to his lodgings in the Strand.

April 1682

Cambridge, England

Pepys could not allow the occasion to pass him by.

The Moorish ambassador had come to Cambridge University. The Mayor and Aldermen had thought it beneath their dignity to receive His Excellency, but Pepys had no such qualms. He needed to visit Magdalene College to discuss his planned legacy of a fully stocked library and this was the perfect occasion to arrange a visit.

DIPLOMATIC FAILURE

It was not beneath his dignity to stand on Regent Walk to watch the history-making procession. The King's coach and six with coachmen in Royal Livery and King's Horse accompanying were followed by half a dozen Moors on horseback. These were brawny men of swarthy complexion, wearing scimitars and knives and carbines. They wore rich mantles of purple and green, their heads were covered with red caps of soft silk, lined with yellow sarsenet that reminded Pepys of night caps. The ambassador stepped from the coach wrapped in a cloak of cloth of gold.

It was not beneath his dignity to grease a few palms to obtain a seat at the banquet in Regent's House. In fact the fish alone had been worth the cost of his place. The soused eel was delicious, the salmon exceptional and the Royal Sturgeon sublime and wasted on the Moors, who ate heartily without showing any appreciation of the subtleties of different cuts each with their own flavour.

Pepys was disappointed to see the ambassador, feeling unwell, retire to the house of the provost of King's College. They being due to leave for Newmarket that afternoon, he would miss any opportunity of speaking personally to Ottor. He had thought it might not be too late to add a few thoughts of his own regarding peace in Tangier. It was rumoured His Majesty had failed to heed the warnings of the Tangier Governor and in consequence had gained nothing on the Governor's agreement and lost much.

Pepys knew it was foolhardy to allow His Majesty to be personally involved in diplomatic discussions – he was much better at laying down objectives for others to attain than achieving them himself. The proponents of Tangier had lost their sway; Sandwich had lost his life, Rupert had lost his conviction and York had lost his influence. The King had refused the Exclusion Bill and Parliament had refused to fund Tangier.

In truth His Majesty always gave away much in return for little or nought, as with his mistresses, and it was probably too late for anyone to make good the damage done by the King.

May 1682

Tangier, Morocco

Stafford Fairborne waved farewell to his mother, his brothers and his sisters.

He did what he could to comfort his mother before she left for England. He was disappointed and sorry to see his family leave, but he was ensign and at sixteen years old was earning enough to keep his creditors at bay. There was no chance his mother would receive preferment from Kirke unless it were in the bedroom and she could do more to prey on the King's conscience from lodgings in London than from their house in Tangier, however comfortable that house might be.

He eyed the ships in the bay, admiring their clean lines, watching the way they rode the waves, counting the gun ports and thinking of the devastating power of a single broadside. He envied the captain who commanded the self-sufficient village, who travelled the world and controlled his own destiny. He had listened to admirals who entertained his father with tales of adventure, he had seen running battles with the Turks and the capture of Algerine corsairs, and heard of taking rich prizes from the Spanish, sailing into new cities, discovering exotic peoples and animals.

He watched the last boats row out from shore, heard the shouted orders and the piping as the ship unfurled her sails and hoisted her flags. His mother stood, holding all her children close as they waved goodbye to him, and he stood long after they had set off in the fresh Levantine, and quickly disappeared around the Spanish coast.

Reluctantly Stafford ascended the cobbled incline to Sandwich Gate, casually wondering whether he would ever have anything named after him. Teviot had a hill, Peterborough a tower, Belasyse a fort. His father, for all his dedication and brilliance, for all his victories, had nothing, at least not yet. Maybe in time, once Tangier was famed throughout the world as a great seaport, there would be a Fairborne lighthouse on the Great Mole of Tangier.

Chapter 15

Tangier Dénouement

September 1683

Tangier, Morocco

She was woken by the heavy throb.

She rolled Pepys' snoring head off her breast.

It was not the sound of cannon. She covered his head with a pillow and listened carefully.

Drums! It was the sound of distant drums.

She slipped out of bed, pulled on her silk pantaloons, dropped the real into her hidden pocket and opened the shutter.

Drums coming from the direction of York Castle. A regiment was on the move.

She shook the Englishman awake, pushed him to the bedroom door, threw on her calico shift, combed her hair, slipped on her shoes and cloak and ran downstairs. She arrived at the market square in time to see the red and white colours of the King's Guards leading the regiment up from Misericordia. A fine display of eight hundred men, and close on their heels was the Tangier Regiment with their familiar green breeches and stockings; then the Dumbartons Scots, saltire waving above, white cuffs on their sleeves and the Second Tangier, now Trelawney's Regiment, with yellow colours. Altogether over three thousand men were making as much noise as possible by the sound of it.

Not the usual stealthy start to a day of battle, trying to catch the Moors unawares. This lot were making enough noise to wake the dead. Clearly they wanted to be heard and seen. A new regiment in what appeared to be brand new uniforms provided another thousand or so men. You might think the noise was to distract the enemy for a surprise attack somewhere else, but there could be no one left to mount an attack elsewhere. Every English soldier south of Plymouth must be marching up the street in front of her.

TANGIER: THE EARLIEST BATTLE HONOUR

This was added to the nine men-of-war in the bay alongside a dozen other assorted ships. Something was afoot. She had learned from Kirke's secretary that Pepys was in Tangier by order of the King of England, and a man of some importance regarding the city, he was to assess the city's defences and report on its merchants and trade, but what that meant was not exactly clear.

Pepys had been asking about the town for a clean whore and when he sidled up to her door she had reassured him she took all precautions, and was perfectly clean, but if he preferred she could service him in ways he could not imagine that would leave him with no uncertainties. At first he had been tentative, but she got him talking about his adventures with maids and theatre women in England and he soon relaxed. He paid in advance and returned often.

Despite his own proclivities he delighted in telling her tales of the Governor's. She knew of Kirke's dallying with soldiers' wives and had heard much of the Governor's harsh discipline and corruption; but the soldiers liked him and stood by him as a worthy commander-in-chief. For certain he knew how to treat with the Moors and nothing was more important for a Governor of Tangier. He had shown he was not afraid of the Qaid or the Sultan. He had visited Sultan Ismail personally and struck a warm relationship, and kept Qaid Benabdala away from the city. The soldiers had no fighting to distract them and spent their time drinking, gambling and visiting her. She had made more money during Kirke's governorship than in the previous twenty years. Now, at last she had enough to buy her wild plot and build her little house.

This man Pepys had asked her many questions about Kirke, trying to find anecdotes to impugn his honour and reputation, and had tried to gather stories to show the people of Tangier to be more dissolute than other places. He spoke of women of loose morals, not recognising the irony in his own visit to her.

In return Pepys had told her, in strictest confidence of course, of the disgraceful treaty agreed by the King himself when the Moorish ambassador visited England, which allowed forty Moors to settle within the city walls. If Ismail had followed the treaty he would have known everything that took place in Tangier and could easily have undermined the security of the town. Fortunately the Sultan, upset by his ambassador's extended stay in England, had refused to ratify the treaty, not realising the advantageous terms he had obtained.

TANGIER DÉNOUEMENT

Pepys spoke of the impossibility of defending the city against the Moors, even though it had not been taken by force in hundreds of years. He spoke of the poor harbour, refusing to accept the growing mole had given safe haven to hundreds of merchantmen and naval frigates. She told him to speak to engineer Shere, who was extending it for more and bigger ships.

Anyway, her militiaman would get her up on to Peterborough Tower for a view of whatever was going on if she promised to waive his next fee. It was beginning to rain again. It had been a wet end of summer and looked likely to continue that way. She ran back indoors to get changed into her new soft leather boots that outlined her legs so well. She packed a small basket of bread and dried fish, added a bottle of small beer and locked her door.

***

There could be no better place to stand. Here she was looking out over the whole of Tangier and all the surrounding countryside. The clouds had been blown away by the fresh Levant and she could see forever, but most of the proud forts she had viewed on her previous visit six or seven years earlier had gone.

The militiamen guarding the upper castle were all watching the regiments streaming out of Katarina Gate and heading towards the Sand Hills.

Already the Guards were formed up on Pole Hill, the Tangier to their left stretched past Belasyse, the Scots fronted the Irish Battery, Trelawney's would form a line to Cambridge Fort, and from there the new regiment of sailors in army uniforms would close the gap to the sea. But why were they there at all?

After a while, beyond the Sand Hills, up on the far slopes where the Moors camped, there was a stirring. The uncertain movement gradually resolved itself into one rider galloping down the hillside kicking up a dust cloud, followed by a group riding somewhat slower and a large group coming more steadily. The lead horseman disappeared into the valley of the Baiom River. When he reappeared on the near side of the valley Dover could see he was carrying a large white flag. He was already halfway to the line of redcoats when the other Moorish riders came over hill and a group of English soldiers, also led by a white flag, rode out to meet him.

The two white flags met and were planted in the ground, marking the place for the first group of Moors to hastily erect a huge green marquee. By the time the dignitaries arrived there were red flags flying from every finial of the tent and large baskets had been carried in. The English soldiers

TANGIER: THE EARLIEST BATTLE HONOUR

erected a flagpole and ran up a massive cross of Saint George in time for the Governor's arrival.

An hour or so later the two groups parted, the tent was dismantled and the regiments, having spent a couple of hours standing in the sun, were led back into the town.

***

It was a meeting, she was informed when the secretary returned for another helping of her special comfort, to show Qaid how expensive any battle would be for his troops if they decided to attack Tangier in the absence of the Sultan's army and especially without months of preparation from siege experts, many of whom had been killed and most of the remainder had run off to join the Ottomans.

October 1683

On the fourth of October the verbal grenade had been thrown into the township.

Governor Kirke's secretary, one of Dover's most frequent customers, had stood on a dais in the market place and read a declaration:

> The King has gone to great expense and trouble to make it a secure habitation, a commodious harbour, and a place for trade to flourish in, yet the results have been so discouraging and so many brave lives have been lost in the defence of the town, which is now in so ruinous a state as to make it dangerous to live in owing to the hostility of the Moors ...

Rumours had been rife ever since the arrival of a dozen virtually empty ships escorted by nine men-of-war. What could such a strange fleet signify? Now all was made clear.

His Sacred Majesty, the King of England, could not keep hold of Tangier in the face of the resistance of uncivilised barbarians! The backward people of Islam had defeated the Christian army of the enlightened English! The Englishmen's lack of purpose was frightening. How could they negotiate when they did not know what they wanted? Why could these ignorant Protestants not at least reach a place of peace with the Muslims?

TANGIER DÉNOUEMENT

The Portuguese had been promised priority evacuation, and were being loaded onto ships even now.

Priority evacuation!

Tangier was Portuguese. Tangier had been Portuguese for two hundred years. Hundreds of Portuguese had died defending it. Hundreds of Portuguese had been thrown out by the English. Now the English were giving it to the Moors.

This pompous Pepys fellow had promised compensation. How do you compensate someone for their life, their country, their living, their history? How to compensate her for the future of her wild plot?

Every Portuguese was angry. They would write to their King requesting he demand the return of Tangier to Portugal. But they knew their pleas would achieve nothing.

They were being evacuated.

She had emptied the house. The cart outside was full of her trunks and her furniture. There were no words to describe how upset she was. She had dressed in black to mourn the passing of her city. She screamed fit to bring the house tumbling down, beat her fists on the walls and stamped until her legs ached, but it did no good. She knew she should have left before, but for her father. At long last the carter got fed up and started off and she had to follow or be left behind to live on the streets. She ran to her wild plot, hugged the orange tree, picked a sprig of blossom and reluctantly dragged herself down to the quayside, hanging back as far as she could while still keeping a watchful eye on her belongings. Tears welled in her eyes and ran down her cheeks to mingle with the rain dripping from her hair, and water ran off her cloak onto her pigskin boots.

It was miserable weather for a miserable day.

What was there in Lisbon for an ageing whore? She opened a final letter from her Jewish contact. The Redemption Fathers had at long last been to Fez, negotiating with Ismail for several hundred Christian slaves. She could only hope her father would be waiting for her in Lisbon.

October 1683

It was ironic, to say the least.

Here he was in the city His Majesty had spent twenty years trying to scrape together enough cash to see it properly defended, and now the King was better funded than ever he was looking for excuses to be rid of it.

TANGIER: THE EARLIEST BATTLE HONOUR

Here he was back in royal favour in the city that had made him rich, ready to condemn it to oblivion. He was Pepys. He was the man who could justify anything.

He had gathered tales to prove Tangier corrupted people, but were Kirke's excesses any worse than His Majesty's? The King, the Sultan, Kirke were all men of power, all sexually rampant, all financially corrupt, all cruel to those who depended upon them. Kirke was a petty tyrant; the King and the Sultan were tyrants on a much greater scale.

He could write of Kirke's immorality and corruption, but His Majesty would shrug it off. His report had to emphasise the poor defensive position of Tangier, the inadequate harbour and to make these credible he had to get the agreement of the very people who had built the walls, the forts and the harbour mole, the people who had sweated and slaved in the defence of this African city, this outpost of England.

Well he would do what he had always done. He would do what the King wanted. Any reservations he might have he would confine to his journal; or maybe not even commit them to paper this time, merely keep them in his own mind.

He started making notes:

> The city is overlooked from the land. More land would need to be enclosed and secured to guarantee the safe defence of the city. This would necessitate a much larger garrison and cost.
>
> Trade and profit had not developed in fact it had declined.
>
> The harbour was not fit for use by His Majesty's navy.
>
> Parliament could be faulted for not providing financial support.
>
> The city and mole should be destroyed to prevent corsairs using it.

Would Kirke agree to condemn the city defences? Would Shere, who had spent so long building the mole, agree to say it did not fulfil its function? The only indisputable fact was that trade had not blossomed, and that was because peace had not been secured with the Moors, and according to Teviot and Fairborne and now Kirke, the army had never been sufficient to threaten the Moors. In fact, whenever the Moors had been soundly beaten in battle or whenever the navy turned up in force the Moors were always willing to agree peace terms.

TANGIER DÉNOUEMENT

It seemed a pity the advantage had not been driven home on those occasions to establish a lucrative trade, bringing great advantage to the Moors, Arabs and Turks as well as the English. Most recently the insistence on trying to force the Sultan to declare and enforce a peace at sea had destroyed any chance of agreeing terms – simply because the Arab dynasty had little control over the corsair towns of the coastal Moors.

Alas what was done was done. Kirke, Shere and the sea captains would have to sign the document declaring the poor situation of Tangier because that was what His Majesty wanted. They would sign it, just as he had to write it, to gain the King's favour, or at least avoid his wrath.

October 1683

Tangier, Morocco

The first explosion confirmed it. It was barely credible.

Over his whole lifetime, Stafford had watched the creature burrow its way under the seabed, tunnelling out from the shore into the bay, pushing the rock up above the water, leaving a trail showing where it had been. The mole had very slowly nosed its way into the sea, into ever deeper water.

He had watched the quarrymen and builders brought out from England with their strange way of talking, seen them construct the lime kiln and operate it. He had watched them build the new settlement on the shore by the quarry and name it Whitby after their home town. Every day he had walked along it, seen Cholmley stood in all weathers supervising the work. He had sympathised with the mole when, battered by the wild Atlantic, it crumbled into the sea. He had seen Cholmley worry over the damage, make plans to restore it, plug the gaps with newly devised towers of rock.

He had seen slaves brought in, olive skins from Barbary, dusky cheeks from France, coffee-coloured dark-haired men from Turkey and mahogany men from New England. He'd watched them build huts for themselves to live in, a drinking house for everyone except themselves, and emplacements for cannon to defend the harbour. He'd seen Shere replace Cholmley, much to his father's approval, and work progress apace.

Every year he had taken his brothers and sisters to watch him add his birthday mark to the mole, and even now Stafford had prayed for the mole, watched it every day; sprung out of bed on mornings after a winter storm to ensure it had survived intact.

Now it had come to this. Over the last few months all the civilians had been evacuated, Tangier was no longer a city; it was a collection of buildings. Now it was down to the engineers and the army to level those. Rather than leave them for the corsairs to use, rather than give the city back to Portugal, rather than gift it to Spain, it was to be destroyed.

The cloud of smoke cleared. Incredibly there was no visible difference to the mole. No hole, no great chunk missing. How much gold had been expended in creating that mole. How much money, how much thought expended on its design and redesign. How much of Stafford's worry. It was going to take more than that to dismantle the construction designed to defy the Atlantic. It was testament to Shere's workmanship and the power of Stafford's love.

Another explosion.

Again no visible damage. Destroying Shere's mole was going to be no easy task. The gunpowder allocated to level Tangier would fall way short of what was required if the resistance being shown by the mole to the first explosion was any indication of what would be needed to destroy the legacy of Tangier.

Tangier his father had died for; Tangier hundreds, no, thousands had suffered and died for, only to be abandoned. Simply given up. No, simply blown up.

After all the bloodshed, all the money spent, money wasted.

His Sacred Majesty was abandoning Tangier.

People speculated on why Sultan Ismail had allowed the four-year truce to stand even after he had gained a hundred cannon from the defeated Spanish in Marmora. People thought he was waiting for the mole to be finished to leave him a valuable harbour. However, secret reports indicated Ottoman Sultan Kara Mustafa had asked Ismail to contribute sappers to his army besieging Vienna. Morocco was not part of the Ottoman Protectorate, and had resisted all efforts of the Algerines to make it so; Sultan Mustafa could not demand but his request from one Muslim leader to another was looked upon favourably. Ismail was left with no miners and no sappers.

However, now Ismail would see the English had no intention of allowing him to keep a harbour, he might feel inclined to send men to help Qaid Benabdala attack what was left of a garrison. Kirke had tried to forestall this with his show of force, in keeping the city walls and cannon manned and retaining ships-of-the-line riding in the harbour with their gun ports open, all big guns ready loaded. He had also, during that parley in the tent under the white flags, threatened the Qaid with a devastating sea-borne attack on Salli. Consequently an uneasy stand-off prevailed, at least for the time being.

Stafford pleaded for permission to stay until the end. If the city was to be knocked down stone by stone he wanted to be the one who took his family home apart, and in some sort of apology to his father's memory, and as a memorial for posterity he would bury English coins in the ground and in the rubble. Anyone rebuilding the city would have tangible proof of the English occupation. Anyone digging foundations would see the ground still belonged to the English.

Up on the hills outside Tangier the Moors were gathering, watching.

February 1684

He had been denied a glorious victory.

Sunset.

Hamut sat on his captured English horse watching the sun casting its last rays on the citadel as it splashed colours across the clouds in a final display.

Truly Allah had spoken through the Imam. The defeat of the Nazarani had come to pass, but not in the crescendo of a final spectacular battle. Hamut's intricately designed system of interconnected, mutually supporting trenches had caused such destruction among the unbelievers that they had decided they could suffer the pain no longer. The English were leaving.

Having been told of the evacuation of the city, in mid-October Sultan Ismail had declared war on the remaining English but he had not pressed any attacks, and was, Hamut thought, wishing to give the impression that the English were retreating in the face of the Sultan's armies rather than leaving because of the threat posed by Hamut's siege warfare. It mattered not at all to Hamut.

There was no more fighting: Moroccan military activity was confined to standing in the rain watching from the surrounding hills as the English soldiers dismantled the buildings of Tangier stone by stone in a prolonged death ritual. The explosions had been reserved for the mole as the greatest engineering work Hamut had ever seen was blasted to pieces. By the end

TANGIER: THE EARLIEST BATTLE HONOUR

of October it was no longer useful, but it had taken another three months to disperse the rocks sufficiently for the English to be convinced the harbour could not be used.

Only now, when all the buildings had been demolished and the harbour was choked with rubble from the magnificent mole, did the Lord Dartmouth for some strange reason parade his remaining troops. The last remnants of the much-feared English Tangier Regiments marched out in full uniform, then after standing a while on silent parade, withdrew to line up in front of Katarina Gate for the last time.

They stood and watched as Pole Fort – fought over for a score of blood-soaked years, the key to Katarina Gate the only land-facing entrance to the city – suddenly erupted. The walls rose several feet into the air before the constituent blocks fell back to earth in disarray.

When the cloud of dust cleared the space in front of Katarina Gate was empty, no fort, no army.

A few moments later all along the city wall, at every tower, explosions blasted masonry in every direction. As the dust settled the remaining wall resembled a mouth with many teeth missing.

Successive explosions rocked the citadel; the bastions shuddered and crumbled; the stables fell like a house of cards, the officers' quarters collapsed in a cloud of dust and rubble; the Governor's Palace, as if in disgust at what it saw, threw itself down into the gardens beneath the seaward bastions. York Castle, the oldest and seemingly the most frail part of the defences, gave in gracefully and fell apart.

Only the lookout tower remained defiant, standing proudly above the ruins all around.

The Grafton sat alone in the Atlantic beyond the reef waiting for the Governor to leave with the last group of Englishmen.

At this very last moment, now it was absolutely clear the hated English had no power to demand or even request anything; Omar had decided to show his mercy. Hamut watched a group of Moorish lancers walking a sorry band of English slaves down from the hills, across Jews' River, and around the shore towards what was left of Whitby.

They walked uncertainly in the darkening evening as if they did not believe they would be permitted to leave, as if it were a last cruel trick played on them by their captors. But the trick was there was no trick. The thirty-eight men walked around the point, past the burnt out wooden redoubt defended to the death by a sergeant and his brave men, past the

TANGIER DÉNOUEMENT

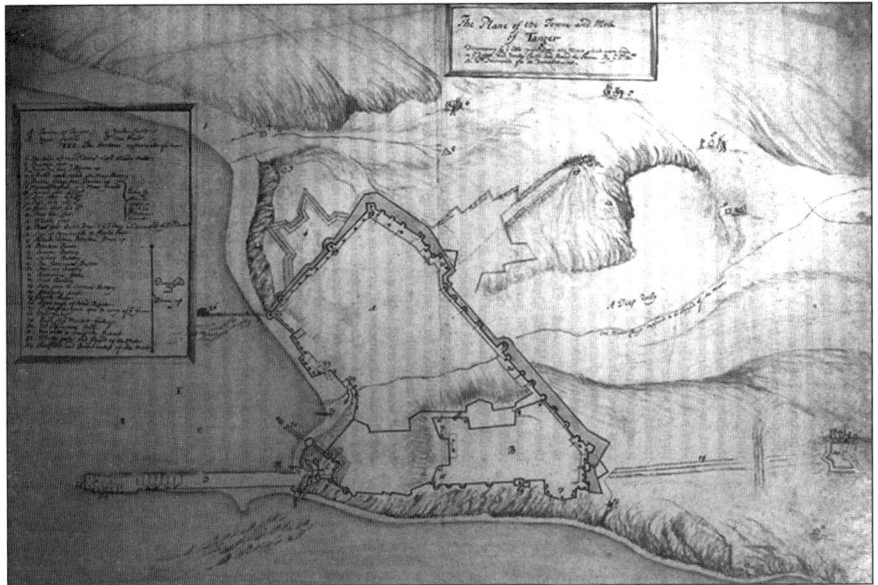

Map of Tangier prior to its abandonment. (Thomas Phillips *The Plane and the Towne and the Mole of Tanger* (1684?) Univ of Toronto, Thomas Fisher Rare Book Library, Wenceslaus Hollar Digital Collection: Public Domain)

ruins of Devil's Drop, again defended to the death. The lancers stopped, cut the bonds of the slaves and waved them on.

Only when they reached the waterfront, with the last rays of the sun illuminating the topsails of *The Grafton*, their transport to England, did they truly believe they would not be used for target practice. At Whitby shore they turned and waved to their ex-captors and almost fell into the waiting longboats in their rush to depart.

Qaid Benabdala received a message that the various parts of the walls still standing were mined and could explode at any minute. Unable to restrain his troops who wished to boast they were the first to enter the recaptured citadel, those who rushed to the tower in triumph had little time to enjoy their fame as the charges belatedly exploded and Peterborough tower fell, crushing all those who had entered.

In the darkness Lord Dartmouth was finally satisfied with the mining of Whitby. He personally lit a long fuse and the last Englishmen to leave Tangier walked down the beach, paddled out over the flat rocks to the waiting longboats and pushed off. A series of booming explosions echoed around the cliffs, signalling the end of the quarrymen's Whitby home.

TANGIER: THE EARLIEST BATTLE HONOUR

Hamut put the spyglass to his eye. The lookout tower, the defensive walls, the stores, the family quarters all fell. A cloud of dust rose high and spread out obscuring the view. He turned the glass to *The Grafton*. Those on board were watching. Dartmouth's face was expressionless, but there were tears on the slaves' cheeks and Shere was wiping his eyes.

Was Dartmouth thinking the English Crown was well rid of such a burden?

And was Tangier well rid of England? She had seen worse days. The English were not Romans. Her conduits were intact. Her streets remained. The building material lay, ready quarried and shaped waiting to be reassembled. Her houses and walls could be rebuilt. The mosque would be restored to Islam. The fields were not sown with salt. Islamic Tangier would rise again as she always had.

Tangier destroyed. ('Tangier in Rewings' Thomas Phillips; Royal Museums Greenwich, Dartmouth Collection L7869 Wikimedia Commons)

Appendix 1

Witness Characters

All of the voices in this narrative history are taken from seventeenth-century sources.

Edward Barlow kept a journal of his many fascinating voyages. The incidents described are consistent with his descriptions, although his encounter with Dover is hypothetical.

Dover is the character with least historical evidence. By his own admission Pepys was constantly looking to extract sexual favours from women within his control, but still managed to take a prudish stance in judgement of others and mentions several women in Tangier he says were infamous for their bawdiness, one of whom was named Dover. There were many reports of spies within Tangier and I have attributed some of their activities to Dover, and used her as witness to various happenings within the town and as a barometer for the well-being of the citizens.

Palmes Fairborne wrote home frequently. All of the incidents involving Fairborne are taken from his letters or other seventeenth-century sources. As he rose from captain to major, was knighted and later became Acting Governor, he was a prominent individual in the small town of Tangier and excited considerable admiration and jealousy. Consequently, the accounts of many others provide rich sources for Fairborne's actions and attitudes.

Stafford Fairborne was the oldest son of Palmes Fairborne, I have deduced his opinions from his later career in the navy.

Hamut is mentioned as a slave Belasyse gifted to James, Duke of York. His rise to Groom of the Backstairs and his infamy in leading Tangier soldiers into an ambush is described in a letter from Fairborne to Williamson several of his interactions with Tangier were noted in original accounts of the city. I have found no evidence for the statement that he turned against Tangier because of a slight by Inchiquin, and I feel it more likely his loyalty was always to his Moroccan compatriots.

Nathaniel Luke was appointed secretary to the governor of Tangier having previously been consul to the ports of Morocco since 1657.

Samuel Pepys is well known as the keeper of a detailed diary. By 1669 when his failing eyesight forced him cease his account of everyday happenings he held the significant posts in the Navy Office and on the Tangier Commission and his actions are recorded by others in various documents. Happily for this history, he wrote a full account of his trip to Tangier and others also commented on his activities. I have been unable to unearth minutes of the Lord's Commission for Tangier; their most significant decisions have been recorded through the actions of the Privy Council.

Appendix 2

Morocco and Moroccans

The seventeenth-century British inhabitants of Tangier did not distinguish between ethnic groups in Morocco – calling all local Muslims 'Moors' or even 'Turks'. For simplicity and consistency I refer to all Africans as Moors or Moorish.

Technically Moors are descendants of African Muslims who invaded the Iberian Peninsula in the eighth century. They were predominantly Berbers, led by Arab rulers. It is said these conquerors took few women to Spain with them and inter-married with the Spanish. Over the centuries the Spaniards gradually resumed control of the country despite several influxes of reinforcing armies of Berbers, Sudanese and Arabs. In the intervening centuries some of these Moors returned to Morocco.

I follow Lancelot Addison who referred to all inhabitants of modern-day Morocco as Moors even though distinguishing several ethnicities at times

Barabars or Berbers: Addison states most inhabitants of the north of Morocco regions of 'the Gharb' and the Rif Mountains were Berbers, native to North Africa. Berber tribes also formed the majority in the Atlas Mountains. Berbers are light skinned, but sun tanned and weather beaten, so may appear darker skinned.

Alarbes or Arabs: The area south of the Gharb was at least partly populated by peoples who had emigrated from Arabia. Addison reports many of these Arabs were nomadic, living in tents or avari (pavilions) rather than permanent houses.

Moriscos: Many Moors remained in Spain through the 'Re-conquista' and into the 1600s, many converting to Christianity at least in name. The majority of these were expelled by Philip III from 1609 onwards, and many of them removed to Salli on the Atlantic coast of Morocco.

TANGIER: THE EARLIEST BATTLE HONOUR

Moriscos could have skin of any colour, depending upon their ancestry, but were mainly of Berber descent.

Sudanese: South of the Sahara, the Sudanese were black skinned. Sudanese were often taken north to Marrakesh and Fez as slaves, but frequently gained their freedom and inter-married with the local inhabitants.

Forces fighting against English Tangier:
Ghailan led a loose federation of city states in 'the Gharb' and 'the Rif' located in the north of Morocco. Addison names twenty-two 'cavilas' or provinces of the Gharb from which Ghailan drew his forces, and adds that Ghailan had intermittent support from four Alarbe (Arab) cavilas.

During the years the Tangier Garrison was fighting Ghailan, his army was almost all Berbers.

Once Sultan Al-Rashid came on the scene the armies of local Qaids were reinforced with the Sultan's men, who would probably have been drawn from the whole of Morocco, and include Berbers, Moors, Moriscos and Sudanese.

Sultan Ismail had a strong contingent of fiercely loyal Sudanese 'slave' soldiers. These did not rely on the vagaries of Berber petty warlords and provided a reliable core for Ismail's army. Ismail also had Turkish mercenaries skilled in siege warfare from their experiences in the eastern Mediterranean. Once again I collectively refer to these as Moorish forces, but occasionally distinguish between them in the way contemporary people might recognise.

Moroccan names and place names in Morocco follow Wilfrid Blunt, *Black Sunrise: The Life and Times of Mulai Ismail Emperor of Morocco (1646–1727)* Methuen, or Addison, Lancelot, *The Moors Baffled*, 1668, and Addison, Lancelot, *The Present State of the Jews in Barbary*, 1675.

Appendix 3

Maps, Views and Fortifications

The maps presented in this book are derived from various seventeenth-century maps with additional information or modifications from written accounts. Seventeenth-century mapping was imprecise, usually copied from other sources – sometimes inaccurately – and names were spelled in a variety of different ways. Views often include proposed buildings rather than existing ones.

Maps of Morocco

The kingdoms and territories of Morocco are depicted to give the reader an understanding of the narrative rather than an accurate detailed record of Morocco.

Maps of Tangier, the Locality and Forts

Contemporary maps of Tangier locality foreshortened the distance between Tangier city and Jews' River, and distorted the positioning of the forts and the defensive ditches or 'lines'.

I have used modern topographical maps to position forts at strategically significant locations, taking note of extant accounts, often imprecise. I have also taken WBT Abbey's on-the-ground observations into account, and I have visited the area myself. Forts were modified over time, some were possibly renamed, and Palmes Fairborne certainly built several blockhouses and wooden forts not shown on any known maps. It seems the Sandhills were constantly shifting and I think it unlikely forts would be built on them.

Hollar's views are generally recognised as accurate, though even he seems quite capable of putting on rose-tinted glasses in the cause of keeping the King happy and selling more prints, by depicting serenity where tensions no doubt existed. These views were all based in his visit in 1669.

Maps and views of Tangier City

Hollar's 1669 views of Tangier are used in most books to represent Tangier throughout the English occupation. Much development took place during the twenty years of the occupation and many accounts do not reflect these improvements.

Ebbl tries to distinguish between Portuguese Tangier and English build. For the purposes of my account it is important to note the work of Beckman and de Gomme on planning improvements to the city walls, Cholmely's road from Whitby to the mole, a new quay in front of York Castle, the Citadel and Governor's Palace under Governor Middleton, and the mole which was often shown completed and enclosing the harbour in a way that was never achieved in practice.

Dates and English names follow Routh, E.M.G., *Tangier, England's lost Atlantic Outpost, 1661-1684*

Acknowledgements

I would like to acknowledge the help I received from Tara Moran and Harriet Fielding of Pen & Sword in bringing my book to fruition, and the staff at The Bodleian, The British Library, The National Archives and the many other libraries and museums all of whom are so knowledgeable and so happy to share their expertise.

Glossary

ablutions	Islamic ritual washing before prayer
adarga	leather shield
Almocaden	Berber leaders of cavilas
arbarello	earthenware jar for medicine
baldric	belt worn over one shoulder reaching to the opposite hip
Barb	Berber horse famed for its stamina
Barbary	the area of Africa between Egypt and the Atlantic, from the Mediterranean coast to the Sahara, (see Map 2)
battalion	a military grouping generally greater than a Company of 50 – 100 men and less than a regiment of 1,000 men
belaying pin	short wooden rod used as repositionable securing for rigging, or as a weapon
Berbers	pre-Arab inhabitant of North Africa
Blue John	a very strong beer brewed in Tangier
brigantine	imprecise seventeenth-century term for two-masted ship, mainmast probably gaff-rigged
Candia	Venetian city modern Heraklion, Crete besieged by Ottomans for 21 years
cavila	administrative area, county
cheich	long scarf worn around neck and face against wind/sand-storms
cheval de fries	portable wooden structure for defence against cavalry

GLOSSARY

Chyhyryn	Cossack Ukrainian city destroyed by besieging Ottomans and in 1678
colours	regimental or company flag; company colours were similar apart from the company number
commissioned officer	officer of rank, captain or above
cornet	the flag of a cavalry regiment, also the rank of the officer carrying it.
corsair	privateer of a Barbary nation, preying on Christian ships
culverin	heavy cannon firing 16lb shot 1500 feet
cutter	large rowboat often with demountable mast
demi-culverin	medium cannon firing 8lb shot up to 1,800 feet
dey	Ottoman title for ruler of Ruler of Algiers, Tunisia and Tripoli
djellaba	loose hooded woollen robe or cloak
doldrums	region of the Atlantic Ocean with long periods without wind
ensign	officer in a Regiment of Foot
Exclusion Bill	attempt to exclude Catholic Duke of York's succession to the English throne
Fajr prayers	Islamic prayers at dawn
falconet	light cannon firing 1lb. shot
fatigue	military labour not involving weapons or battle
Foot	soldiers not cavalry
forlorn hope	the vanguard or advance party of troops
frigate	imprecise seventeenth-century term for fast, manoeuvrable warships, less than 50 guns
gaff-rigged	a means of securing a four-cornered sail aligned with the length of the boat, using a pole, or gaff to support its top-side
galley	a ship mainly or exclusively powered by oars
grenade	a hollow metal ball filled with gunpowder

TANGIER: THE EARLIEST BATTLE HONOUR

groat	coin of value four pence (240 pence to the pound)
groyne	breakwater
guidon	flag of cavalry troop
Horse	cavalry
houri	a beautiful virgin some Muslims believe lives with the blessed in paradise
jihad	religious war against non-Muslims
kaftan	long belted tunic
lancer	mounted Moorish soldier armed with lance, scimitar and often a musketoon
lateen rig	a triangular sail hung from a long pole mounted on the mast at an angle
Levant	easterly wind from the Mediterranean, when channelled through the Straits, made it difficult for sailing ships to enter the Mediterranean
Maghreb	broadly synonymous with Barbary
minbar	pulpit in a mosque
miner	Soldier whose task is mining
mining	digging of mines to destroy fortifications with explosives
mobilis	disorderly crowd, rabble (=> mob)
mole	breakwater
Monmouth cap	knitted brimless hemispherical hat skull-cap worn by sailors or soldiers when a brimmed hat was inappropriate
Morisco	a mixed race Spanish/Moroccan or a Moroccan expelled from Spain
musselman	English name for Muslims
musketoon	musket with short barrel for easier use on horseback
Nazarani	Muslim name for Christians

GLOSSARY

petronel	long barrelled pistol, shorter than a musketoon
pieces of eight	Spanish silver dollar value of eight reales, approximately five English shillings
pistole	French name for Spanish gold coin worth 16 reales
Pope's effigy	expression of disdain for Catholicism, often paraded and burned on bonfire
powder-play	random firing of muskets showing approval, esp. of military excellence
pressed	forced into military service
privateer	pirate operating under licence preying on enemies of the licensing state
Qaid	Military governor of Berber town
Ramadan	Islamic month of daylight fasting
real	Spanish silver coin, see 'pieces of eight'
repast	meal
Rif	Mountain range in north-east Morocco, and the region they occupy
Sanhaja	Berber tribes typically inhabiting the Rif and Middle Atlas mountains
sally	sudden charge from a besieged town
sapper	soldier who digs trenches
sapping	digging trench for protection during attack or to undermine fortification
Sarhawi	area of western Sahara south of Morocco
shamshir	scimitar
snaphaunce	fore-runner to flintlock musket, alternative to matchlock
stadtholder	leader of the United Provinces assembly and Commander of the army
swagger stick	short stick carried by soldiers to show their authority

TANGIER: THE EARLIEST BATTLE HONOUR

tabourida	exhibition of horse riding skill involving a line of mounted warriors charging at the audience and firing muskets in the air simultaneously
Tuareg	Berber tribe from the Sahara
Tarris	mixture of Roman mortar and lime designed to set underwater
tuppence	two English pennies
touareg	Berber headdress of long wrapped scarf
United Provinces	The Netherlands
xebec	sleek fast Mediterranean sailing vessel with lateen sails
Zellij tiles	distinctive clay tiles in traditional colours, typically made in Fez

Bibliography

Primary Sources

Bodleian Library Oxford

MSS Carte 53, 75, 232, 243, 268; MSS Rawlinson A112; 185; 189; 190; 339; B 339; C 502; 859; D916A; 1139-40; 1216; Tanner MSS 44; 49; 239; 259; 292; 297

British Library

Add MS 10119, 11597, 15551, 41590, 5755, 5936, 9302, 15896, 28078, 158920, 280940; MSS Egerton 2542-3; MSS Harley 1223, 1243, 1898, 3876; Lansdowne Papers 1054; MSS Sloane 1425, 2902, 2906, 3329, 35120; MSS Heathcote
Map of Tangier and environs by Beckman. K. Top CXVII.77

National Archives, London

CO 279/1 - 48 (Colonial Office Papers 1661 - 1684)
MPH 1/1/1 – 1/1/54 (Maps and Plans of Tangier)
PC 2; 6 (Privy Council Papers)
PRO 30, 31 (Public Record Office); GD24 Shaftesbury Papers
SP 9, 28, 29, 30, 44, 46 (State Papers Domestic, Charles II)
SP 71 (State papers Foreign, Barbary States); SP 89, 209 (State papers Foreign, Portugal)
Treasury T 33-4; T48 (Secret Service Accounts); T51; T60
WO 4/1; 5/1; 24/1-24/3; 55; 78 (War Office)

National Maritime Museum

Cholmley, Sir Hugh, Account of Tangier and Journal at Tangier 614 K15 2

TANGIER: THE EARLIEST BATTLE HONOUR

Rijkarkivet, Sweden

Planta von Tanger 0406:07:009:002

Royal Collection Windsor

Plan showing position of the forts at Tangier 1676 now held in the National Archives MP1/1.

Printed Material

Addison, Lancelot, *West Barbary* (Oxford John Wilmot, 1671)

Addison, Lancelot, *The Moors Baffled* (London: William Crooke, 1681)

Barlow, Edward, *Barlow's Journal of his life at Sea, transcribed by Lubbock, Basil (London: Hurst & Blackett, 1934)*

Elliot, Adam, *A Narrative of my Travels, Captivity and Escape from Salle in the Kingdom of Fez 1682*

Philips, George, *The Present State of Tangier* (London: H Herringman, 1676)

Halkett, Sir James, 'The Diary of Sir James Halkett', Ed. McCance, H.M., *The Journal of the Society of Army Historical Research* Vol 1 December 1922

Johnson, Captain, *An Account from Fez 1682*

Luke, John, *Tangier at High Tide:* The Journal of John Luke 1670-1673, Ed. Kaufman, H. A. and Kaufman, P. (Geneva Libraire E, Droz, 1958)

Sandwich, Edward Montagu, Earl of, *The Journal of Edward Montagu*, 1659-1665 Ed Anderson. R.C., (London: Printed for the Navy Records Society 1929)

Montague, Edward, Earl of Sandwich, *The Journal of Edward Montague*

Pepys, Samuel, *The Diary of Samuel Pepys*, Ed. Latham, R., and Matthews, W. 1983

Pepys, Samuel, *Life, Journals and Correspondence of Samuel Pepys, including a Narrative of his Voyage to Tangier* 1841. Ed. Smith, Rev. John

Ross, John. *Tangers Rescue* (London: Henry Hills 1681)

G.P., (only initials given) *The present State of Tangier* (London: Henry Herringham, 1676)

Unattributed, *A Particular Narrative of the Great Engagement at Tangier* (London: Newcomb, 1680)

BIBLIOGRAPHY

Secondary Sources

Abbey, W.B.T., *Tangier under British Rule 1661-1684* (Channel Islands: J.T. Bogwood, 1940)

Aylmer, G.E., 'Slavery Under Charles II: The Mediterranean and Tangier', *The English Historical Review*, Apr., 1999 Vol. 114 No. 456 pp378-388

Barbano, Matteo, *Within the Straits: Tangeri, gli inglesi e il Mediterraneo occidentale nella seconda metà del XVII secolo*, (Palermo: Palermo University Press/New Digital Frontiers, 2019)

Beach, Adam R., 'Baffled Colonial Discourse', Restoration: *Studies in English Literary Culture 1660-1700* Fall 2007, Vol 31. University of Maryland

Bejit, Karim, *English Colonial Texts on Tangier, 1661-1684*, (Farnham: Ashgate 2015)

Blunt, Wilfred, *Black Sunrise*, (London: Methuen, 1951)

Chandaman, C.D., *The English Public Revenue 1660 – 1688*, ( )

Childs, J., *The Army of Charles II*, (London: Routledge & Kegan Paul, 1976)

Corbett, Julian S., *England in the Mediterranean*, 2 Vols. (London: Longmans & Co. 1917)

Davis, Lieut.-Colonel John, *The History of the second Queens' Royal Regiment Vol. 1, The English Occupation of Tangier*. (London: Bentley & Son, 1887)

Davis, J.D., 'The Navy, Parliament and Political Crisis in the Reign of Charles II', *The Historical Journal*, Jun 1993 Vol 36, No. 2 pp271-288

Drenth, Weinand, *The First Colonial Soldiers*, (Eindhoven: Drenth Publishing, 2014)

Elbl, M.M., *Portuguese* Tangier (1471-1662) Colonial Urban Fabric as Cross-Cultural Skeleton, (Peterborough, Ontario: Baywolf Press 2013)

Glickman, Gabriel, 'Empire, "Popery", and the fall of English Tangier 1662-1684'. *The Journal of Modern History* 87 (June 2015): pp247-280

Haley, KHD., *Politics in the Reign of Charles II* (New York: Basil Blackwell, 1985)

Konstam, Angus, *The Barbary Pirates*, (Osprey Elite 2016)

Matar, Nabil and Vitkus, Daniel J., *Piracy, Slavery, and Redemption: Barbary Captivity Narratives from Early Modern England*, (Columbia University; 2001)

Matar, Nabil, *Britain and Barbary 1589-1689*, (Gainsville; Univ. Press of Florida, 2005)
Meakin, J.E.Budgett, 'The Morocco Berbers', *The Journal of the Anthropological Institute of Great Britain and Ireland*, 30 Jan 1894
Meakin, Budgett, *Moorish Empire* (London: Swan Sonnenschein & Co., 1899)
Mercer, Patricia, *Palace and Jihad* 1977: The Journal of African History, October 1977, Vol 18, Issue 4 pp. 531-553
Routh, E.M.G., 'The English at Tangier', *The English Historical Review*, July 1911 Vol. 26 No.103 pp 469-481.
Routh, E.M.G., *Tangier, England's Lost Atlantic Outpost* (London: John Murray, 1912)
Saunders, Andrew, *Fortress Builder: Bernard de Gomme, Charles II's Military Engineer,* (Liverpool: Liverpool University Press, 2004)
Tapsell, G., *The personal Rule of Charles II, 1681–1685* (Woodbridge: Boydell & Brewer, 2007)
Tinniswood, A, *Pirates of Barbary* (London: Jonathan Cape, 2010)

Online Sources

www.pepysdiary.com Pepys Diary
www.academia.edu/38395440/Tangier Fortress Article A pdf
www.academia.edu/38395439/Tangier Fortress Article B pdf
Beckmann P.E., *Martin Beckman and the English Occupation of Tangier 1662-1684* Pt 1&2

For supplementary information on Tangier or to contact the author please visit my website:
www.englishtangier.co.uk

Index

Addison, Lancelot, 38-41, 207-208
Admiralty *see* Pepys, admiralty
Aidill, xv-xvii, xix, 8
Alcohol, 69, 79, 101
   see also Beer; Genever
Algeria:
   against Morocco, 143, 200
   French in, 53, 78
   prizes, 129, 189, 192
   treaty enforcement, 76-80, 92
Al Kasr, 14, 33, 65-7, 108, 188
   see also Haddu, Qaid Omar bin
Allin, Admiral, 76-7, 80, 92, 98, 118, 173
Al-Rashid, Mulay Arsheid, Zerif:
   army, 83, 96, 208
   character, 60, 82, 85
   death, 101-3
   negotiations, 85, 93, 95
   rise, 60, 65-7, 73, 82-3, 90
   Tangier, 65-68, 77, 79, 82-6, 90
Ambassador, embassy, envoy:
   Ben Haddu Ottor, 188-91
   Don Diego, 38, 40-2
   from Queen Luisa Maria of Portugal, 21
   Howard, Lord Henry, 79, 85-8, 93
   Kirke, Percy, 182-6, 194-97
   Leslie, Major, 152, 183, 185, 187
Ambush:
   Baker's Folly, 14, 17
   Fiennes, 17-8

Hamut's treachery, 112-5
Teviot's Hill, 47-52
Angera, 14, 103
Arlington, 1st Earl of, Henry Bennet, 57, 69, 89, 189-90
Artillery, 1, 14, 16-7, 27-8, 41-2, 61, 65, 130, 137, 142-4, 150, 151, 164-5
   captured in battle, 179-80
   enemy, 44, 47, 98, 160, 170, 172-3, 176, 200
   fire-master, master gunner, 22, 137, 165
   fort cannon 28, 84, 132-3
   lost to the enemy, 136, 144-5, 150
   mole cannon, 59, 61, 137
   shortage & unreliability, 6, 114, 125, 126, 169
   salute, 3, 129, 160, 189
   ships, xvii, 59, 63
Arzila:
   as Anglophile cavila, 77, 82, 103
   Ghailan's cavila, 14, 33, 40, 66-7, 73

Bank:
   Goldsmith Bankers, 71, 100
   merchant bankers, 100
Barbary, xxii, 10, 21, 33, 130, 199
Barb ponies, 30, 178
Barclay, Capt., 156, 162-3, 166
Barlow, Edward, xvii, xviii, 1-3, 6-7, 76-7, 79-81, 115-7, 205

Battle of Solebay, 105
Bear Inn, 92
Beckman:
  engineer, *see* Engineer, Beckmann
  spy, 37, 38, 44
Beer, 4, 20, 59-60, 71, 104, 150, 195
  Blue John, 104
  small ... , 195
  .... tax, 71
Belasyse, Earl of, John Belasyse, 54–65, 72, 192
  fort, 192, 195
  Hamut, 68, 77, 85, 94, 205
Benabdala, Ali, Qaid, 188, 194, 200, 203
Ben Abu Bakr, 14, 32, 49, 111, 115
Beniharos, 67
Bennet, Henry *see* Arlington
Berber, xvi, 29, 53, 132
  ethnicity of Moroccan armies 207-8
Black Guard, 107-108
Blaney's Bottom, 128
Blockade, 59, 62
Blue John *see* Beer, Blue John
Boar Tavern, 19
Bombay, xxii, 21, 23
Boundary, 47, 89, 95, 122, 160
Bowes, Captain George, 174
Boynton, Major, 114, 146-7, 155-6, 174
Bridges, Capt. Tobias, 30, 52-3, 56
Bull-fight incident, 35
Butchers Row, 35
Bye Street, 4

Calico, 129, 193
Cambridge University, 190
Candia, 7, 12, 21, 89, 143
Cannon *see* Artillery
Cape Malabata, 137
Cape Spartel, 61, 73

Castelo Novo, 8
  see also York Castle
Cathedral, xviii, xx, 9, 34, 35, 150
Catherine of Braganza, xxii, 6, 13
  dowry, xxii, 21-3, 71
Catholic:
  cathedral, 35
  Catholic Plot, 138
  Dominican, priests, xx, 16, 77
  governors, 24, 72, 138
  politics, 99, 105, 139
  regiments, 8, 98, 160
  Royal family, 21, 98, 139
Cavalry charge:
  Bridge, Tobias 29-30
  Pole Fort, 162
Cavila, 14, 18-9, 32, 60, 67, 208
Chapel, xviii, 4, 47
Charles II:
  colonisation, xxiii, 10, 11, 87
  dowry, *see* Catherine of Braganza
  finances, xxiii, 10, 21-2, 71-2, 93, 99, 100, 105, 116, 182
  mistresses, 71, 93, 99, 159, 185, 187
  Parliament, 100, 105-6, 140, 181, 191, 198
  Tangier diplomacy, 18, 42, 79, 169, 183, 187, 190-1,
  Tangier, influence over, xxiii, 21, 46, 52, 141, 181
  Tangier policies, 10, 31, 44, 46, 62, 191, 194
Chatham, 136-8
Cheval de fries, 170
Cholmley, Sir Hugh, 54–6, 61, 63, 71, 88–9, 199
Christmas, 78, 88-91
Citadel, 1-3, 17, 46, 137, 198, 200, 210
  battery, 59, 61, 63, 129
  destruction, 202-3

INDEX

strengthen defences, 98, 154, 170, 189
Coldstream Guards *see* Regiments, King's Battalion
Colonisation *see* Charles II, colonisation
Committee for the Affairs of Tangier, 22, 52, 97, 130, 187
   commissioners, 23, 72, 98
   see also, Pepys, Tangier Commissioner
Convent, xviii, xx, 4
Convoy, 61-3, 105, 116-7
Corruption:
   Charles II, 72
   colonels, 79
   commissioners, 78, 93, 187
   deductions from soldiers' pay, 25, 118
   governors, 25, 58, 61, 72, 87, 110, 198-9
   Pepys, 25, 78, 79, 93, 98, 118, 130
Corsair, xxii, 58, 80, 88, 199
   actions against, 2, 12, 54, 76, 80, 92, 173, 192
   political control, 199
   Tangier, xxii, 54, 58, 64, 74, 102, 115, 160, 198
Countryside:
   fauna, 36, 77
   flora, xvii, 2, 6, 19, 37, 48, 73, 81, 96
   rivers, 3, 48, 96, 125
   sandhills, 34, 83, 90, 209
Court of Admiralty, 11
Court Martial, 17, 109, 110, 118
Crown v Parliament, 106, 140, 204
Cudgel, 86
Culverin *see* Artillery, culverin

Dartmouth, Baron, George Legge, 202–4
Declaration:
   free port, 43
   Tangier abandonment, 196
   Tangier occupation, 12
Declaration of Indulgence, 105
De Gomme, 46-7, 210
Deserter, 90-1, 145, 155
Dog Place, 75
Dominican *see* Catholic, Dominican
Don Luis, Governor, xix, 5, 8
Dover (Portuguese prostitute):
   building plot, xx, 37, 60 73, 102, 116, 125, 129, 135, 194, 197
   father, xiv, 5, 19, 43, 60, 87, 101-2, 105, 135, 182, 187, 197
   politics, 45, 88, 95, 100-1
   public events, 136-8, 154-6, 181-4, 195-6
   spying, 19, 34, 38, 41-2, 65, 75, 103, 116-7, 186-7
   whoring, 35, 59-60, 95, 101
Draa, 108
Drinking house, 4, 60, 103, 199
   Bear Inn, 92
   Boar Tavern, 19
   Mole Tap, 103
   Tavernos Street, 4
Drunkenness, 88, 117
   Middleton, 88, 95, 111, 116
   Rashid, 101
Duel, Fairborne and Fitzgerald, 70
Duke of York:
   Catholic, 139, 140, 181
   Hamut, 93, 109, 205
   Lord High Admiral, xxi, 99, 120
   Pepys, 138-9
   Royal African Co., xxii, xxiii, 11, 35, 160

TANGIER: THE EARLIEST BATTLE HONOUR

Tangier Commissioner, 11, 17, 23-4, 72, 78, 98, 130, 187
Dutch Republic:
   1st Dutch War, 54, 56, 72, 78
   2nd Dutch War, 99, 105, 109, 116
   actions vs. corsairs, 92
   Dutch fleet, xxi
   Tangier blockade, 61-64, 102, 105-6, 116
   Tangier city attacks, 59-60
   threat against Tangier, 57, 64, 71, 75, 89
   trade, xxii, 35, 37

Embassy *see* Ambassador
Engineer, 87, 89,
   Beckmann, 22, 26-7, 31, 36, 162, 167, 170, 175, 210
   Cholmley, 55, 61
   de Gomme, 46-7
   destruction of Tangier, 200, 201
   forts, 162, 167
   miners, 56, 157
   Shere, 104, 120-1, 123, 136, 162, 167
   siege, 143, 152
Ensign:
   flag, 34, 129, 162
   officer, xviii, 148, 166
   Stafford Fairborne, 119, 138, 173, 191
Entrepot *see* Tangier, entrepot; Trade, entrepot
Envoy *see* Ambassador
Escape:
   escape from Charles, 146-51
   Turkish prisoners, 136-8
Escort *see* Convoy

Fairborne, Marjory, 7, 13, 17, 90, 110, 170
Fairborne, Palmes, 7, 12, 179
   acting governor, 117-121, 123-134, 136-138
   care for his men, 112-5, 130, 145-50
   court martial, reinstatement, 109-111
   duty & honour, 70-1, 90-1, 117-9
   family, 13, 68-9, 70, 90, 109, 119, 138, 170
   letters, gifts, 85, 111, 130, 205
   military competence, 123, 136-8, 143, 173-9
   promotion & knighthood, 55, 57, 110, 111, 205
   slaves, 119-121
   strategy & treaties 136, 138, 209
   Tangier Relieved, 156-166
   visit to England, 138, 141
Fairborne, Stafford:
   career, 119, 149, 173-4, 180, 188-9
   family, xii, 109, 119, 179, 191
   mole, 121, 199, 200
Farmers:
   tax collectors, 100
   workers on the land, 152
Farrell's Regiment *see* Regiments, Irish
Fawtrey, Captain James, 174
Fez:
   city, 197, 87, 102, 111-2, 135, 197, 208
   headwear, 29, 74, 165
   kingdom, xxiii, 10, 14, 18, 60, 65, 102, 115, 130, 190, 216
   King of, 190
Fiennes, Major *see* Ambush, Fiennes
Fire-master, 22, 26
Firing squad *see* Punishment, military, firing squad
Fitzgerald, Edward, 70

INDEX

Fitzgerald, James, 70
Fitzgerald, John, 24, 34-5, 38, 41-2, 45, 48, 52, 55
Fitzgerald's Regiment, *see* Regiments, Irish
Forlorn Hope, vanguard:
   escape from Charles, 147-9
   Hamut's raid, 112-4
   Pole, 159-63, 167-8, 173-6, 179
Forts:
   Anne, 47, 55, 83, 96, 133, 142, 144, 167, 172, 175
   Cambridge, 83, 90, 195
   Charles, 46, 55-6, 95, 123, 125-6, 132-4, 163
   Devil's Drop, 56, 125, 127, 133, 203
   escape from Charles, 146-151
   Fountain, 152, 172, 188
   Giles, 151
   Henrietta, 56, 95, 123, 126-7, 136, 151
   Henrietta, capture, 132-4, 143
   Henrietta, destruction of, 144-6
   isolating trenches, 142
   James, 83-4, 90-1, 163, 167, 172, 175-7,
   Kendal, 47, 96, 134, 136
   labour, 120, 130
   manning of, 95, 135
   Monmouth, 83-4, 90, 163-5, 175-6
   need for, 22, 44, 52, 112, 141
   Norwood, 30, 152
   Palmes, 136
   Pole, 26-30, 36, 47, 48, 56, 83, 167
   Pole rebuilding, 159-163
   Pole relief of, 169-70, 175-6
   Pond, 123, 132-4, 142, 144
   siting, 22, 44, 46-7, 55, 209
   undermining, 142-4, 151, 170
   Whitby, 52, 56, 122, 126-7, 133, 199, 202-3

Whitehall, 174
York, 164-7, 176
   see also Maps of, 46, 55, 126, 203, and Plates P2 6-8
France:
   alliance, 99, 105
   expansion, xxii, 21, 23, 53
Free port *see* Trade, entrepot, free port
Frigate, 1, 34, 62, 80, 123, 154, 189
   convoy, 61-4, 102, 116-7
   protection, 58, 59
   safe port, 76, 195

Galley, 58, 68, 74
   slaves, 54, 58, 92, 102, 120, 145
   see also, Salamander, Tangier privateer
Gallows, 117
Gambia, xxii, xxiii, 35
Garrison:
   adequacy, 47, 95-6, 117, 135
   cost, 23, 52, 72, 78-9, 118
   establishment, size, 3, 46, 52, 57, 59, 75, 78, 87, 111, 113, 132, 135, 171
   pay, 25, 86
      deductions from pay, 25, 118
      in arrears, 37, 53, 58-9, 62, 86, 91, 95, 98, 105, 111, 117-8, 123, 130, 155, 182
   regiments *see* Regiments
Genever, 101
Gentlemen Volunteers *see* Regiments, Gentlemen Volunteers
Ghailan, 6, 12, 14, 18-9, 28
   against Ismail, death, 102, 107-8
   army, tactics, battles, 18, 28-32, 47-51, 52, 65
   character, 27, 31-3, 37, 41
   in Arzila, 66-8

in Tangier, 74-7, 82
strategy, 18, 37-8, 40-44, 48, 65
treaties, 6, 17, 34, 42, 67-8, 77, 82-3, 103
Gharb, 14, 18, 60, 65, 79, 103, 108, 111, 125, 130, 143, 169
population of, 207-8
Gift:
colt from Fairborne, 70, 85
from King Charles, 22, 93, 183
Hamut, 54, 94
slave boy, 186
to Ghailan, 12, 41
Giles, Lt. Colonel, 163, 165
Golden Horse see Prize, Algerine
Goldsmith bankers, 71, 100
Governance:
civil authority, 47, 72, 73
court martial, 17, 109-10, 118
governors, vii, viii
Mayor, 86, 95, 136, 189
mayor and councillors, 47, 72-3, 87, 116, 128
under attack 58-63
Governors *see* Governance, governors
Governors' palace, 12, 22, 61, 75, 111, 118, 123, 151, 189, 202, 210
Guidon, 30, 161, 166
Grenade, 28, 30, 49, 51, 83-4, 96, 127, 142, 147, 166, 174-7
captured, 133, 174-7
glass, 136
pouch, 132, 158
Grenadier:
establishment, 26, 188
in battle, 49, 51, 83, 147
shock troops, 158
Grenadier Regiment, *see* Regiments, King's Battalion
Great Valley, xvi, 113-4, 128

Guinea, xxiii, 35
Gunner *see* Artillery, master gunner
Gunpowder, 31, 122
demolition, 200
for peace treaty, 44, 183, 188
quarrying, 122
siege mining, 144
Haddu, Qaid Omar bin, 112, 125, 143, 188-9
Halkett, Sir James:
Pole Fort, 155-6, 159, 162-7
The Final Battle, 172, 174, 179-80
Hampshire, 189
Hamut:
betrayal, 109, 112-5
early years, xvi, 13-6, 32-3, 39-41
English career, 93-4, 106-9, 111
jihad, 128, 142-5, 175-8, 184-5, 189, 201-2, 204-5
slavery, 53-4, 61-4, 66-8, 75, 77, 85
Hand drake, 165
Hangar sword, 30
Harem:
Ghailan's, 77
Ismail's, 186
Harley's Regiment *see* Regiments, Harley's
Herbert, Admiral Arthur, 146, 154-6, 158, 166, 172-4
Holmes, John, Capt., 102
Holmes, Robert, Major, xxi-xxiii, 34-8, 99, 173
Horse, as animal:
Fairborne's, 90-1, 113
Ghailan's five horses, 107-8
stabling & fodder, 2
Horse, as cavalry:
establishment, xxiii, 10, 46, 62, 78, 82, 96, 151-3, 159
Horse in support, 14, 17, 128, 133-4
Ismail's, 107

INDEX

lancers, 29
  Moorish, 6, 28-9, 50-1, 107, 114-5, 125, 127, 134, 149
  Moorish General of Horse, 32, 48
  Rashid's, 83, 96
  see also Cavalry charge;
    Regiments, King's Horse;
    regiments, Tangier Horse
Hospital, 16, 31, 64, 95, 149-50, 180
Howard, Lord Henry, 79, 85-8, 93
Hume, Captain George, 146-150, 158, 174

Inchiquin, Earl of, William O'Brien, 111–3, 116–8, 128, 130, 138
  leave of absence, 118
  military competence, 112-3, 116, 138, 141-6, 149
  negotiations, 145, 151–2, 159, 181
  removal, 155, 157
  strategy, 141–3, 145–6, 149
  treaties, 145, 151-2, 159, 181
Irish Battery, 3, 16, 83, 90, 163-5, 195
Ismail, Mulay Ibn Zerif:
  army, 130, 136, 141-3, 152, 183, 200, 208
  character, 111, 145, 150, 179, 185-6, 188, 194, 201
  rise, 102-3, 105, 107-8, 111, 115, 125, 130
  Tangier, 109, 111, 125, 171
  treaties, 169, 181, 183, 186, 188, 194, 197, 200

Jacob, 103-5
Jewish Quarter, 4
Jews' Lane, 6, 102
Jews' Mount, 49-51
Jews' River, xvi, 47-8, 52, 125, 142-3, 146, 163, 202, 209
Jihad, 106, 127, 143-4, 169, 186

Katarina Bastion, Ravelin, 26, 165, 167
Katarina Gate, xv, 2-4, 9, 16, 18, 26, 28-30, 36-6, 41, 85, 89, 97, 132-135, 147, 149-50, 154, 159, 162, 170, 172-3, 182, 189, 195, 202
Katarina Street, 9, 149, 159, 182
King's Battalion *see* Regiments, King's Battalion
Kirke, Percy:
  character, 182, 184-6, 192, 194, 198
  friendship with Ismail, 184-6
  governorship, 187-8, 194, 198-9
  negotiations, 182, 184, 186, 188-9, 200
Knights of Malta, 58, 102

Lancers, Moorish, 29, 91, 107, 202-3
  ambush, xvi, 15-7, 18, 113, 115, 134
  against cavalry, 30-1
  against forts, 125-8
  against massed soldiers, 84, trap
  escape from Charles, 146-50
  Tangier Relieved, 156-168
  Teviot's stand, 49-51
  The Final Battle, 171-178
Lasin el Phut, 67
Leslie, Major (Sir) James:
  1st Tangier, 114, 133-4, 187
  cavalry officer, 183
  diplomat, 152, 183-4, 186
Levantine wind, Levant, 56, 60, 123, 192, 195
Livorno, 56, 89, 102
Louise de Kerouialle, 93
Louis XIV, 10, 21, 140
Lucas, Mohammed, 103-5
Luke, John, 85, 98, 102-4, 109, 111
Luke, Nathaniel, 6, 19, 38, 43, 47-51
Lundy, Captain Robert, 174

TANGIER: THE EARLIEST BATTLE HONOUR

McCracken, 174
McKenny, Captain Alexander, 172
Maghreb, 58
Malnutrition, 45, 62, 64, 92, 95-6, 118
Man-of-war, 34, 61
Marigold, 115-7
Marines *see* Regiments, Marines
Marjory *see* Fairborne, Marjory
Market, activity, 34-5, 37-8, 95, 116, 123, 129, 188
Market place, xviii, 9, 156, 159, 182, 188, 193, 196
Marl, 27, 88
Marshan Plateau, 46, 56, 142, 146, 170, 172
Mayor *see* Governance, Mayor
Medals, 52
Mequinez, 105, 135, 184
Mercedarians, Order of *see* Redemption Fathers
Merchants, prospects in Tangier, xx, 36, 44-5, 54, 79, 88, 95-6, 102, 116, 135, 155
Merchant shipping, 34, 58, 76, 116, 129, 195
Merlyn, 64
Middleton, Earl of, John, 72, 78–9, 87, 102–3, 210
  character, 88, 95, 110–11, 116
  defences, 97–8
  Fairborne, 110
  Hamut, 109
  negotiations, 103
Militia:
  Moroccan, 8, 152
  Tangier, 62, 154-7, 162, 172-3, 195
Mining *see* Siege, tunnel, undermine
Mole:
  construction method, 89, 121-4
  contractors

Cholmley, 54
  Shere, 120, 121, 136
  damage, 88
  defence, 59-65, 137-8
  delays, 55-6, 96
  destruction, 198-202
  growth, 74, 76, 97, 152, 195
  need for, 57
  quarrying, 56
  workers, 54, 85, 118, 120, 129
Mole Tap, 103
Monmouth cap, 1, 7, 26
Morale, 15, 53, 55, 57, 66
Morisco, xxii, 207-8
Morocco:
  fragmented, 14, 18, 19
  unified under Ismail, 103, 111, 115, 130
  unified under Rashid, 60, 65, 73, 82-3
Morocco Company, 10
Mutiny, 118-9

Native American, 120
Nell Gwynne, 99
Newcastle, 94
New Model Army, 8, 21
Norwich, 1
Norwood:
  Ghailan, 66, 68, 74-5, 77
  Lt.-Governor, 34-8, 71-2, 78, 82, 86
  Pole Fort, 28-31

Old Tangier, 3, 34, 52, 97, 167
Omar, Qaid *see* Haddu
Order of Mercedarians *see* Redemption Fathers
Ossory, Earl of, Thomas Butler, vii
Ottoman, 132, 136, 143, 196, 200

228

INDEX

Palisade, 90, 125-7, 134, 165, 168, 173
Parliament:
   conflict with Crown, 72, 100, 104-6, 140, 181, 191
   Pepys speech, 138
   Tangier, 23, 140,181, 191, 198
Pay *see* Garrison, pay
Peace treaty:
   Algerine, 76
   benefits, 36-7, 152
   Dutch, 78
   Fitzgerald, 52
   Ghailan, 17-9, 38, 42, 52, 67, 82, 103
   Ismail, Omar Haddu, 125, 145, 151-2, 159, 181
   Peterborough, 17
   Portuguese-Spanish, 89
   Rashid, 79, 95
   Teviot, 38
Pepys, Samuel:
   admiralty, xxi, 9, 20, 22, 73, 78, 99-100
   arrest & dismissal, 138-9
   corruption, 25, 78, 93, 98, 118, 130
   prize money, 129, 130
   Sandwich, Earl of *see* Sandwich, Pepys
   Tangier Commission, xxiii, 22, 52, 98, 160, 206
   Tangier treasurer, 11, 23, 72-3, 78-9, 95, 98, 118
Peterborough, 2nd Earl of, Henry Mordant:
   governor, xxi, 1, 7, 8, 11, 12, 17, 18, 20-23, 31, 48
   remit, xxiii, 10, 12
Peterborough Tower, 48, 61, 122, 146, 172, 195, 203
Pieces of eight, xx, 4-5, 19-20, 41, 80, 86

Piso Nobre, 86
Plague, 62, 64-5, 89, 135
Plymouth, Earl of, Charles FitzCharles, 159, 162-3, 193
Portuguese Brigade, 56, 79
Portuguese Horse *see* Regiments, Portuguese Horse
Postal service, 60
Post Office revenues, 71, 93
Powder play, 39, 189
Pressed men, 7, 76, 80, 146
Privateer:
   Salamander, 74
   Tangier, 54, 58-9, 62, 74, 102, 118, 129
   see also Corsair
Prize Officer *see* Fairborne Palmes, court martial
Prize ships, 68, 92, 102
   Algerine, *Golden Horse*, 189
   Dutch, *Swan*, 117
   official licence conditions, 11, 79, 129-30
   Tangier finances, 58, 102, 110, 118, 129-30, 187
Punishments, military:
   firing squad, 110, 119, 131, 117
   hanging, 119, 144
   whip, 131
   wooden horse, 117, 119

Quarry, 56, 76, 96, 122, 125, 133, 199
   see also Whitby
Quarrymen, 56, 133, 150, 152, 199, 203
Queen Regent Luisa Maria of Portugal, xix, 6, 21, 23
Queen's Steps, 69, 75, 88, 94, 104, 136

Rashid *see* Al-Rashid
Ravelin, 2, 27, 29, 36, 161-2, 165, 167

Redemption Fathers, 5, 101, 120, 135, 187, 197,
Regiments:
  1st Tangier, 83-85, 96-7, 112-115, 119, 142, 168, 174, 182-3, 193, 202
    colours & uniforms, 147, 156-7, 193
    escape from Charles, 146-7, 149
    Tangier Relieved, 156-7, 167
    The Final Battle, 171-178
  2nd Tangier
    colours, 193
    Tangier Relieved, 156, 158-9, 162-8
    The Final Battle, 177-182
  Dumbartons Scots, xii, 182
    colours & uniforms, 142, 147, 156, 162, 193
    escape from Charles, 146-50
    Tangier Relieved, 156-168
    The Final Battle, 171-178
  Gentlemen Volunteers
    colours & uniforms, 159
    Inchiquin's, 111, 113
    Tangier Relieved, 156-168
    The Final Battle, 171-178
  Harley's Regiment, 8, 15-6, 26-31, 37, 47-51
    colours & uniforms, 7
  Irish Regiments, 8, 26-31, 47-51
  King's Battalion, Grenadier, Coldstream Guards
    colours & uniforms, 159, 162-3, 179
    Tangier Relieved, 156-168
    The Final Battle, 171-178
  King's Horse
    colours, 161
    Tangier Relieved, 161-7
    The Final Battle, 173-5
  Marines, seamen
    colours & uniforms, 158, 162
    escape from Charles, 146-9
    Tangier Relieved, 156-166
    The Final Battle, 174
  Portuguese Horse, xv, xvi, xix, 8, 17
  Spanish Horse, 170, 178
  Tangier Horse, xi, xii, 8, 30, 48, 53, 83, 128, 133-4
    colours, 161
    establishment, 75, 78, 82, 96
    Pole, charge, 30
    escape from Charles, 147-51
    Tangier Relieved, 161
    The Final Battle, 172-7
Reserve, 34
Resolution, 92
Rif, 14, 60, 103, 108, 136
  definition, 215
  population of, 207-8
Robinson, Lieutenant, 174
Royal African Company, xxii, 35, 160
Rua de la Duana, 149
Rua de Misericordia, xvii, xix, 34, 136, 182, 193
Rua de Sainte Roque, 75
Rua de Tavernos, 4, 20

Sackville, Lt.-Colonel Edward:
  acting governor, Colonel 183, 186-7
  Tangier Relieved, 156, 158-9
  The Final Battle, 171-4, 179
St John, Capt. Thomas, 138, 147-50
Salamander, Tangier privateer, 74, 102, 120
Salli, xxii, 19, 65, 73, 201, 207
Salli Rovers, 116
Sandhills, 34, 83, 90, 172, 175, 178, 188, 209

INDEX

Sandwich, Earl of, Edward Montague:
  diplomacy, 13, 23
  equipping Tangier, 2, 8, 19, 22, 56
  naval career, xxi, 105
  Pepys, xxiii, 9, 10, 21, 22, 23, 25, 92-3
  securing Tangier, xv, xvii,, xxi, 1, 9
  support for Tangier, 2, 8, 10, 13, 22, 23, 78
  Tangier Commission, xxiii, 11, 22-3, 25
  Tangier report, 72, 78
Sandwich Gate, 75, 80, 88, 104, 133, 136, 192
Scots *see* Regiments, Dumbartons Scots
Scrope, Captain Stuart, 130-1
Seamen *see* Regiments, Marines, seamen
Secretary of State, *see* Arlington
Shaftesbury, Lord, 98, 138, 160
Shere:
  fort building, 162, 167, 169, 179
  mole building, 120-1, 123-4
  mole destruction, 195, 198-9, 200
  propaganda, 181
  womaniser, 56, 101, 104, 136
Siege warfare, 135-6, 141, 143, 145, 208
  counter-mine, 142
  tunnel, undermine, 143-5, 152, 200
  sally, 142, 145-6, 175
  sapper, spade men, trenching, 130, 142-4, 167, 200
  siege tower, ladder, 29, 142, 126, 133-4, 136
  speaking trumpet, 145
  trench, 142-9, 174-9, 185, 201

Slaves:
  Barbary, xxii, 5, 54, 66, 120, 185, 197, 202-4, 208
  in Tangier, 54, 102, 118, 120-1, 129, 167, 199
  Ismail, 125, 143
  Rashid army 82,
  slave trade, xxii, 35, 62, 80, 102, 119
Spanish Horse *see* Regiments, Spanish Horse
Spanish Plot against Tangier, 1-2, 19, 38-41
Spotswood, Surgeon, 170
Square, pike and shot, 50, 112-5, 117
Stables:
  Ghailan's 32
  Ismail's 145
  Tangier, 2, 202
  Whitby, 56
Stafford, *see* Fairborne, Stafford
Sudanese foot, 96, 148, 161, 166-7, 175-8, 182, 207-8
Suffocation bomb, 134
Surgeon, 17, 77, 84, 110, 131, 149-50
Sus, 10, 108
Swan, 117

Tafilalt, 60, 103, 108, 125
Tangier:
  city finances, 23, 45, 72, 89, 93, 97-8, 121, 140, 198-9
  entrepot, free port, xxiii, 35, 45, 56, 87
  everyday life, 35-8, 45, 68-70, 73, 86-91, 96, 104-5, 151,
  governors see Governance, governors
  parades, 73-4, 155, 188
  public events, 122-4, 136-8, 181-4, 195-7

231

rule of law, 109, 117-9, 130-1
taxes, free city, free trade, 11, 43-4, 47, 188-9
the city, xviii, xx, 2-4, 9, 13, 19, 22, 34-5, 73-6, 154
trade, 21, 33, 38, 48
treasurer, *see* Pepys, Tangier treasurer
see also Corruption; Prize ships, Tangier
Tangier Horse *see* Regiments, Tangier Horse
Tarpaulin admiral, captain, 92
Tarris *see* Mole, construction method
Taxes see Charles II, finances; Tangier, taxes
Taza, 66, 103, 107, 111
Terrace, xxi, 81
Test Act, 105
Tetuan:
    Ghailan, 6, 14, 19, 33
    Ismail, 111
    Tangier, 6, 19, 38, 39-41, 65, 103
Teviot, Earl of:
    corruption, 25, 37, 46-7
    Ghailan relationship, 32-3, 42
    military competence, 26-7, 31, 43-4, 46-8
    reputation, 25, 27, 41, 45, 48
    Teviot's Hill stand, 48-51
Tollemache, Captain Thomas, Coldstream, 159, 162-3
Torre Principal, 1
Torre do Sino, 3
Tower of London, 139, 160
Trap *see* Ambush
Treasurer *see* Tangier, treasurer
Treaty *see* Peace treaty
Treaty of Dover, 99
Trelawney Charles, Col., 182, 193, 195

Trelawney Francis, Capt., 142, 148-150
Trelawney's boy, 149-50
Trench, lane, 22, 26, 28-31, 125-6, 162-3, 166-7
    siege trench *see* Siege, trenches
Truce *see* Peace treaty
Turncoat, 103, 116, 189

United Provinces *see* Dutch Republic

Vanguard *see* Forlorn Hope
Victualler, 25, 118
Victuals, 129

War without quarter, 45, 51
Water:
    conduit, 2, 204
    fountains, wells, 2, 152
    river, 2
Whitby, 56, 122, 126-7, 199, 203
    see also Quarry
Whitehall *see* Forts, Whitehall
White, Surgeon, 68-70
William of Orange, 105
Williamson, Under Secretary of State, 69, 85, 205
Wilson, James:
    friend of Duke of York, xxiii
    spy, 6, 19, 20, 23, 27
Wilson, Lt., 142
Wooden horse *see* Punishment, military, wooden horse
Wren, Christopher, 98

Yarmouth, 76, 79
York Castle, 61, 73, 75, 85-6, 94, 134, 154, 189, 193, 202
    location, view, x, 210
    renamed, 8, 34

Bridges to Messiah Yeshua

Bridges to Messiah Yeshua

The Sacred Calling of the Messianic Believer

Copyright © 2019 William & Frances Kuik
All rights reserved.

No part of this publication may be reproduced, stored in a retrieval system, or transmitted in any form or by any means without prior written permission of the publisher, except for brief reviews in magazines, or as quotations in another work when full attribution is given.

Cover illustration by Frances Kuik

First Edition Published 2019
ISBN – 978-0-578-44863-3

Additional Resources.

- Accompanying PowerPoint Slide Presentation with notes designed for Teaching, Sermon, Bible Study, or Lecture.

- Website: Tree of Life in Yeshua; www.byeshua.org

- ebook available through Amazon.com

- Other Messianic Topical Studies available

Published by:
CSCI Publishing
PO Box 1404
Cortez, CO 81321

Dedication

Deep gratitude is given to my wife, Fran, for her patience and her devotion. She is an excellent wife and mother. Her steadfast dedication to God's work and to her family are what makes material like this possible. Her many edits and recommendations make this a better product for you and a better witness for the work of God's Kingdom. It is an honor and a privilege to present this work to you. Our prayer is for your walk and faith to be strengthened by what God has put on our hearts for your learning, edification, and understanding.

Contents

Dedication ii

Table of Figures iv

Introduction v

As a Bridge 1

What Caused This Rift? 8

Antioch 17

Persecution Starts at Antioch 26

Titus Vespasian 29

Hadrian Visits Antioch 32

Hadrian Declares War on God's People 34

The Jewish nation rebels 38

Rabbi Akiva endorses Bar Kokvah as the Messiah of Israel 39

Hadrian Underestimates the Force of the Rebellion 41

A little history 44

The Diaspora (The Scattering) 48

Persecution in Europe From Then Until Now 50

Bridges Connect two places together 52

Yeshua's Parable of the Wedding Feast 54

Do You See Why We Are A Bridge? 57

About the Author 58

About the Editor and Illustrator 59

Table of Figures

Figure 1 David Ben-Gerion, Wikipedia Commons 4
Figure 2 Mikvah Second Temple period; Also see Mikvah path at Davidson Center Archaeological Park (Assaf Peretz, Israel Antiquities Authority)/Photo flicker.com 13
Figure 3 Pool of Siloam Steps, ritual bath and location of the blind beggar in John 9:7. This was recently excavated in the ancient City of David. 14
Figure 4 Graphic of the Pool of Siloam at the time of Yeshua......... 15
Figure 5 Reconstructed 3D model of ancient Antioch. In antiquity, the course of the river divided to form an island. This was one of the larger cities in the Roman Empire. /http.//followinghadrian.com/2017/08/11/11th-august-117-ad-hadrian-is-hailed-emperor 21
Figure 6 The first coin issued at the mint of Aelia Capitalina about 130/132 CE. (The founding of Colonia Aelia Capitolina) 34
Figure 7 Apostle Paul's First Missionary Journey 44-46 A.D............ 36
Figure 8 Rabbi-Akiva, Wikipedia Commons 38
Figure 9 Old City of Jerusalem, 1928 by Kosel & Pustet, Munchen; The Jewish National & University Library, Hebrew University, Dept. of Geography. 43
Figure 10 Old photograph from around 1900 CE. This view is from the South-South-West showing the fields south of the Temple Mt. 44
Figure 11 Original City-of-David shown in red, Photo Google Maps. 45
Figure 12 Persecution, Wikipedia Commons 50
Figure 13 Longest Sea Bridge https://www.youtube.com/watch?v=N63mEBOcIpA 52

Introduction

At Firekeepers Fellowship in Farmington, NM[1] Adam Parker[2] did a really good job of explaining the Messianic Community as a 'bridge.' His message was the inspiration to perform this research and expand it into this book.

We are a bridge between the Jewish[3] community and the nations (Gentile communities). The testimony of God's Word rests on the Hebrew Scriptures. We are a bridge between Christian communities who are followers of Yeshua (Jesus) but have a need to know the cultural and historical context of the Scriptures, the Jewishness of the Scriptures, as well as the Jewish background and context of Yeshua HaMashiach (Jesus the Christ).

We are a bridge between the Word of God as presented in the Bible, and the individual Jewish people who have not yet come to know Yeshua (Jesus) as their Messiah. 'Yeshua Ha-Mashiach' is the Hebrew way to say, 'Jesus the Christ.'

Yeshua is the way you say Jesus in Hebrew. In Luke 1:31 and Matthew 1:21 the angel Gabriel was sent from God to a virgin of Israel named Miriam who was engaged to a man named Joseph, who was of the line of David. The angel told her she would conceive in her womb and bear a son, and you shall name Him Yeshua, for He will save His people from their sins. Yeshua means 'God Saves' or 'Salvation.' Christians are more familiar with *Christ*, which comes from the Greek language, meaning 'anointed.' *Ha-Mashiach* is from

---

[1] Four Corners Firekeepers Fellowship, Farmington, NM is a satellite of Firekeepers International, Blountville, TN, USA. https://www.firekeepersinternational.org/

[2] Adam Parker is the Senior Pastor of Firekeepers Farmington, NM

[3] Jewish: In this text Jewish is a modern way of saying "The Whole House of Israel", the 12 tribes of Jacob.

the Hebrew transliteration for a similar word meaning 'Messiah' or 'the Anointed One.'

This knowledge of Messiah originates in the Tanakh, which Christians call the Old Testament. Understanding and further clarification is provided through the New Testament. Most people have never learned that the New Testament contains many quotations which originated in the Old Testament, and Scripture verifies Scripture. The traditional Christian Church has distanced itself from the Jewish foundation of God's Word. This separation has led to many problems over the years.

This bridge extends to non-believers of every walk of life because of the connection between the individual and the Word of God presented in its entirety, complete and for today. Before I explain that connection, I must first give a brief explanation about why these two communities are disconnected. The purpose of this booklet is to provide historical background as to why a rift exists between the Jewish people and the traditional Christian Church. I will give a historical overview about how the Roman Empire tried to destroy the people of God, why the Christian Community was forced to distance itself from its heritage, and how God has manipulated this persecution through time as a tool to distribute His Word throughout the world. God is placing Jewish and Gentile Messianic Believers right in the middle of this rift to bridge a spiritually starving world with the Word of God, through Yeshua.

As a Bridge

As a bridge we connect the Jewish people to Messiah. Romans 11:25 tells us a partial hardening of Israel has happened until the fullness of the Gentiles comes in. We know Israel's heart is softening because of prophecy, because Israel is back in the land and because many, many Jewish people are coming to know Messiah Yeshua. This has only happened one other time in history, and that was at the time of Messiah. The 'fullness of the Gentiles' is close at hand4. In fact, it is at our door. Yes, there have been Messianic Believers since Yeshua's earthly ministry and, as we are learning, the original Church was Messianic in nature. Or, if I can be so bold, the believers in Messiah Yeshua were a distinct sect within Judaism.

As a bridge we connect the Jewish people to Messiah. As a bridge we connect modern Christians to the heritage and wisdom of the ancient Hebrew Scriptures; the very revelation into which they have been grafted.

It seems a strange irony that in the First Century when the Jewish believers spread out from Jerusalem and spread God's Word across the nations, they were the bridge to the nations. They taught about Yeshua through the wisdom and teaching of the ancient Hebrew writings written on parchment scrolls and shared through the spoken word. These parchment scrolls are compiled today into the pages of the

---

[4] Fullness of the Gentiles; Romans 11:25; Luke 21:24; John 10:16; Rom 11:12

Tanakh.[5] In these end times, the Believers in the nations are the bridge to Israel. In both cases the foundation has been the Word of God.

Many Christians do not realize how far from the Jewish foundation they have been removed. This rift between the two is no accident. For centuries Satan has brought up barriers to deepen and to widen this gap. No sooner had Yeshua laid down His life for us than the adversary started trying to separate mankind from their salvation. His tactics are to divide and to conquer through deceit, ultimately separating the people of God from the foundation of God. This scheme is as ancient as the Garden of Eden, where the serpent said to Eve,

Gen 3:1
'Has God said, you shall not eat from every tree in the garden?'
- First, he exaggerated and distorted the truth and misled Eve.
- The serpent then directly calls God a liar. *"You surely will not die!"*
- With the fall came separation from Yehovah[6], separation from the Creator who made us.

With separation we inherited a fallen nature. Maybe a more direct way of saying it is that there is no way to have a fallen nature if you are in direct contact with, or if you are one with your Creator. Separation from God manifests a fallen nature.

---

[5] Tanakh is an acronym with the first two letters of each of the Hebrew words: Torah, Neviem, and Ketuviem; Law (or instructions, 5 books of Moses), Prophets, Hagiographa (Writings). Most people would simply know this as the "Old Testament".

[6] Yehovah: In most English translations the tetragrammaton (Hebrew 4 letter name of God YHVH יהוה) is translated LORD. Many people say this name as: Yahweh. I personally like the work of Nehemia Gordon, Shattering the Conspiracy of Silence as a work talking about the name of God.

In the Torah portion Va'etchanan[7] we looked at Deuteronomy 5:25-27; the children of Israel told Moses they did not want to have God speak to them again. They said, "if we hear the voice of the LORD our God any longer, then we will die…You go and talk to the LORD, then come back and tell us what he said."

The voice of the LORD thundered through their very being. They truly believed they would die if God spoke to them again. This is one of the few times we realize just how far we have fallen. If we would only listen to our Creator.

Deut. 5:29
> 29 "Oh that they had such a heart in them, that they would fear Me and keep all My commandments always, that it may be well with them and with their sons forever!"

For people to fall they need to be separated from God's Word. The further we can be separated from God and from his plan for our lives, the more Satan has created a rift between us and our creator. History is about this struggle. Just as importantly though, history shows us how God has utilized the human condition to work His plan.

This teaching is to provide an explanation and a history of how a rift formed between the people chosen by God[8] to deliver his message and the people who received that message. It is a lesson of human nature. It is a lesson of God's plan for humanity. It provides understanding of how and why the Messianic Community is a "bridge" between Jew and

---

[7] Va'etchanan (And I besought), Deu 3:23. The first significant word in the Torah portion provides the name of the portion. Every Synagogue around the world utilizes the same Torah portions and dates on the calendar for reading.

[8] Hebrew Nation formed through Abraham (Abram), See Genesis 12:1—3; And in you all the families of the earth will be blessed. NASB

Gentile, between the Church and the Word of God[9] through Yeshua Ha-Mashiach, Jesus the Messiah.

Figure 1 David Ben-Gerion, Wikipedia Commons

It is said by the Rabbis, 'Coincidence is not a kosher word.' The end times formation of the Messianic Movement, worldwide, has been directly in conjunction with, and coincident with, the formation of the nation of Israel. On May 14, 1948 God placed Israel back in the land. David Ben-Gurion signed the documents for a Jewish state to be officially formed and recognized by the United Nations. It is the nation of Israel. Jewish people from around the world began returning to the land given to them by God Himself over 3,400 years earlier.

David Ben-Gurion quotes Ezekiel 37 as the official authentication of the declaration. Another significant verse is Isaiah 66:8, which says:

Isaiah 66:8
   8 Who has heard such a thing? Who has seen such things?
   Can a land be born in one day?
   Can a nation be brought forth all at once?

This was by the finger of God. We see His fingerprints in these prophetic verses. But I love how God works His miracles. As evening

---

[9] Word of God: Tanakh & Brit Chadashah (Old and New Testament); references here in are from the New American Standard Updated Version (NASU); The Lockman Foundation

approached the day Israel became a nation, it became Shabbat on the Jewish calendar. May 15th, 1948 was a Sabbath; a day of rest.

The haftarah text read in synagogues around the world that Shabbat was Amos 9:11-15, which prophesied:

> Amos 9:11-15
> 11 "In that day I will raise up the fallen booth of David,
> And wall up its breaches;
> I will also raise up its ruins
> And rebuild it as in the days of old;
> 12 That they may possess the remnant of Edom
> And all the nations who are called by My name,"
> Declares the Lord who does this.
> 13 "Behold, days are coming," declares the Lord,
> "When the plowman will overtake the reaper
> And the treader of grapes him who sows seed;
> When the mountains will drip sweet wine
> And all the hills will be dissolved.
> 14 "Also I will restore the captivity of My people Israel,
> And they will rebuild the ruined cities and live in them;
> They will also plant vineyards and drink their wine,
> And make gardens and eat their fruit.
> 15 "I will also plant them on their land,
> And they will not again be rooted out from their land
> Which I have given them,"
> Says the Lord your God.

To summarize, it is Friday May 14th as it is heading toward evening when the news of Israel being restored begins to be heard throughout the land of Israel and the world. It is the Sabbath,[10] (Friday evening at sunset, May 15) the ancient schedule for the reading of God's Word in

---

[10] Sabbath traditionally starts Friday evening after 3 stars can be seen in the sky and lasts until Saturday evening.

the Synagogue is the Torah portion *Kedoshim* which means 'Holy' Leviticus 19:1—20:27 and Amos 9:7—15, the prophet declares the LORD will raise up the fallen tabernacle of David, restore the nation, and plant the people directly into the land, never again to be uprooted.[11] After almost two thousand years, God chooses that very scripture to restore his people.

It has been said that at the time of the forming of the current state of Israel, only a handful of people in the nation were Messianic Jews.[12] Today, the primary evangelistic work in Israel is not through missions. It is being done through local Messianic congregations. The larger ones are in Tiberias, K'far Saba, Netanya, Jerusalem and Jaffa. There are 150-plus congregations in Israel with as many as 15,000 Messianic Jewish believers, of whom about 60 percent speak Russian as their first language.

These Messianic Jewish congregations are now led by Israelis, even though they may have a mix of Jews and Gentiles. Most services are in Hebrew (sometimes Russian, Amharic, French or Spanish). The music too is indigenous, as is the style of worship —very Israeli. The melodies have a distinctly Middle Eastern tone to them. Most meet on Saturday when Jews generally hold worship services. These congregations of Yeshua-followers are clearly Jewish.[13] There are thousands of Messianic Congregations across the world. The United States has many, many congregations, especially if you include the smaller groups meeting in almost every city or town (Lord we pray for you to unite these groups). One part of the passage of Amos just quoted is to restore the tabernacle of David, Yeshua is in the direct line of David,

---

[11] Jonathan Cahn, "The Book of Mysteries," p. 67, Charisma Media, Florida 32746, 2016

[12] Messianic means, 'Like Messiah Yeshua' or like Jesus the Christ, same words different languages. So, saying you are Messianic just means you are following in the footprints of the Messiah Yeshua.

[13] Https://www.charismanews.com/world/46304-messianic-judaism-gaining-momentum-in-israel

from the tribe of Judah.[14] Restoration of the Jewishness of the Gospels and the Jewishness of the Messiah coincide directly with the restoration of Israel as a nation.

---

[14] Matthew 1:1-17 through the line of Joseph, Yeshua's Earthly (step) Father; Luke 3:23-38 through the line of Miriam, Yeshua's Mother.

What Caused This Rift?

What caused the rift between the Jewish people and the Messiah, and between the new believers and the Jewish people? The seeds of Rabbinic Judaism were already planted at the time of Yeshua, we know this from the Pharisees and the Sadducees and the dialog between them and Yeshua. But Rabbinic Judaism as we know it today sprang up from the sword of the Roman Empire. To understand this, you really must go back to the time of the Maccabees and move forward, however, for our purposes we will start just after the Messiah's resurrection from the dead.

So, what was going on at that time and how is the stage set?
Look at Acts 1:1-1:14; 2:1-2:47. This is simply amazing.

> 1 The first account I composed, Theophilus, about all that Jesus began to do and teach, 2 until the day when He was taken up to heaven, after He had by the Holy Spirit given orders to the apostles whom He had chosen. 3 To these He also presented Himself alive after His suffering, by many convincing proofs, appearing to them over a period of forty days and speaking of the things concerning the kingdom of God. 4 Gathering them together, He commanded them not to leave Jerusalem, but to wait for what the Father had promised, "Which," He said, "you heard of from Me; 5 for John baptized with water, but you will be baptized with the Holy Spirit not many days from now."
> 6 So when they had come together, they were asking Him, saying, "Lord, is it at this time You are restoring the kingdom to Israel?" 7 He said to them, "It is not for you to know times or epochs which the Father has fixed by His own authority; 8 but you will receive power when the Holy Spirit has come upon you; ***and you shall be My witnesses both in Jerusalem, and in all***

Judea and Samaria, and even to the remotest part of the earth."

The Ascension

9 And after He had said these things, He was lifted up while they were looking on, and a cloud received Him out of their sight. 10 And as they were gazing intently into the sky while He was going, behold, two men in white clothing stood beside them. 11 They also said, "Men of Galilee, why do you stand looking into the sky? This Jesus, who has been taken up from you into heaven, will come in just the same way as you have watched Him go into heaven."

The Upper Room

12 Then they returned to Jerusalem from the mount called Olivet, which is near Jerusalem, a Sabbath day's journey away. 13 When they had entered the city, they went up to the upper room where they were staying; that is, Peter and John and James and Andrew, Philip and Thomas, Bartholomew and Matthew, James the son of Alphaeus, and Simon the Zealot, and Judas the son of James. 14 These all with one mind were continually devoting themselves to prayer, along with the women, and Mary the mother of Jesus, and with His brothers…

The Day of Pentecost (Feast of Weeks; Shavuot Leviticus 23)

2:1 When the day of Pentecost had come, they were all together in one place. 2 And suddenly there came from heaven a noise like a violent rushing wind, and it filled the whole house where they were sitting. 3 And there appeared to them tongues as of fire distributing themselves, and they rested on each one of them. 4 And they were all filled with the Holy Spirit and began to speak with other tongues, as the Spirit was giving them utterance.

5 **Now there were Jews living in Jerusalem, devout men from every nation under heaven.** 6 And when this sound occurred, the crowd came together, and were bewildered because each one of them was hearing them speak in his own language. 7

They were amazed and astonished, saying, "Why, are not all these who are speaking Galileans? 8 "And how is it that we each hear them in our own language to which we were born? 9 *"Parthians and Medes and Elamites, and residents of Mesopotamia, Judea and Cappadocia, Pontus and Asia, 10 Phrygia and Pamphylia, Egypt and the districts of Libya around Cyrene, and visitors from Rome, both Jews and proselytes, 11 Cretans and Arabs - we hear them in our own tongues speaking of the mighty deeds of God."* 12 And they all continued in amazement and great perplexity, saying to one another, "What does this mean?" 13 But others were mocking and saying, "They are full of sweet wine."

Peter's Sermon
14 But Peter, taking his stand with the eleven, raised his voice and declared to them. "Men of Judea and all you who live in Jerusalem, let this be known to you and give heed to my words. 15 "For these men are not drunk, as you suppose, for it is only the third hour of the day; 16 but this is what was spoken of through the prophet Joel.
17 'AND IT SHALL BE IN THE LAST DAYS,' God says, 'THAT I WILL POUR FORTH OF MY SPIRIT ON ALL MANKIND; AND YOUR SONS AND YOUR DAUGHTERS SHALL PROPHESY, AND YOUR YOUNG MEN SHALL SEE VISIONS, AND YOUR OLD MEN SHALL DREAM DREAMS; 18 EVEN ON MY BONDSLAVES, BOTH MEN AND WOMEN, I WILL IN THOSE DAYS POUR FORTH OF MY SPIRIT and they shall prophesy. 19 'AND I WILL GRANT WONDERS IN THE SKY ABOVE AND SIGNS ON THE EARTH BELOW, BLOOD, AND FIRE, AND VAPOR OF SMOKE. 20 'THE SUN WILL BE TURNED INTO DARKNESS AND THE MOON INTO BLOOD, BEFORE THE GREAT AND GLORIOUS DAY OF THE LORD SHALL COME. 21

'AND IT SHALL BE THAT EVERYONE WHO CALLS ON THE NAME OF THE LORD WILL BE SAVED.'[15]

22 "Men of Israel, listen to these words. Jesus the Nazarene, a man attested to you by God with miracles and wonders and signs which God performed through Him in your midst, just as you yourselves know - 23 this Man, delivered over by the predetermined plan and foreknowledge of God, you nailed to a cross by the hands of godless men and put Him to death. 24 "But God raised Him up again, putting an end to the agony of death, since it was impossible for Him to be held in its power. 25 "For David says of Him,

'I SAW THE LORD ALWAYS IN MY PRESENCE; FOR HE IS AT MY RIGHT HAND, SO THAT I WILL NOT BE SHAKEN. 26 'THEREFORE MY HEART WAS GLAD, AND MY TONGUE EXULTED; MOREOVER, MY FLESH ALSO WILL LIVE IN HOPE; 27 BECAUSE YOU WILL NOT ABANDON MY SOUL TO HADES, NOR ALLOW YOUR HOLY ONE TO UNDERGO DECAY. 28 'YOU HAVE MADE KNOWN TO ME THE WAYS OF LIFE; YOU WILL MAKE ME FULL OF GLADNESS WITH YOUR PRESENCE.'[16]

29 "Brethren, I may confidently say to you regarding the patriarch David that he both died and was buried, and his tomb is with us to this day. 30 "And so, because he was a prophet and knew that GOD HAD SWORN TO HIM WITH AN OATH TO SEAT one OF HIS DESCENDANTS ON HIS THRONE,[17] 31 he looked ahead and spoke of the resurrection of the Christ, that HE WAS NEITHER ABANDONED TO HADES, NOR DID His flesh SUFFER DECAY. 32 "This Jesus God raised up again, to which we are all witnesses. 33 "Therefore having been exalted to the right hand of God and having received from the Father the promise of the Holy Spirit, He has poured forth this which you both see and

---

[15] Quoting Joel 2:28-32. In the NASB (New American Standard Bible) New Testament scripture in Capital letters are direct quotes from the Old Testament.

[16] Psalm 16:8-11

[17] Psalm 132:11

hear. 34 "For it was not David who ascended into heaven, but he himself says.
'THE LORD SAID TO MY LORD,"SIT AT MY RIGHT HAND, 35 UNTIL I MAKE YOUR ENEMIES A FOOTSTOOL FOR YOUR FEET."'[18]
36 "Therefore let all the house of Israel know for certain that God has made Him both Lord and Christ - this Jesus whom you crucified."

The Ingathering

37 Now when they heard this, they were pierced to the heart, and said to Peter and the rest of the apostles, "Brethren, what shall we do?" 38 Peter said to them, "Repent, and each of you be baptized in the name of Jesus Christ for the forgiveness of your sins; and you will receive the gift of the Holy Spirit. 39 "For the promise is for you and your children and for all who are far off, as many as the Lord our God will call to Himself." 40 And with many other words he solemnly testified and kept on exhorting them, saying, "Be saved from this perverse generation!" 41 So then, those who had received his word were baptized; and that day there were added about three thousand souls. 42 They were continually devoting themselves to the apostles' teaching and to fellowship, to the breaking of bread and to prayer.

43 Everyone kept feeling a sense of awe; and many wonders and signs were taking place through the apostles. 44 And all those who had believed were together and had all things in common; 45 and they began selling their property and possessions and were sharing them with all, as anyone might have need. 46 **Day by day continuing with one mind in the temple**, and breaking bread from house to house, they were taking their meals together with gladness and sincerity of heart, 47 praising God and having favor with all the people. And the

---

[18] Psalm 110:1

Lord was adding to their number day by day those who were being saved. (NASU; Headings and Bold/Italics not in original text)

Figure 2 Mikvah Second Temple period; Also see Mikvah path at Davidson Center Archaeological Park (Assaf Peretz, Israel Antiquities Authority)/Photo flicker.com

When Yeshua told the disciples to wait until the Ruach HaKodesh (Holy Spirit) comes upon them, it was only ten days until the Feast of Weeks, a pilgrimage celebration God had prescribed in Leviticus 23. Many people know this as Pentecost. This is a First-Fruits celebration of the wheat harvest. Jewish people from around the Mediterranean would have been present in Jerusalem. Jerusalem was a metropolitan city and as mentioned above, Jews from many places lived there. On the day prescribed by God as a foreshadowing, the Holy Spirit was poured out as a First-Fruits. Three thousand men were baptized in Yeshua, through the Holy Spirit of God, that day. There were Temple

Mikveh's (Ritual Baths) all around the Temple Mount at that time, these were used by the people who made pilgrimage to Jerusalem three times a year. Two hundred of these baths have been found around Jerusalem.[19]

A recent discovery, in the last ten years, has been the actual Pool of Siloam. Figure 3 is a picture of the actual steps of the spring. King Hezekiah built a water tunnel from the Gihon Spring that feed water directly into the Pool of Siloam. This was the location Yeshua sent the blind beggar to wash in when he healed him.[20]

Figure 3 Pool of Siloam Steps, ritual bath and location of the blind beggar in John 9:7. This was recently excavated in the ancient City of David.

The Pool of Siloam has a path of paving stones up to the Temple. Pilgrims and visitors to the Temple would wash in this pool.

In Acts Chapter 4 we are told the number of men who had believed the message was about five thousand. Don't forget this was a typical method of counting at the time and this means woman and children

---

[19] At the Davidson Center Archaeological Park in Jerusalem is a path running among two-thousand-year-old Mikveh's used by pilgrims visiting the Temple Mount. Reference Leviticus 16:4 and other places.

[20] John 9:7—12

included in these numbers would have brought the number of believers to well over fifteen thousand people. This is only months after the resurrection of Yeshua. It is sad to me how our English translations downplay this. In Acts 21:20 in the Greek text it says. *"You see, brother, how many tens of thousands there are among the Jews of those who have believed..."*.

Figure 4 Graphic of the Pool of Siloam at the time of Yeshua.

This is extremely important for understanding what was happening and what we are describing on the next pages. Yeshua's words in Acts 1:8 above are being fulfilled rapidly and it is the chosen people, the people of God, the Jewish people who are carrying this out. We have just learned these are individuals from Parthia, Elam, Mesopotamia, even Egypt and Libya, all around the known world at the time. Residents of distant lands who have pilgrimaged to Jerusalem and are making an extended stay and now they have become believers.

Through the Holy Spirit they are testifying to all the people around them. Notice the progression—Yeshua prophesies His Word is going to spread to Jerusalem, Judea, Samaria, and even to the remotest part of the earth.

Antioch

Acts Chapters 11-13 is a brief history representative of many other places around the Mediterranean and around Judea. This is known as Paul's First Missionary Journey 44-46 CE.[21] With a Messianic background or with a little forethought, you will be amazed at some of the things that jump out at you in the book of Acts. This is about twelve years after the resurrection of Yeshua.

> Acts 11:19-26
> 19 So then those who were scattered because of the persecution that occurred in connection with Stephen made their way to Phoenicia and Cyprus and Antioch, **speaking the word to no one except to Jews alone.** 20 But there were some of them, men of Cyprus and Cyrene, who came to Antioch and began speaking to the Greeks also, preaching the Lord Yeshua. 21 And the hand of the Lord was with them, and a large number who believed turned to the Lord. 22 The news about them reached the ears of the church at Jerusalem, and they sent Barnabas off to Antioch. 23 Then when he arrived and witnessed the grace of God, he rejoiced and began to encourage them all with resolute heart to remain true to the Lord; 24 for he was a good man, and full of the Holy Spirit and of faith. And considerable numbers were brought to the Lord. 25 And he left for Tarsus to look for Saul; 26 and when he had found him, he brought him to Antioch. **And for an entire year**

---

[21] AD vs C.E. Anno Domini is Latin for "Year of our LORD", C.E. is Common Era. The secular world didn't like saying AD because of the implications, because of this they made the change to C.E. But what defines the "Common Era"? Yeshua is the only thing: he died for our sins, rose from the grave so we could have life. The very idea of a common era invokes the message of the cross. For anyone who asks, it is a segue for the Gospel!

they met with the church and taught considerable numbers; and the disciples were first called Christians in Antioch.[22]

When Stephen was stoned in Jerusalem a great persecution began. Many Believers were scattered and fled. These believers were Jewish men and woman who had accepted Yeshua. Put this into perspective with what we just read above in the first chapters of Acts. These were Jewish Believers from virtually every land and tongue, people who in many cases lived in distant lands and only temporary residency in Jerusalem. Many had seen the risen Messiah, Yeshua personally.[23] 1 Cor. 15:6 tells us over 500 saw Him at one time.

Where did these believers go?

In many cases they went home! In other cases, they went into the towns and villages around the Mediterranean and around Judea. Specifically, they went to Phoenicia, Cyprus, and Antioch. But more importantly they went into the synagogues. Acts 11:19 says the brethren were "speaking the word to no one except to Jews only." They did the same thing Paul was doing in all the cities he visited.[24]

Acts 11:20-21
> 20 But there were some of them, men of Cyprus and Cyrene, who came to Antioch and began speaking to the Greeks also, preaching the Lord Yeshua. 21 And the hand of the Lord was with them, and a large number who believed turned to the Lord.

---

[22] NASU; bold-italics not in the original text
[23] 1 Cor. 15:6 After that He appeared to Cephas, then to the twelve. After that He appeared to more than five hundred brethren at one time, most of whom remain until now, but some have fallen asleep; then He appeared to James, then to all the apostles; and last of all, as to one untimely born, He appeared to me also.
[24] Acts 13:5, 14, 43; 16:13; 18:4

In Antioch, where were the believers in Yeshua meeting?
At the synagogues.
What day of the week was it?
Shabbat! (Saturday)

Acts 11:26
> And for an entire year they met with the church and taught considerable numbers and the disciples were first called Christians in Antioch.

For an entire year Barnabas and Paul met at the Synagogues in Antioch and they brought considerable numbers of new believers to the LORD. Afterward, Barnabas and Paul took a collection to help support the Believers in Jerusalem because a famine had been prophesied, and then they returned to Antioch. The brethren, through the Holy Spirit sent Barnabas and Paul to Cyprus and again they entered the synagogues of the Jews in Cyprus. This theme is repeated over and over all through the New Testament teachings and the epistles (letters) of Paul (Acts 13:5, 14, 43; 16:13; 18:4). It is odd that the Church will cite 1 Cor. 16:2 as a text to show the Church was meeting on the first day of the week (Sunday), when it is a well-known fact, that Jewish people traditionally will not handle money on the Sabbath (Saturday).[25]

The "church" (*ekklesia*) was still meeting in the synagogues.[26] The English translation distances us in our thinking from what Paul would have been saying. There was only one place anyone at this time would have thought of to meet, that is the synagogue.

How do you know? Paul tells you in Acts 13:14 and on the Sabbath day they went into the synagogue and sat down. ***After the reading of the Law and the Prophets the synagogues officials sent to them,***

---
[25] 1 Cor. 16:2 On the first day of every week each one of you is to put aside and save, as he may prosper, so that no collections be made when I come.
[26] Ekkleesian: Strong's 1577; a calling out..., especially a religious congregation (Jewish synagogue or Christian community)

saying, "Brethren, if you have any word of exhortation for the people, say it." I want to point this out because people don't think about it. The timeframe here was after Paul and Barnabas had spent a year in Antioch teaching. This was after they had left and returned, being instructed to go to Cyprus. Now they have come back. Where do they go? To the synagogue. Who asks them to stand up and teach? The synagogues officials. Did the synagogues officials have anything bad to say about them? No, rather they were invited to address those in the synagogue.

Beginning in Acts 13:16
Paul stood up, and motioning with his hand said, "Men of Israel, and you who fear God, listen…

Paul gives them an overview of the history of God's people beginning with the Hebrew captivity in Egypt and he takes them all the way through to the Resurrection of Messiah Yeshua. We know many Gentiles were present at the synagogue because they told everyone they met about the teaching so that the next Sabbath, at the same synagogue, almost the entire city of Antioch was there (Acts 13:44). This is important. Antioch was one of the larger cities in the Roman Empire. It had many more Gentile people than Jews. Paul's teachings about Yeshua was well-received, clearly endorsed even by the synagogue officials.[27]

---

[27] The synagogue officials had to have been believers in Yeshua. This is the only conclusion possible. Several things make this obvious: 1. If the ekklesia (church) had been driven out of the synagogue and Paul and Barnabas had continued to teach for an entire year, they would have been at enmity with each other, this is clearly not the case. 2. The synagogue officials asked them to speak, knowing full well who they were. 3. Significant numbers of Gentile believers were present because the entire city of Antioch became aware Paul and Barnabas had returned to teach.

Figure 5 Reconstructed 3D model of ancient Antioch. In antiquity, the course of the river divided to form an island. This was one of the larger cities in the Roman Empire. /http.//followinghadrian.com/2017/08/11/11th-august-117-ad-hadrian-is-hailed-emperor

You can picture the scene. Paul and Barnabas were both well respected, and now they have returned from Cyprus. Many have just heard what the LORD had placed on their hearts to teach. When the people left the synagogue, they told anyone they saw: "you must come and hear the good news being presented, *Paul has returned, he is going to teach again next week, you must come and hear him speak.*" This is amazing, think about this, almost the entire city came to the synagogue to here Paul speak.

This history lesson has several facets.
- It is important to notice the early Church first met in Jerusalem, and then was scattered throughout the known world.

- Peter and many others still were worshiping in the Temple even after the persecution started.[28]
- The believers in Messiah Yeshua spread out to the surrounding cities and worshiped in the synagogues with all the other God-Fearing people as a sect of Judaism. In many cases these families went back to their home town synagogues and began teaching about Yeshua.[29]
- The synagogue of Antioch was filled with believers, both Jew and Gentile alike. The believers in Antioch were strong and numerous, the first to be called Christians (Messiah-like or followers-of-Messiah).[30]
- The 'Home Church' or 'Underground Church' only appears in locations with extreme persecution, otherwise believers followed the traditions and teachings of Moses as had been taught from ages past and assembled with a hierarchy of leadership in the synagogues.

I want to emphasize this point about the 'Home Church.' Many times, people will state that the First-Century Church, the original believers in Yeshua, were small groups meeting in homes, and this was the intention of Messiah. This is simply not true. In fact, what you see is the opposite. We are to congregate together building the surrounding community, together we can pray for one another and utilize our spiritual gifts in service to God's people. All of scripture testifies to this. The book of Acts testifies to this. In every case, the Believers started in the Temple or in the synagogues. Only under persecution did they regroup in homes. Now having said this, home fellowship, Bible study groups, church plants, etc., all are blessed by

---

[28] James the brother of the Messiah Yeshua became the head of the church in Jerusalem and was martyred there in 62 or 69 AD. James the brother of John, son of Zebedee, was also martyred in Jerusalem by Herod in 44 AD.

[29] Acts 2:9; 2:14 Peter: "Men of Judea and all you who live in Jerusalem"; 11:19

[30] Acts 11:26

God and all have incredible rewards for fellowship, prayer, learning, and outreach. In Acts 2:46 God shows us this principle: "Day by day **continuing with one mind in the temple**,[31] *and breaking bread from house to house*, they were taking their meals together with gladness and sincerity of heart…" We need to have a corporate place of worship, prominent in the community and prominent in the culture. In fact, it should drive the culture. The culture and governance of the synagogue is a model we should study. Point in fact, God has kept the Jewish community together in foreign lands for two thousand years without them losing their identity. Place Yeshua into the middle of this picture; breath life, wisdom, and understanding into the Word through the Ruach Ha-Kodesh (Holy Spirit); follow Yeshua's command and it will change the culture.

Matthew 28:19—20
"Go therefore and make disciples of all the nations, baptizing them in the name of the Father and the Son and the Holy Spirit, teaching them to observe all that I commanded you; and lo, I am with you always, even to the end of the age".

Leviticus 23:2
Speak to the sons of Israel and say to them, 'The LORD's [Appointed Times (מוֹעֲדֵי Mow-a'deey)] which you shall proclaim as [holy convocations. מִקְרָאֵי קֹדֶשׁ miqraa'eey Kadesh], - My Appointed Times are these…

The first Appointed Time listed is the Sabbath. It always surprises me how many pastors will quote Leviticus 23 as having seven (7) appointed times. It describes eight (8); the Sabbath being the first one and the one omitted from the list.

---

[31] Bold Italics not in original text. Notice they were of one mind in the temple. They were eating and having fellowship at individual people's homes.

How can you omit the first of God's Appointed Times?[32]

That word, *Mow-a'deey,* properly means 'an appointment', specifically 'a festival'. It implies an assembly for a specific purpose; and technically a synagogue or congregation is a place of meeting. *Miqraa'eey* is something called out; i.e., a public meeting. It also has the meaning of 'a rehearsal' (Strong's 4744). And of course, *Kadesh* is 'holy', which means set apart from common.

Do you realize the Sabbath is a time for us to corporately meet[33] in preparation (a rehearsal)?

Preparation for what?...

Rehearsal for what?...

Now you know why Paul says in Col 2:15 that the Sabbath is, [present tense] a shadow of what is [present tense] to come!

A shadow, a preparation, a rehearsal, for what?...

If you read the entire Bible from cover-to-cover, you will have a pretty good idea of what we are preparing for. This is the journey of a lifetime and the rewards are astonishing.

In conclusion, the idea of a 'home church' or 'home synagogue' should be viewed as a seed meant to grow into a full-fledged congregation with extensions and ties throughout the community. Believers who stay at home, or only meet in very small groups, often state they only follow Yeshua directly through his Word. They typically

---

[32] The Sabbath is first mentioned in Genesis 2:1-3..., 3 Then God blessed the seventh day and sanctified it, because in it He rested from all His work which God had created and made.

[33] Luke 4:16 And He came to Nazareth, where He had been brought up; and *as was His custom*, He entered the synagogue on the Sabbath..., (italics not in original) NASU

claim the original believers in Yeshua were small bands of home groups. This is a false claim often used to justify not having to submit to authority. "But know this first of all, that no prophecy of Scripture is of one's own interpretation," (2 Peter 1:19). Iron sharpens iron, so one man sharpens another (Proverbs 27:17). Tithes, offerings, time, and commitment are utilized by God through the community of believers, the synagogue or church. [34]

---

[34] Synagogue simply means assembly, church means assembly. בית כנסת Bet Kenesset "House of Assembly" or בית תפילה Bet Tefila "House of Prayer" in Hebrew. In Yiddish you call this a shul, "school".

Persecution Starts at Antioch

At that time, the non-believing Jews in the area began persecuting the followers of Yeshua.

   Acts 13:45-47 says:
>45 But when the Jews saw the crowds, they were **filled with jealousy** and began contradicting the things spoken by Paul and **were blaspheming**. 46 Paul and Barnabas spoke out boldly and said, "It was necessary that the word of God be spoken to you first; since you repudiate it and judge yourselves unworthy of eternal life, behold, we are turning to the Gentiles. 47 "For so the Lord has commanded us...

   This tells us of the hearts of those who had not believed. Filled with jealousy, they were contradicting Paul and blaspheming. Blaspheming? Think about this! I believe this tells us several things about these people. They were Jewish by lineage, but not the observant Jews normally attending the synagogues. They had come with the rest of the town to hear Paul. These people were not worried about the things of God and they obviously did not know their own scriptures. You know this from the text. Devout or Orthodox Jews would not have been blaspheming (this is a little obvious). The other reason you know this is because of what I mentioned earlier. Paul and Barnabas had been teaching there for over a year, the people in the synagogues already knew their teaching. Having been gone for only a short time, upon their return the synagogue officials invited them to speak. The normal attendees of the synagogue not only invited them back to speak the next Sabbath, but they also invited virtually the entire town. That is when the trouble started. I find this amazing to think about!
   Paul quotes verses from Isaiah 42 and 49 in rebuking them.

Isaiah 42:6-7
6 "I am the Lord, I have called You in righteousness,
I will also hold You by the hand and watch over You,
And I will appoint You as a covenant to the people,
As a light to the nations,
7 To open blind eyes,
To bring out prisoners from the dungeon
And those who dwell in darkness from the prison.

Isaiah 49:6
6 He says, "It is too small a thing that You should be My Servant To raise up the tribes of Jacob and to restore the preserved ones of Israel;
I will also make You a light of the nations
So that My salvation may reach to the end of the earth."[35]

One of the functions of the people of Israel, the Hebrew People, is to be a light to the nations by bringing them the Word of God.[36]
Yeshua was telling the people of Israel these same words.

Matthew 5:13-15
13 "You are the salt of the earth; but if the salt has become tasteless, how can it be made salty again? It is no longer good for anything, except to be thrown out and trampled under foot by men.
14 "You are the light of the world. A city set on a hill cannot be hidden; 15 nor does anyone light a lamp and put it under a

---

[35] NASU; bold Italics not in original text.
[36] Word of God is Yeshua; John 1:1-5 In the beginning was the Word, and the Word was with God, and the Word was God. He was in the beginning with God. All things came into being through Him, and apart from Him nothing came into being that has come into being. In Him was life, and the life was the Light of men. The Light shines in the darkness, and the darkness did not comprehend it.

basket, but on the lampstand, and it gives light to all who are in the house.

In the book of Deuteronomy, Moses warned the children of Israel what would happen if they did not follow God's ways. He cautioned the people that they would be dispersed out of the land and sent away to the ends of the earth for their disobedience. I firmly believe the events I am getting ready to talk about were a direct result of two things:

1. Israel began following their own ways instead of the scriptures.[37]
2. They were selfish in not obeying God to be a light to the nations. Scripture is clear, God chose a specific people and entrusted them with His Word and they were then to be an example and a light to bring the entire world to the knowledge and salvation of God. When they stopped being a light, God dispersed them across the world to all nations.[38]

---

[37] This concerns the leadership and the nation, not necessarily individuals. Interesting note: In Antioch it was the regular attendees of the synagogue, the ones familiar with the Hebrew Scriptures, who believed in Yeshua.

[38] To understand part of why this nationalistic pride happened, a study of the time of the Maccabees and of the persecution under Antiochus Epiphanes needs to be performed. In the process of restoring the nation, there was a lot of animosity toward the outside world. This manifested as Roman oppression.

Titus Vespasian

In 70 AD Titus Vespasian placed the Fifth, Twelfth, and Fifteenth Legions on the west side of Jerusalem; and the Tenth Legion was located on the east side of Jerusalem, on the Mount of Olives. He then commanded his armies to lay siege to Jerusalem and burn the Temple. You must remember the Roman rulers worshiped the Pagan Pantheon of the Greeks. They mandated and enforced Pagan worship. Titus strategically surrounded Jerusalem with his army. He then let the Jewish people who had pilgrimaged in from foreign lands enter the city for Passover.[39] After the pilgrims entered the city, He closed the gates and laid siege on Jerusalem. These were the most devout and affluent of the people. They had the means to make such a pilgrimage and they felt it was important to make the trip. Acts 2:9 above gives us some idea of the people making pilgrimage for the Passover. If you and I can figure this out, it is easy to see Titus Vespasian had a clear military strategy worked out. This was not an accident. From a military standpoint. the overpopulation in the city immediately strained the food and water supply. From a political and religious standpoint, he had captured many of the most devout and affluent Jewish people, even from distant parts of the empire. The accounts of what followed are brutal, Josephus and other historians of the time record the events leading to the destruction. It is estimated 1.2 million (1,200,000) people were killed. Some estimates are as high as 1.5 million. The Temple was destroyed, and Jerusalem was left desolate.[40] Titus orders the remaining walls of the city to be

---

[39] Passover is one of the three Pilgrimage Feasts listed in Exodus 23:14. These are the Feast of Unleavened Bread (Passover & Unleavened bread are celebrated together); Shavuot ("weeks;" occurs midsummer); Sukkot ("booths;" occurs in the fall).

[40] Leviticus 26:43; Deuteronomy 28:49—68; Jeremiah 12:7—17; Matthew 23:37—39.

torn down and the remains of the Temple are removed stone by stone. Matthew 13:2 and Luke 19:44 are fulfilled as literally as can be imagined.

> Luke 19:41—44
> 41 When He approached Jerusalem, He saw the city and wept over it, 42 saying, "If you had known in this day, even you, the things which make for peace! But now they have been hidden from your eyes. 43 "For the days will come upon you when your enemies will throw up a barricade against you, and surround you and hem you in on every side, 44 and they will level you to the ground and your children within you, and they will not leave in you one stone upon another, because you did not recognize the time of your visitation."

Much of the gold lining the inside of the Temple was melted during the fire and ran down through the stones of the building. When every stone was removed to recover the gold, The Temple was completely gone. Jerusalem, the City of David, with its walls were in ruins. This was the city and walls originally built by Melchizedek, the Righteous King, he was the first priest of God, and first built an alter there, and called the city Salem, later the name became Jerusalem.[41]

> "From King David, who was the first of the Jews who reigned therein, to this destruction under Titus, were 1179 years; but from its first building, till this last destruction were 2177 years;

---

[41] Genesis 14:18 is the first mention of Melchizedek. (It is my opinion Melchizedek was responsible for the first construction of Jerusalem and the Jebusites later conquered it for themselves. Ref needed) King David took the city from the Jebusites around 3000 BCE (2 Samuel 5:6—10). David's son Salomon built the first temple and on the 9th of Ave Nebuchadnezzar of Babylon destroyed it (2 Kings 25:9). The Temple was rebuilt on its original foundation at the decree of Cyrus II the Great, King of Persia. Herod the Great continued construction (refurbishment) at the time of Yeshua. This was the Temple Titus Vespasian destroyed.

yet hath not its vast riches, nor the diffusion of its nation over all the habitable earth, nor the greatness of the veneration paid to it on a religious account, been sufficient to preserve it from being destroyed. And thus ended the siege of Jerusalem."[42]

At this point in my research it is my opinion that Melchizedek was not of Canaanite descent, but was Noah's son, Shem.[43] The walls of the original city were not rebuilt. As we move forward we find this original site was covered over by Hadrian and remained hidden until now. Archaeologists are just now finding and unfolding the ancient City of David. Read on!

Eventually, the Jewish people resettled in Jerusalem and began again. They were hoping for a repeat of Jeremiah 25, where Yehovah tells B'nei Yisra'el[44] after 70 years he will restore the nation. Daniel[45] prayed for God to fulfill the words of Jeremiah to restore the land and through Cyrus the Great, Jerusalem was restored in 539 BC. However, this was not what was going to happen.

---

[42] Josephus; Wars of the Jews Book VI, Chapter X, page 856, David McKay Publisher, Washington Square.

[43] It is beyond the scope of this book to go into any detail about Shem.

[44] B'nei Yisra'el: Sons of Israel

[45] Daniel 9:2

Hadrian Visits Antioch.

In the year 129 AD Hadrian was ruler of all the Roman Empire. Rome had conquered most of their known enemies, and Hadrian was basically going around the empire as The Supreme Ruler or as a deity. He was building Pagan temples to the gods of the Greeks in cities he was visiting.[46]

When Hadrian gets to Antioch, he finds a very large number of Jews and Gentiles worshiping together in the synagogues. They are part of a religious sect that follows the tenets of Judaism, which includes resting and worshiping on the Sabbath, and practicing the Feasts of Yehovah, the God of Israel. He sees that many of the people of Antioch have joined this sect of Judaism, known as Nazarenes or Followers of the Way. These are the disciples of Yeshua.

He is told by these people of Antioch that they will not bow down to him or to his Pagan gods. They reject his Pagan temples and will not participate in Pagan practices.[47] Hadrian spent his life worshiping, elevating, and promoting these Pagan practices.

---

[46] https://followinghadrian.com/2017/08/11/11th-august-117-ad-hadrian-is-hailed-emperor-in-antioch-hadrian1900/; Cassius Dio 69; Historia Augusta, The Life of Hadrian; Birley, Anthony R. (1997). Hadrian. The restless emperor (p. 77-80); J. Bennett, Trajan Optimus Princeps, A Life and Times, London – New York, 2005.; Eusebius, The Ecclesiastical History, Book 4; The Princeton Encyclopedia of Classical Sites: Antioch on the Orontes; Glanville Downey, A History of Antioch From Seleucus to the Arab Conquest pp. 218-223; Richard H. Chowen, The Nature of Hadrian's Theatron at Daphne. American Journal of Archaeology, Vol. 60, No. 3 (Jul. 1956), pp. 275-277

[47] Acts 11-13, in context, makes it very plain what was being taught and the response of the people. In Acts 13 Paul and Barnabas sat until after the reading of the Torah and the Haftorah portions. Torah is often translated as 'Law', but is best translated as 'Instructions', the 5 books of Moses specifically. The Haftorah portion is the reading of the Prophets and the Writings. Together these comprise what we

_____

call the Old Testament. The Synagogue Officials were using the exact same order of service used in Synagogues around the world to this day. After reading the Torah and Haftorah portions Paul got up to speak.

Hadrian Declares War on God's People

What is the very next thing Hadrian does after encountering the Christians at Antioch? Hadrian immediately goes to Judea and declares Jerusalem to be the location he is going to turn into a Pagan place of worship, declaring war on the God of Israel and on his People. Hadrian sets the course to build a new city over the remains of Jerusalem, renaming it Aelia Capitolina. The orders are given to build a new temple dedicated to Jupiter on the Temple Mount. He changes Israel's name to Palestine, a name we hear repeatedly to this day. The name comes from the Philistines in the Bible, the enemies of the Jews. The exact order of these events is disputed by historians. We do know he was in Jerusalem in 130 AD. We know he ordered the temple to Jupiter built at that time. One of the evidences of this is the first coin minted in Aelia Capitolina 130-132 AD. It has on its back-side Hadrian plowing the field with bulls. This is a symbol to the people he is plowing over the old city and building a new one.

Figure 6 The first coin issued at the mint of Aelia Capitalina about 130/132 CE. Reverse side COL[ONIA]AEL[IA] CAPIT[OLINA] COND[ITA] (The founding of Colonia Aelia Capitolina)

It is reported from Historia Augusta[48] Hadrian banned circumcision (*brit milah*).[49] It is likely Hadrian also banned most Jewish practices at this time.

Reading a history of Hadrian, it becomes very clear what his intentions were: To force the people of Israel to assimilate until there was no more Israel. The war against God would be over. Essentially, he was doing the exact same thing Antiochus Epiphanes did almost 300 years earlier. He was making every effort to eliminate the Word of God from the people.[50]

---

[48] Augustine History is a Roman collection of biographies, written in Latin, of the Roman Emperors and junior colleagues from 117 to 284 CE. A compilation of 6 different authors written during the reigns of Diocletian and Constantine I.

[49] The Historian Cassius Dio gave written account of Hadrian visiting Jerusalem in 130 AD. This fact was confirmed in 2014 with the Israel Antiquities Authority uncovering an inscription bearing the name and title of Hadrian and commemorating a visit he made to the city in 130 AD.
http://www.thetower.org/article/remembering-hadrian-destroyer-of-the-jews/

[50] Discovered in Jerusalem is a tribute to Emperor Hadrian in the year 129/130 CE. Strong evidence Hadrian visited Jerusalem that year triggering the revolt. https://en.wikipedia.org/wiki/Bar_Kokhba_revolt, Reference 81, Roman Imperial inscription in Jerusalem. Cassius Dio Volume 8 makes it very clear in his work from 215 AD Hadrian started Aelia Capitolina during his visit in 130 AD.

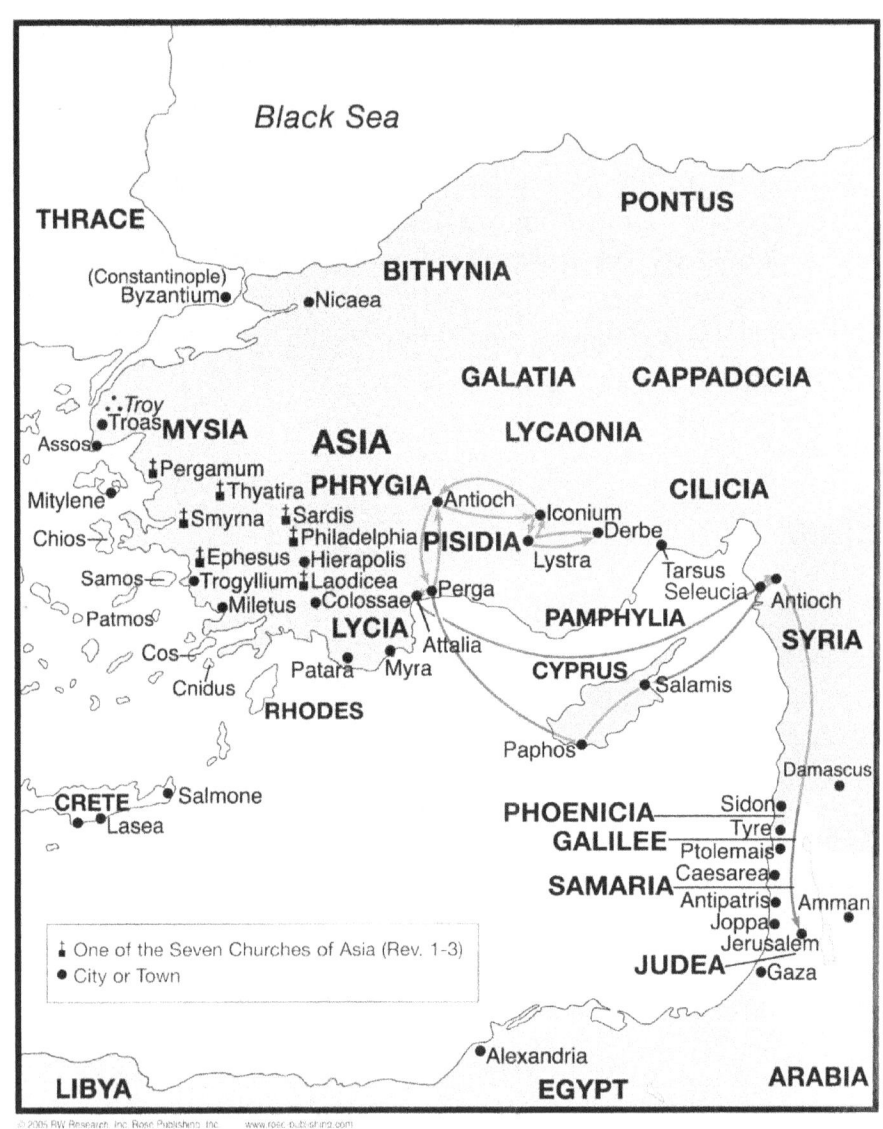

Figure 7 Apostle Paul's First Missionary Journey 44-46 A.D.

Paul had spent a year in Antioch around AD 45. There was dissention in the synagogues in AD 46, but virtually everyone in the entire city showed up to listen to Paul and rejoiced at what he said. Hadrian visited in AD 129, about 83 years later.

What Hadrian didn't count on was how serious God was when he made Israel in the first place.
Deut. 4:10
> 10 "Remember the day you stood before the Lord your God at Horeb, when the Lord said to me, 'Assemble the people to Me, that I may let them hear My words, so they may learn to fear Me all the days they live on the earth, and that they may teach their children.'

Instilled in the very being of the Jewish people is the Word of God. In spite of great adversity, one thing has never changed—the Hebrew people have never stopped protecting the Word of God.

The Jewish nation rebels

In 131 AD the people began to revolt. By 134 AD the Bar Kokvah Revolt led to the final diaspora of the Jewish people.[51] This is the main event that triggers the dispersal of Israel, the Jewish people around the entire world.

Figure 8 Rabbi-Akiva, Wikipedia Commons

By 136 CE Hadrian had completely stopped the rebellion. This is one of the most significant events in human history and most people are not even aware of it or its impact.

In this same time period Rabbi Akiva is extremely significant. He is the "Chief of the Sages". He leads the largest Rabbinic School at the time of the revolt. Estimates range from 12,000 to 48,000 pupils. Rabbi Akiva is responsible for the Mishnah, the first major written collection of Jewish oral traditions known as the Oral Torah. He also is responsible for the Midrash Halakha, ancient Judaic rabbinic method of Torah study involving the 613 Mitzvot (commandments).[52]

The Mishnah is regarded with great admiration by almost all people. Most oral tradition provides insights into the thinking and historical background of the Tanakh as people thought about it at the time of Yeshua.

---

[51] https://en.wikipedia.org/wiki/Bar_Kokhba_revolt
[52] https://en.wikipedia.org/wiki/Rabbi_Akiva

Rabbi Akiva endorses Bar Kokvah as the Messiah of Israel

Rabbi Akiva declared Bar Kokvah as the Messiah. This is one of the reasons the majority of Judea and the surrounding Jewish people rallied around him to fight the Roman assault on the land, and on the assault directed on the God of Israel. Several key consequences of this revolt are as follows.

- Believers in Messiah Yeshua did not follow Bar Kokvah. He was not the Messiah and they knew it. This caused huge arguments and dissention between the different sects of Judaism.
- Believers in Yeshua were kicked out of the synagogues. The Jewish people were looking for someone to help them in the war against the Romans. They did not appreciate the arguments from the believers in Yeshua that the Messiah had to pay for our sin, redeeming mankind, before he would return to rule the world.[53]
- Under these circumstances, believers could not support Bar Kokvah, the leadership was clearly flawed. Also, it is possible the prophetic messages Yeshua had given about the Romans was still prevalent in the minds of the believers. Many Nazarenes, followers of The Way (believers in Yeshua), fled from the coming destruction.

THIS IS THE RIFT THAT HAS SEPERATED BELIEVERS FROM THEIR ROOTS TO THIS DAY.

---

[53] Isaiah 53:1-12 All Rabbis prior to Rabbi Rashi (1040 to 1105 CE) had confirmed Isaiah 53 as a Messianic prophecy. It was Rashi who tried to make this prophecy a reference to Israel as a way of distancing it from its clear Messianic implication. For a list of 300 Messianic Prophecies fulfilled by Yeshua see: All the Messianic Prophecies of the Bible, Herbert Lockyer, Zondervan, Copyright 1973

This event is a turning point in all history. The believers in Yeshua were on their own, separate from the Jewish community. As the distance between them grew, doctrines diverged, and the rift grew larger. So far, the discussion has been about the Jewish community and how the rift developed between the believers in Yeshua and Rabbinic Judaism. At this same time the Jewish believers in Yeshua were dispersing into the nations around them and teaching the gentile community. This dynamic is important because the number of non-Jewish believers was increasing exponentially. In a future booklet "We Are Bridges, Part 2", it will be shown how the Christian Church diverged from its biblical Judaic Roots. The events being discussed are shaping history. These events are critical to an understanding of how we ended up where we are today.

Hadrian Underestimates the Force of the Rebellion

Put yourself in this time for a moment to get a feel for what happened and the mood in the Roman Empire. They have conquered most of the known world. Hadrian is building Pagan Temples all around the empire to honor himself and the Greek pantheon. The Jewish rebellion starts. In the first part of the war, Hadrian suffers extreme losses. The legion from the Roman province of Britannia (Britain) is virtually eliminated. Reinforcements from Syria, Egypt and Arabia don't help. An independent state of Israel is established. To my knowledge, the losses to the Roman army are the largest of any war they ever fought. 90,000 Roman solders lose their lives in this war, this is right in the middle of the Roman Empire.

Hadrian responds by assembling legions from around the empire. He amasses a huge army and systematically begins regaining all of Judea. 580,000 Jews perish in the war, and many more die through hunger and disease. This is nothing short of genocide. This is the third war with the Jewish people and Hadrian follows through with his decision to remove Judea from the map along with the Jewish people.

- Hadrian enslaves an unknown number of people, in addition to the slaves Titus Vespasian had taken in 70 A.D. (80,000 to 100,000)
- He renames Judea as Palestine, the name Israel is removed from the map
- He builds a temple to Jupiter on the Temple Mount in Jerusalem
- Jerusalem is renamed Alia Capitolina
- All Jewish practices of Israel are outlawed.
    - Reading the Hebrew Scriptures
    - Hebrew calendars designating Sabbath and Festivals

- Meetings of the Sanhedrin or distribution of Jewish Articles including the setting of the dates of the Jewish Calendar
- The Name of God is forbidden to be spoken
- Jewish people are not allowed in Jerusalem at all; however, a concession is made to allow them once a year on Tisha B'Av, the day the Temple was destroyed.

Hadrian continued what Titus Vespasian had started sixty years earlier. He makes sure the original City of David is turned into farmers fields. This is something basically unrealized until very recently. Micah three is an interesting prophecy about Jerusalem and the temple.

Micah 3:12
12Therefore, on account of you
Zion will be plowed as a field,
Jerusalem will become a heap of ruins,
And the mountain of the temple will become high places of a forest.

Micah of Moresheth prophesied in the days of Hezekiah king of Judah[54] that Jerusalem and the temple would become ruins, plowed as fields and the mountain of the house of the LORD as the high places of a forest. When king Hezekiah heard this prophecy, he made changes and the LORD relented and did not allow the destruction at that time. However, look at Micah Chapter 4, the verses directly after the quote we just read. It is about the "last days". It is about the end times when God again will establish the mountain of the house of the LORD and peoples from many nations will come to Jerusalem. For from Zion will go forth the law, even the word of the LORD from Jerusalem.[55]

---

[54] Jeremiah 26:18 describes specifically this prophecy by Micah the prophet and states Hezekiah the king did not put him to death because of it, even though Micah was prophesying about the destruction of the city and the temple.

[55] Micah 4:1—4

This is astonishing to me in light of the things that have been unfolding in recent years. Most people are not aware that the south side of the temple mount has been open vacant fields since the time of Hadrian.

During the time around 200 BC several aqueducts were made bringing water to the upper part of Jerusalem. This made it possible to expand the city to the west and to the north. Titus Vespasian and afterward, Hadrian, made sure the original city was literally plowed over. Figure 8 below shows what the city looked like in the year 1928. Notice the south side is farm land. The water supplied externally from the aqueducts made it possible to build away from the Gihon Spring.

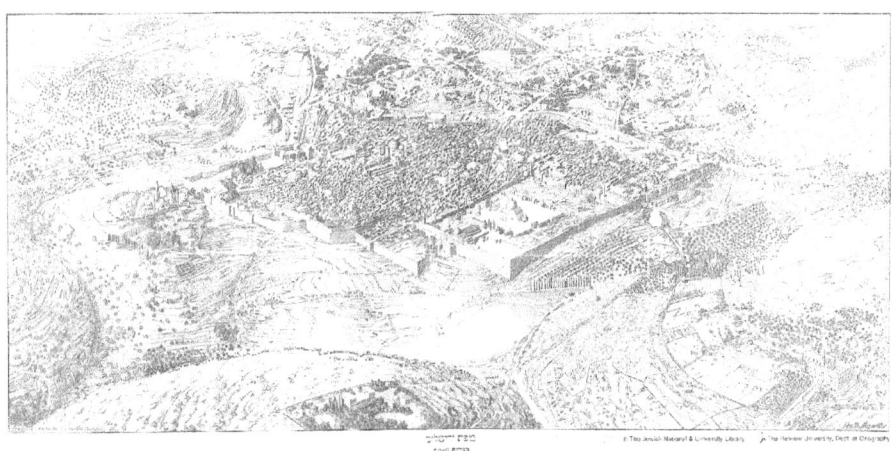

Figure 9 Old City of Jerusalem, 1928 by Kosel & Pustet, Munchen; View looking from the South-East, the city extends North and West from the Temple Mount; The Jewish National & University Library, Hebrew University, Dept. of Geography.

There have been at least twenty archaeological projects on the south side of the temple mount over the last ten or fifteen years (through 2018). This has proven beyond any doubt, the City of David, the old original city of Jerusalem, was on the south side of the area called the Temple Mount.

A little history

In the year 1867 Queen Victoria of Great Britain commissioned Captain Charles Warren to perform archaeological work in Jerusalem and the temple mount. To his disappointment, he was not allowed to dig on the temple mount itself and so made excavations on the south side. He found many ancient artifacts dating much older than expected. His work went mostly unnoticed. However, we have photos of the south side of Jerusalem from when he arrived (See figure 9). There is nothing but open fields down the south slope. Jerusalem was rebuilt, conquered, and rebuilt several times on the west, and north sides.

Figure 10 Old photograph from around 1900 CE. This view is from the South-South-West showing the fields south of the Temple Mt.

What no one has realized is the south side is where the actual city ruins are located. Dr. Eilat Mazar is responsible for finding King David's palace in this location. Figure 10 shows a current photo of the south side with the original location outlined in red. Visitors to Israel today can visit King David's Palace and the Pool of Siloam.

The size of the Roman Empire was immense, stretching from Britannia down through Northern Africa, and across Egypt. It was for all practical purposes the entire known world at the time. It continued in one form or another, for at least the next 400 years, some would argue it still exists to the present day.

The Romans' focus was on the Hellenistic culture and Greek mythology. By the time of Constantine in the fourth century, there were also four sects of sun worshipers predominant across the empire.

Figure 11 Original City-of-David shown in red, Photo Google Maps.

Stereotypically, the Romans hated the Jewish people. Having fought three wars in which thousands of lives were lost in battle, they had little tolerance for the rebellious behavior of the Hebrews. The Jews absolutely would not submit to the Pagan cultural and religious practices of the Romans: the worship of Greek idols, including sun worship; temple prostitution, and other deviant sexual activities which were aspects of their religion. The Roman Emperor continued to persecute the Jewish people; the assumption was that under extreme pressure they would eventually assimilate into the Roman cultural traditions.

Now, after the Bar Kokvah revolt the Jewish people were banned from entering Judea, it was turned into Palestine. There were Roman solders from every land in the empire killed in the Jewish wars. As the Jewish refugees were pushed from place to place, they moved to more distant lands. They also stayed together in small enclaves anyplace they found refuge.

The new believers in Yeshua who were not Jewish lived noticeably different lifestyles than the Romans around them. Their morality and ethics created a separation between themselves and their Pagan neighbors. They worshipped on the biblical Sabbath and followed the Feasts of God which were prescribed in Leviticus 23. When these early Christians did not join in with the Pagan festivals and practices, they stuck out like sore thumbs. While they surely had been as discreet as possible, they would not have escaped notice, either by their neighbors or by the Roman government.

It must also be understood the Jewish believers in Messiah Yeshua were very numerus. In Acts 21:20 it says: *"You see, brother, how many tens of thousands there are among the Jews of those who have believed, and they are all zealous for the Law"*.[56] As discussed above, eighty-five more years had passed since Acts 21. We know God moved the hearts and minds of hundreds of thousands of people, Jew and Gentile alike, who accepted the gospel of the Messiah Yeshua. Many of the Jewish believers in Yeshua had warned their brothers Bar Kokvah was not the Messiah and had fled the persecution that had been foretold. These people were not welcome in the synagogues and had banded together with other believers. All of this, though, was illegal in the eyes of the Roman government and the Pagans around them. These are the believers who were fed to the lions, and who were killed in the circuses around the Roman Empire.

---

[56] Most English translations state "thousands"; look up the original Greek text, it clearly says: "tens of thousands".

It was punishable by death for a Jew to proselytize a Gentile. It was also punishable by imprisonment or death for a Gentile to proselytize other Gentiles in the ways of Judaism. Remember, at that time Believers were a sect of Judaism; the government and the Pagan world saw no difference.

Observing the Sabbath, the Feasts, and most importantly, The Word of God in the Scriptures, made an undeniable contrast between you and others who only knew the Roman way of life. You risked imprisonment and death for rejecting the Pagan gods of your ancestors. Your life was also in danger for following Yeshua with His Jewish or Biblical roots. Your work week gave you one day off on Sunday, which was the Pagan day for worshiping the sun god.

Hadrian implemented many laws and policies to stop the spread of Judaism across the empire. These laws were enforced for many centuries.[57]

---

[57] https://en.wikipedia.org/wiki/Religious_persecution_in_the_Roman_Empire; Tiberius forbade Judaism in Rome, Claudius expelled them from Rome, (multiple articles in Wikipedia, follow links); https://primolevicenter.org/printed-matter/roman-policy-towards-the-jews-expulsions-from-the-city-of-rome-during-the-first-century-c-e/ Suetonius makes the remark: they (Jews) constantly made disturbances at the instigation of Chrestus (many believe this to be early Christians). Acts 18:2 confirms that Claudius expelled the Jews from Rome at that time. Notice there is no distinction between the believers in Yeshua and the rest of the Jewish community. Domitian condemned Judaism as atheism (rejecting the pagan gods). From 70 AD on Rome instituted a Jewish Tax, requiring the tax be paid to practice Judaism.

The Diaspora (The Scattering)

Before I go any further, it must be understood I am reporting the history regarding the Jewish people and how it affects all of history. Paul warns everyone in the book of Romans:

Romans 1:19-22
> 19 You will say then, "Branches were broken off so that I might be grafted in." 20 Quite right, they were broken off for their unbelief, but you stand by your faith. Do not be conceited, but fear; 21 for if God did not spare the natural branches, He will not spare you, either. 22 Behold then the kindness and severity of God; to those who fell, severity, but to you, God's kindness, if you continue in His kindness; otherwise you also will be cut off.

If you are called by God's Name, if you are a believer in Yeshua, you better realize all of Scripture teaches us God is just. All of us are judged individually, but God also judges nations and leadership. The consequences are real and affect everyone.

Deuteronomy 28:64
> 64 "Moreover, the Lord will scatter you among all peoples, from one end of the earth to the other end of the earth.

The last chapters of the book of Deuteronomy make it clear that Israel will be led astray. When this happens, they are told that they will be dispersed from one end of the earth to the other. This is amazing in its prophetic significance.
- Israel is Holy (set apart), different from all other people.
- Israel is charged with the scriptures of God.
- Israel is to be a light to the nations for God.

Who is supposed to make the nations aware of their history, their relationship with God, and how they are supposed to live in righteousness? Israel.

What does God do when they refuse to bring His Word, His Yeshua to the nations? He distributes Israel and His Word to every nation on earth!

Do you remember Yeshua telling Peter, *"I also say to you that you are Peter [bed-rock], and upon this rock I will build My church; and the gates of Hades will not overpower it?* (Matthew 16:18, NASU)

I believe one aspect of revelation from God is the foundation of His Word, and the foundation of His Word is Yeshua. *Upon this rock I will build My assembly*. The Jewish people hold The Word of God in their hands, treasure it, and guard it; as stated earlier, it is in their DNA to hold onto it. When the events above forced the people to flee, they went to every nation on earth. There is not a place on earth where the nation of Israel hasn't put their feet. This "Rock" the Torah, the Tanakh, has been in every place on earth for the last 1900 years. I find that amazing.

Persecution in Europe From Then Until Now

With the history we gave of Antioch, with the knowledge many Jewish believers had spread the good news of Yeshua across the Roman Empire, picture what was going on in Europe, Asia, and the Roman Empire at the time. Many Jewish people had come to Messiah and believed, even more Gentiles had heard and believed. Christianity was growing across the empire despite the persecution from the laws and culture of the Pagans they lived among.

Figure 12 Persecution, Wikipedia Commons

Picture yourself as a Believer at the time. You worship on the Sabbath, follow the Feast Days, and you recognize that God created the heavens, the earth, the sea, and all that is in them.

You can easily see why the Gentile believers distanced themselves from the Jewish communities. With the above background you can also understand why the non-believing Jewish communities distanced themselves from the Christians.

As time passed and the number of believers increased in the empire, it became easier to follow customs less foreign to the people. Syncretism between Paganism and Christianity became more common. By the time of Constantine in 325 AD, half of the empire had converted to Christianity. Constantine was trying to unite the empire and performed a political move declaring Christianity to be a sanctioned religion. He called together a meeting called the Council of Nicaea and invited over 1800 Bishops from around the Roman Empire. Less than 300 showed up, and of them there were no Messianic Rabbis invited or present at the meeting. The Appointed Times of Leviticus 23 were strictly forbidden, including worshiping on the Sabbath. What was allowed was worshiping on the "venerated day of the Sun". This was the day Mithra (the sun god) was worshiped. One place of research on this subject is to look up the Quartodeciman Disputes, this shows the wide spread disagreement with the policies coming down from the Emperor.

Bridges Connect two places together

Everything changed when Israel became a nation again, and prophetically the time clock has restarted.

Figure 13 Longest Sea Bridge https.//www.youtube.com/watch?v=N63mEBOclpA

Look at all the hearts, minds and souls being opened to the fullness and rich substance of the scriptures. In 1948 there were maybe five people who would call themselves Messianic in the entire nation of Israel; today there are about 150 Messianic Congregation in Israel. The hearts and minds of the Jewish people are being softened toward Yeshua, the Jewish Messiah. God is doing amazing work.

Look at the Gentile nations, it is nothing short of remarkable what God is doing around the world. There are thousands of Messianic

Jewish congregations worldwide, and television channels teach Messianic principles from Messianic Rabbis on worldwide media outlets. For the first time since the times we have been talking about, the nations are learning about their Biblical Judaic Roots. The fullness of the Gospel message comes to life with each new element put into its Biblical perspective.

Once you realize God's timing takes centuries and millennia to unfold, then you begin to understand that many things have been interacting together over the course of time.

Satan and mankind in rebellion have done everything possible to stop God's people, both Jew and Gentile, from growing the Kingdom of God. Each step of the way, God has used these things to further his plan in spite of what people thought they were doing. God works all things together for good to those who love Him, to those who are called according to His purpose. (Romans 8:28).

Yeshua's Parable of the Wedding Feast

Read below as Yeshua tells the parable of the wedding feast.

Matthew 22:8-14

22 Jesus spoke to them again in parables, saying, 2 "The kingdom of heaven may be compared to a king who gave a wedding feast for his son. 3 "And he sent out his slaves to call those who had been invited to the wedding feast, and they were unwilling to come. 4 "Again he sent out other slaves saying, 'Tell those who have been invited, "Behold, I have prepared my dinner; my oxen and my fattened livestock are all butchered and everything is ready; come to the wedding feast."' 5 "But they paid no attention and went their way, one to his own farm, another to his business, 6 and the rest seized his slaves and mistreated them and killed them. 7 "But the king was enraged, and he sent his armies and destroyed those murderers and set their city on fire.

8 "Then he said to his slaves, 'The wedding is ready, but those who were invited were not worthy. 9 'Go therefore to the main highways, and as many as you find there, invite to the wedding feast.' 10 "Those slaves went out into the streets and gathered together all they found, both evil and good; and the wedding hall was filled with dinner guests.

11 "But when the king came in to look over the dinner guests, he saw a man there who was not dressed in wedding clothes, 12 and he said to him, 'Friend, how did you come in here without wedding clothes?' And the man was speechless. 13 "Then the king said to the servants, 'Bind him hand and foot, and throw him into the outer darkness; in that place there will

be weeping and gnashing of teeth.' 14 "For many are called, but few are chosen."

In a case like this it was customary for the king to provide the wedding clothes for the guests. His guests would not have provided their own clothes. This means the man didn't bother to put them on.

In the parable, what are the wedding clothes the king provided for his guests?

The wedding clothes are the Word of God, which is the embodiment of Yeshua:

- Torah (instructions)
- Prophets
- Writings
- Brit Chadashah (New Testament)

The Christian Church today is representative of the man without the wedding clothes, having no understanding of the root of the tree they have been grafted into.[58] Even worse, the average Christian today doesn't understand *why* they need to put on the wedding clothes. *"Friend, how did you come in here without wedding clothes?" And the man was speechless.*

Matthew 7.21-23
> 21 "Not everyone who says to Me, 'Lord, Lord,' will enter the kingdom of heaven, but he who does the will of My Father who is in heaven will enter. 22 "Many will say to Me on that day, 'Lord, Lord, did we not prophesy in Your name, and in Your name cast out demons, and in Your name perform many

---

[58] Romans 11:15—16

miracles?' 23 "And then I will declare to them, 'I never knew you; DEPART FROM ME, YOU WHO PRACTICE LAWLESSNESS.'[59]

Put on the wedding clothes, pray for Yehovah to breath life into you. Repent and walk in the grace and admonition of the LORD.[60]

---

[59] Psalm 6:9
[60] Ephesians Chapter 2

Do You See Why We Are A Bridge?

Yeshua uses us to connect the Word of God[61] with the People of God.

Yeshua uses us to connect the Word of God with the People of All Nations Everywhere.

**I pray you take up the challenge to be a bridge
for the Kingdom of God.**

---

[61] John 1:1 In the beginning was the Word, and the Word was with God and the Word was God, He was in the beginning with God. All things came into being through Him, and apart from Him nothing came into being that has come into being. In Him was life, and the life was the Light of men. The Light shines in the darkness, and the darkness did not comprehend it.

About the Author

William J. Kuik is a Messianic Believer walking with Yeshua in Southern Colorado with his wife, Fran, and their son. Bill has a Bachelor of Science degree in Aerospace Engineering from the University of Colorado, Boulder. He has been studying the Tanakh and Brit Chadashah (Old and New Testament of the Bible) for over 25 years.

About the Editor and Illustrator

Frances Kuik has a Bachelor of Fine Arts degree in Illustration from Rocky Mountain College of Art & Design in Lakewood, CO. She has also been studying Scripture for about 25 years.

Lightning Source UK Ltd.
Milton Keynes UK
UKHW041819040123
414830UK00001B/4